T0373883

Gospel Thrillers

What if the original teachings of Jesus were different from the Bible's sanitized "orthodox" version? What covert motivations might inspire those who decide what the text of the Bible "says" or what it "means"? For some who ask conspiratorial questions like these, the Bible is the vulnerable victim of secular forces seeking to divest the United States of its founding identity. For others, the biblical canon suppresses religious truths that could upend the status quo. Such suspicions surrounding the Bible find full expression in Gospel Thrillers, a 1960s fictional genre that endures and still commands a substantial following. These novels imagine a freshly discovered first-century gospel and a race against time to unlock its buried secrets. They also reflect the fears and desires that the Bible continues to generate. Andrew Jacobs reveals, in his authoritative examination, how this remarkable fictional archive opens a window onto disturbing biblical anxieties.

ANDREW S. JACOBS is Senior Fellow at the Center for the Study of World Religions at Harvard Divinity School. Editor of *the Elements of Religion in Late Antiquity* series (published by Cambridge University Press), and the writer and coeditor of five previous books, he is in addition author of *Epiphanius of Cyprus: A Cultural Biography of Late Antiquity* (2016), which in 2017 was awarded the Philip Schaff Best Book Prize from the American Society of Church History.

Gospel Thrillers

Conspiracy, Fiction, and the Vulnerable Bible

ANDREW S. JACOBS
Harvard Divinity School

CAMBRIDGE
UNIVERSITY PRESS

Shaftesbury Road, Cambridge CB2 8EA, United Kingdom

One Liberty Plaza, 20th Floor, New York, NY 10006, USA

477 Williamstown Road, Port Melbourne, VIC 3207, Australia

314–321, 3rd Floor, Plot 3, Splendor Forum, Jasola District Centre,
New Delhi – 110025, India

103 Penang Road, #05-06/07, Visioncrest Commercial, Singapore 238467

Cambridge University Press is part of Cambridge University Press & Assessment,
a department of the University of Cambridge.

We share the University's mission to contribute to society through the pursuit
of education, learning and research at the highest international levels of excellence.

www.cambridge.org
Information on this title: www.cambridge.org/9781009384612

DOI: 10.1017/9781009384605

First published 2024

Printed in the United Kingdom by TJ Books Limited, Padstow, Cornwall

A catalogue record for this publication is available from the British Library.

Library of Congress Cataloging-in-Publication Data
Names: Jacobs, Andrew S., 1973- author.
Title: Gospel thrillers : conspiracy, fiction, and the vulnerable Bible / Andrew S. Jacobs,
    Harvard Divinity School.
Description: Cambridge, United Kingdom ; New York, NY, USA : Cambridge University
    Press, 2024. | Includes bibliographical references and index.
Identifiers: LCCN 2023015512 (print) | LCCN 2023015513 (ebook) |
    ISBN 9781009384612 (hardback) | ISBN 9781009384599 (paperback) |
    ISBN 9781009384605 (epub)
Subjects: LCSH: Bible–In literature. | Suspense fiction, American–History and criticism. |
    Christian fiction, American–History and criticism. | Conspiracies in literature. |
    American fiction–20th century–History and criticism. | American fiction–21st
    century–History and criticism. | LCGFT: Literary criticism.
Classification: LCC PS374.B53 J33 2024 (print) | LCC PS374.B53 (ebook) |
    DDC 813.009/3822–dc23/eng/20230519
LC record available at https://lccn.loc.gov/2023015512
LC ebook record available at https://lccn.loc.gov/2023015513

ISBN 978-1-009-38461-2 Hardback

For Catherine

Contents

Preface

We live in a time of rampant conspiracy theories and exuberant biblical "discoveries"; an era of Truthers and of a Museum of the Bible in the US capital. This book is about how biblical desires and conspiratorial fears are illuminated, amplified, and ultimately contained in an unnoticed genre of fiction: the Gospel Thriller.

I discovered my first Gospel Thrillers browsing in a used bookstore in Northern Virginia that no longer exists (another sign of the times). There were just a few of these books, all from the 1960s and 1970s, shelved with "historical fiction" alongside fictional versions of biblical stories like *Ben Hur* and *The Robe*. But these novels weren't historical; they imagined a lost gospel resurfacing in the present day and the desperate lengths shadowy forces would go to in order to suppress their dangerous truths or promote their insidious lies. They were *thrillers*, fast-paced suspense novels that pitted protagonists stumbling upon a shocking truth against ruthless antagonists determined to stop them.

I thought these few books were a curiosity from the 1960s and 1970s, a period rife with "Jesus fiction" and "Jesus theories," forgotten companions to *Jesus Christ Superstar* and *The Passover Plot*. I thought they were a strange window into what a reading public decades earlier thought of the Bible and biblical studies (and scholars of biblical studies). I even gave an amusing after-banquet talk about them at one of my professional society meetings.[1]

Over time, however, I became aware that this was not a brief publishing blip but rather an ongoing publishing phenomenon, particularly (although not uniquely) in the United States. These novels all share formulas, plot devices, even settings. The first one I have found appeared in 1964; the most recent I consider here was published in 2020. They comprise a distinct genre; I call that genre "Gospel Thrillers."

---

[1] Later published as "Gospel Thrillers," *Postscripts* 1 (2005): 125–42.

I am by training a historian of early Christianity, but the longer I sat with these novels (in conjunction with teaching college courses in biblical studies) the more I saw connections between the imaginary worlds conjured within them and the assumptions (not to mention fears and desires) that animated the professional guilds in which I spent my time. These novels are not just a window into the minds of the biblically curious general reader; they provide insight into the ways US cultures have fantasized about the Bible and how those fantasies emerge from and are embedded in the bedrock of the scholarly study of Christian origins.

In almost all of these novels the lost gospel that has resurfaced, or threatens to resurface, is described as a "bombshell," "earth-shattering," "beyond anything that could be imagined by the mind of man."[2] Robert Ludlum has one character say at the outset of his 1976 Gospel Thriller, *The Gemini Contenders*:

Within that vault are documents that would rend the Christian world apart, so devastating are their writings. They are the ultimate proof of our most sacred beliefs, yet their exposure would set religion against religion, sect against sect, entire peoples against one another.[3]

In truth, as I discuss toward the end of *Gospel Thrillers*, the "devastating" secret of the lost gospel rarely ends up having much effect at all: status quo generally prevails. But this certainty that a newly found gospel would "rend the Christian world apart" speaks to the central place that Bible holds in the US imaginary: it is the pillar of an imagined "western" civilization of which the United States is the vanguard. At the same time, this indispensable pillar is uniquely vulnerable to unsavory secrets from the past or clever forgeries perpetrated in the present (not to mention the inability to tell the difference between the two). Gospel Thrillers confront their readers with the enormity of the Bible and the thrill of imagining it under threat; they magnify and dramatize the biblical fears and desires that permeate so much US culture.

---

[2] "Bombshell": Gold, *The Lost Testament* (1992), 7; "earth-shattering": Rabb, *The Book of Q* (2001), 110; "beyond anything that could be imagined by the mind of man": van Greenaway, *The Judas Gospel* (1972), 84. Throughout this book I cite the novels by author, brief title, and page number of editions consulted. Full bibliographies for the novels can be found in the Appendix.
[3] Ludlum, *The Gemini Contenders*, 15–16.

Like the "bombshell" secrets they narrate, these novels have had little effect. They are a niche genre, a minor footnote in the publishing world. But if Gospel Thrillers do not "change the world," they do illuminate it, shining light on the particular fears and desires that the Bible continues to produce well into the twenty-first century.

Acknowledgments

In a project like this one, which has lasted more than a decade, the accumulation of debts is monumental. I must above all thank the many patient audiences who have heard me ruminate on the topics in this book over the years. In 2005, I delivered a semi-humorous talk on some quirky novels at the North American Patristics Society at the invitation of the Society's Vice President, Maureen Tilley (of blessed memory). Elizabeth Castelli, who was in the audience, then invited me to submit a written version of my talk to a new journal that she had founded. As my collection of quirky novels grew, so did my opportunity to deliver more measured thoughts on them throughout the 2000s: at my home institutions (first University of California, Riverside, then Scripps College); at other colleges and universities (Michigan State University, Bowdoin College, Williams College, Brown University, University of Oklahoma); and before international audiences (MF Center for Advanced Studies, Oslo). It was the reassurance of these audiences, over more than 15 years, that gave me courage to pursue a study whose parameters and implications seemed to grow year by year.

Gospel Thrillers was, for much of this time, a back-burner project while I published other articles, essays, and books. Around 2016 (only a decade or so after I began!), I moved it to the front burner, inspired by the changing world around us and a professional move that took me from California to New England. I am especially grateful to Charles Stang and the Center for the Study of World Religions at Harvard Divinity School for making room for an academic émigré. Encouragement from old friends and new, especially on social media where I could test out new ideas, helped me bring the project, at long last, to completion. I must thank those colleagues who in the final sprint gave me feedback on significant portions of the manuscript: Laura Salah Nasrallah, Christopher Douglas, and David Brakke. Catherine Allgor, my spouse – to whom I gratefully and happily dedicate this book – read it from end to end and pronounced, "It's a book!"

I want to express appreciation to the people who made this book technically possible. The crackerjack staff of the Special Collections at Honnold-Mudd Library of the Claremont Colleges – especially Carrie Marsh, Ayat Agah, and Ashley Larson – gave me access to the Wallace Family Archives, including a bounty of notes and artifacts related to Irving Wallace's *The Word* (I wish I could have incorporated more of this amazing treasure trove!). Thanks are also due to my editor at Cambridge University Press, Beatrice Rehl, who found the book intriguing enough to send out into the world, and to the three anonymous readers who gave me feedback that made the book much better.

Introduction

Two Headlines

Two headlines appeared in very different publications, several decades apart. Together these headlines frame the story I want to tell about conspiracy, fiction, and the vulnerability of the Bible in *Gospel Thrillers*.

In March 1972, the millions of subscribers to the *Ladies Home Journal* opened the new issue to find, on p. 127, the following headline taking up the top third of the page:[1]

Christ Survived Calvary, Lived to Age of 54: Archeologist's Amazing Find Casts Doubt on the New Testament

Astute readers might have noted the "Book Bonus" header at the top of the page; they might also wonder that such a giant headline, with such a shocking story, was found so far near the back of that month's issue (the cover of which featured Sophia Loren peddling her new Italian cookbook; the "Christ Survived Calgary" story is teased at the top left). Upon closer inspection, even less astute readers would have realized they were reading a synopsis of a newly published bestseller by potboiler author Irving Wallace disguised as a headline:

The newspaper headline above is fascinating but fictional ... This controversial theory is the theme of a sweeping new novel by one of the world's most widely read authors ... The *Journal* believes that his latest book, also destined to climb the best-seller lists, is so challenging, so provocative and enthralling that we will publish our condensation in three installments.

---

[1] In 1972, the *Ladies Home Journal* was the eighth most popular magazine in the United States (between *National Geographic* and *Playboy*): Richard Campbell, Christopher R. Martin, and Bettina Fabos, *Media and Culture: An Introduction to Mass Communication*, 8th ed. (Boston, MA/New York: Bedford/St. Martins, 2012), 268.

For three months in 1972 readers of the *Ladies Home Journal* could enjoy a condensation of Wallace's "sweeping" (several hundred page) novel *The Word* which would, indeed, remain one of the top-selling novels of the year. Its marketing here as "fascinating but fictional," with a central plot described as "a controversial theory," encourages readers to imagine the "amazing find" not merely as a novelist's invention but as a "provocative and enthralling" possibility.[2]

The second headline appeared on the front page of the *New York Times* on September 18, 2012:

A Faded Piece of Papyrus Refers to Jesus' Wife

While lacking the sensationalism of the headline in the *Ladies Home Journal*, the bare simplicity of the *New York Times* headline is just as "provocative and challenging" as the Wallace teaser. After all, how out of place would it be to put the *Journal* subheadline – "Archeologist's Amazing Find Casts Doubt on the New Testament" – below the *New York Times* headline? The *New York Times* article reports that Dr. Karen King of Harvard University had revealed the "faded papyrus" at an international conference in Rome. According to the *New York Times*, King tried to rein in overly exuberant speculation: "She repeatedly cautioned that this fragment should not be taken as proof that Jesus, the historical person, was actually married."[3]

Nonetheless the article's author notes the papyrus "could reignite the debate over whether Jesus was married" and concludes by comparing the papyrus's mention of "Jesus's wife" to "the bestseller and movie *The Da Vinci Code*." Even as the introduction in the *Ladies Home Journal* nudged a piece of fiction into the realm of "controversial theory," so the *New York Times* article placed a material artifact in the realm of fictional bestsellers and blockbusters. Subsequent reporting on the Gospel of Jesus's Wife, culminating in a deeply reported piece in *The Atlantic* and a book-length nonfiction exposé, continues to press the more inflammatory aspects of this papyrus

[2] *The Word* debuted at ninth place on the *New York Times* Best Sellers list on March 26, 1972, and stayed on the list for thirty-one weeks, making it to number one twice (May 14 and June 4). According to *Publishers Weekly*, *The Word* was the fifth highest selling novel for the year ("Best Sellers: The Year of the Bird and the Bible," *Publishers Weekly* 203.6 [February 5, 1973]: 41).
[3] Laurie Goodstein, "A Faded Piece of Papyrus Refers to Jesus' Wife," *New York Times* (September 19, 2012): A1 and A21, quoted at A21.

"discovery" (I discuss this event and the ensuing fracas in more detail in Chapter 6).

There are many differences between these two headlines; most notably, of course, one purports to be about a piece of fiction and the other about a historical artifact. (As it will turn out, both stories will end up being about forgeries.) Nonetheless, both headlines speak to the same fears and desires about the Bible, centered on a tantalizing possibility: What if some new gospel emerged that could challenge and disrupt the Bible, Christian beliefs, even the age-old institutions of Christianity itself? What hopes and fears might be generated by the possibility of a vulnerable Bible? This book is about those fears and desires; the chapters that follow interweave real-world thinking about the Christian Bible in popular and academic press with their exaggerated and magnified fictional representations in the Gospel Thrillers.

We find versions of the story of a new and disruptive gospel reaching back to the earliest centuries of Christianity itself. In the next chapter, I trace the modern origins of the "lost gospel" narrative in the colonialist and evangelical contexts of the nineteenth and early twentieth centuries. But these two headlines point to a more recent version of this story that is specific to the culture and politics emerging after World War II in the United States. As the Cold War dawned, and even after it petered out and transformed into a global "war on terror" at the end of the twentieth century, the Bible became an object of conspiratorial thinking. What lies was our Bible perpetuating and what truths were being concealed in texts excluded from its covers? What if some new gospel emerged – from the deserts of Israel, from the "secret libraries" of the Vatican, from a hillside monastery, from some lost corner of the third world – that could uncover the Bible's shocking, hidden truths or threaten its integrity with a twisted forgery?

The furor surrounding the Gospel of Jesus's Wife, as well as other new gospel finds from recent decades, such as the Gospel of Judas or the Secret Gospel of Mark (to which I also turn in Chapter 6), make clear that the Bible remains in US culture a distinctive object of fear and desire because of its importance and its vulnerability. This fear and desire are explored in great depth in a genre of novel that was born during the Cold War and continues to appear, almost annually, on US bookshelves. Wallace's *The Word* was but one example of dozens of what I call Gospel Thrillers.

Gospel Thrillers and Lost Gospel Fiction

Gospel Thrillers are a large subset of "lost gospel" fiction, a catch-all category that has received some analytical attention. Robert M. Price, a theologian who gained notoriety for the theory that Christ should be understood as mythical rather than historical, wrote a 2011 survey of what he called "lost gospel" novels. He included a number of novels I exclude from my own study and is more interested in the aesthetic and theological problems with the works surveyed. Historian Philip Jenkins briefly mentions a few of the works I include here as part of his larger invective against popular obsession with finding (or inventing) lost gospels to displace the canonical New Testament. He mentions some early examples of a "fictional genre revolving around rediscovered gospels, genuine or false, and the perplexing world of subterfuge, conspiracy, and assassination in which New Testament scholars seem to operate."[4]

Unlike Price and Jenkins, I am not interested in lodging theological or aesthetic critiques against these novels. My interests lie in how they emerge at a particular moment in US religious politics and how they can in turn inform our understanding of the Bible's complicated place in those religious politics. I trace in Chapter 2 how the Gospel Thrillers emerged out of two intertwining contexts of US culture: biblical authority and conspiracy theory. In this brief introduction, I offer a preliminary definition of Gospel Thrillers and give a sense of their scope.

Gospel Thrillers are English language novels, published primarily in the United States, that follow a common formula: they recount the story of a newly discovered first-century gospel whose shocking contents promise to overturn everything we thought we knew about Christ, Christian origins, and western civilization. In some novels, this lost gospel is revealed completely while in others it is merely discussed or rumored. It always comes from the hand of an eyewitness to the events of Jesus's life or even from Jesus himself. In these novels our

---

[4] Robert M. Price, *Secret Scrolls: Revelations from the Lost Gospel Novels* (Eugene, OR: Wipf & Stock, 2011); Philip Jenkins, *Hidden Gospels: How the Search for Jesus Lost Its Way* (New York: Oxford University Press, 2001), 182. For a partial look at what he calls "discovery novels," including several Gospel Thrillers, see John Kissinger, "Archaeology as 'Wild Magic': The Dead Sea Scrolls in Popular Fiction," *Journal of American Culture* 21.3 (1998): 75–81.

protagonist (usually a man, often with a woman sidekick) finds himself in a dangerous race against time to find the gospel and find the truth. Shadowy antagonists oppose him, often allied with sinister international political or religious institutions (Nazis and the Roman Catholic church feature prominently in many novels). The protagonist travels to exotic locales to learn the truth, embodying at once western privilege and postmodern rootlessness.

This formula is fairly stable, although details vary: sometimes the gospel is a forgery, but more often it is authentic; sometimes the protagonist is an academic, but more often he is an outsider drawn into the intrigues of international antiquities markets; sometimes the "shocking" secret of the new gospel is revealed, sometimes it remains forever hidden. But key elements persist across these novels: the new gospel; the race against time; the protagonist facing off against conspiratorial forces motivated by greed and desire for power.

This description leaves out a small number of related lost gospel novels that may be familiar to readers but which I omit from my study. (I may also have unintentionally left out other novels that do fit these parameters.) I do not discuss novels that are not part of the thriller genre, such Wilton Barnhardt's 1993 comic novel *Gospel* or Simon Mawer's 2002 meditation on loss, *The Gospel of Judas*. In these novels, along with more straightforward mysteries (like Laurie King's *A Letter of Mary* [1996] or Mary Higgins Clark's *The Lost Years* [2012]), the lost gospel often functions as a MacGuffin, a plot device that is ultimately peripheral to the novel's main action. As I explain in Chapter 2, the *thriller* aspect is crucial to the cultural work of these novels: thrillers are the classic narrative form of the conspiracy, in which the discovery of secret knowledge forces protagonists (and readers) to confront the unreliability of their most fervently held beliefs and cherished institutions. Gospel Thrillers place the Christian Bible at the center of a world of secrets and conspiracies, and they comprise the vast majority of lost gospel fiction since the 1960s.[5]

---

[5] For a trenchant analysis of several literary lost gospel novels, see Magdalena Mączyńska, *The Gospel According to the Novelist: Religious Scripture and Contemporary Fiction*, New Directions in Religion and Literature (London: Bloomsbury, 2015), 96–106. The term "MacGuffin" was invented by director Alfred Hitchcock to describe an object of desire that seems central to a story's plot but is really a device to bring particular characters together in conflict: see Todd McGowan, "Hitchcock's Ethics of Suspense: Psychoanalysis and the

Left Behind: Evangelical Thrillers and *The Da Vinci Code*

In addition to focusing solely on *thrillers*, I have also restricted myself
to Gospel Thrillers published by secular presses. This decision means
I have excluded the handful of Gospel Thrillers published by self-
identified Christian (usually evangelical) presses since the late 1990s.
The most successful of these evangelical novels is probably Paul
Maier's *The Constantine Codex*. Maier, a history professor, has writ-
ten a series of novels featuring fictional Harvard biblical studies pro-
fessor Jonathan Weber. In *The Constantine Codex*, Weber and his wife
Shannon discover a copy of a fourth-century codex of the New
Testament containing an "original" lost ending of the Gospel of
Mark as well as an addendum to the Acts of the Apostles ("Second
Acts") recounting Paul's successful trial before the emperor Nero. The
novel posits a tight link between biblical restoration and global
Christian ecumenism: the discovery of the codex, hinted at by earlier
manuscript discoveries in the novel, is made by Jonathan and Shannon
while in Istanbul preparing for an internationally televised debate
between "Christianity" and "Islam," with Jonathan as the spokesman
for Christianity. The novel ends (after the theft of the precious codex
and its recovery from Islamic terrorists) with an ecumenical council of
Protestant, Catholic, and Orthodox Christians voting to "restore" the
recovered texts to the "official" Christian Bible. *The Constantine
Codex*, like all of Maier's novels, was published by Tyndale House,
an evangelical publisher perhaps best known for publishing the wildly
successful *Left Behind* series. The "shocking" finds made in Maier's
novel do not threaten the traditional Christian Bible but rather affirm
it: Mark's "lost" ending provides an early witness for the resurrection
of Christ and Second Acts affirms Christianity's natural place as a
triumphant global religion.[6]

Other novels published by religious presses, like Paul Nigro's *Q*,
similarly take the basic plot of the Gospel Thriller and use it to comfort
Christian readers who might feel unease at the possibilities of biblical
"discovery," revision, and vulnerability: in Nigro's telling, the lost

Devaluation of the Object," in *A Companion to Alfred Hitchcock*, ed. Thomas
Leitch and Leland Poague (Malden, MA: Wiley Blackwell, 2011), 493–528,
at 513–15.
[6] Paul Maier, *The Constantine Codex* (Carol Stream, IL: Tyndale House
Publishers, 2011).

gospel source "Q" (which I discuss in Chapter 6) affirms the accuracy and reliability of the canonical gospels. *Q* and *The Constantine Codex* certainly inhabit the same world of conspiratorial fears and desires that we will see in secular Gospel Thrillers. These evangelical novels also share similar tropes with their secular counterparts: Vatican conspirators are central to Gary Parker's *The Ephesus Fragment*; anxieties about Israeli politics occupy much of Evan Drake Howard's *The Galilean Secret*; secret codes and international travel are central to Terry Brennan's *The Sacred Cipher*.[7]

Despite these aesthetic overlaps, however, evangelical Gospel Thrillers operate in a different literary ecosystem from their secular counterparts. Recent work on the rise of evangelical publishing in the United States, especially its push into fiction, has emphasized how much evangelical fiction promotes a special sense of community among its readers. Amy Johnson Frykholm's qualitative study of *Left Behind* readers uncovers a "longing for community relationships." Daniel Silliman's more recent study of "Christian fiction" explores the "imagined community" of evangelicalism that emerges in "the evangelical book market and Christian bookstores." Of course, it makes sense that a publishing industry grounded in a desire to spread the "good news" of the Bible would similarly market and promote fiction to an audience of biblical believers set apart. While we might imagine various communities of readers for secular Gospel Thrillers (fans of archaeological fiction or of particular authors) their appeal does not come in the creation of a special community set apart from the world. The power and the vulnerability of the Bible in secular Gospel Thrillers emerges, as we shall see, out of the broader currents of US culture during and after the Cold War. If the small handful of evangelical Gospel Thrillers speak in a specialized, insider language, their more plentiful secular cousins speak in a broad, easily accessible colloquial language.[8]

---

[7] Paul Nigro, *Q: A Novel* (Tulsa, OK: River Oak Publishing, 2002); Gary Parker, *The Ephesus Fragment* (Minneapolis, MN: Bethany House, 1999); Evan Drake Howard, *The Galilean Secret* (New York: Guideposts, 2010); Terry Brennan, *The Sacred Cipher* (Grand Rapids, MI: Kregel Publications, 2009).

[8] Amy Johnson Frykholm, *Rapture Culture:* Left Behind *in Evangelical America* (New York: Oxford University Press, 2004), 180–81; Daniel Silliman, *Reading Evangelicals: How Christian Fiction Shaped a Culture and a Faith* (Grand Rapids, MI: Eerdmans, 2021), 218; on the way evangelical publishing markets have actively produced "evangelical publics," see Daniel Vaca, *Evangelicals*

Dan Brown's *The Da Vinci Code* does speak in this broad cultural colloquial language but I nonetheless also exclude it from my study. While I do discuss it a bit in Chapter 2, it differs from Gospel Thrillers in key ways. This blockbuster 2003 novel (made into a blockbuster movie three years later) draws on some of the same themes as Gospel Thrillers and speaks to many of the same fears and desires. It remains a touchstone of cultural anxieties about the Bible and truth (note its casual invocation in the *New York Times* piece about the Gospel of Jesus's Wife I cite above) and often features in post-2003 marketing for and reviews of Gospel Thrillers. But *The Da Vinci Code* does not revolve around newly discovered (or rumored) gospel from the time of Jesus. Instead, Brown uses surviving noncanonical early Christian texts to reconstruct a hidden history of Jesus and Mary Magdalene. The fictional gospels in the novels I am considering give authors and readers space to imagine new biblical possibilities while at the same time allowing readers, at the end of the novel, to set aside those possibilities. Telling readers that Jesus was really married and had children is very different from inventing a fictional gospel recounting his domestic life; Gospel Thrillers give readers an out, an escape valve ("What a clever invention!") that Dan Brown did not allow.[9]

Political, Theological, and Personal Stakes

Even setting aside mysteries, literary novels, evangelical offerings, and *The Da Vinci Code*, we are still left with dozens of novels that have appeared since the 1960s, published by mainstream US and Anglophone presses that continue to be published today. (See this book's Appendix.) They do not seem to be aware of each other: that is, an author of a Gospel Thriller in 2020 does not refer, either in their text or in marketing materials, to previous novels of the same genre. Even the genre label, "Gospel Thrillers," is my own invention. The genre's persistence, then, shows how deeply themes around the Bible and conspiracy run in US culture. What are these themes?

In short: Gospel Thrillers reveal in vivid narrative form the political, theological, and personal tensions that the vulnerable Bible evokes in the US public.

Incorporated: Books and the Business of Religion in America (Cambridge, MA: Harvard University Press, 2019).
[9] Dan Brown, *The Da Vinci Code* (New York: Doubleday, 2003).

That the Bible is a political artifact in the United States may go
without saying. But even beyond the explicit use of the Bible for
legislative or judicial ends, the Bible evokes anxieties about the political
relationship between the West and the East. On the one hand, the
postcolonial Middle East in US politics is a site of unrest and conflict;
on the other hand, it remains a generative place of origins for Judeo-
Christian (i.e., white, western) culture. Would a new gospel from this
ambiguous zone reaffirm and renew Judeo-Christian dominance or
would it prove, once and for all, the foreign strangeness of the Bible?
How Jewish can Jesus be before he unsettles US Christian assumptions? Much of this biblical discomfort with the East has its roots in
broader Euro-American contexts of the nineteenth and early twentieth
centuries, contexts I explore in Chapter 1. During the age of "Bible
Hunters" and colonial missionaries, notions of race, religion, and
politics were deeply entangled in the efforts to produce a more reliable
(i.e., western) biblical text. Those older racial and colonial politics
continue to weave through US biblical fears and desires, coded in the
fictional Gospel Thrillers through generic tropes of exoticism, travel,
and "discovery."[10]

The Bible has also produced theological fears and desires among its
US readers. How do we understand the moral and metaphysical messages of a text that has undergone so many layers of translation and
transmission, often in the hands of untrustworthy religious institutions? Does the Bible reveal sacred truths or is it concealing religious
truths long suppressed? What if the biblical history, morality, and
dogma preached in churches is not telling the whole story? What forms
of belief and practice deemed heretical might flourish if a lost gospel is
found to emend or even supplant the Bible we have? Alternatively:
What dark and subversive moralities and beliefs might rise up from a
strange and distant past?

The Bible as it exists in modern US culture is at once a coherent and
totemic artifact ("the Bible") and the result of centuries of painstaking,
ongoing work executed by an array of scholars ("biblical studies").
While the guild of biblical studies often presents its own work as
objective and depersonalized, Gospel Thrillers probe the human

---

[10] On the ways religion has been and continues to be racially inflected throughout
   US history, see Kathryn Gin Lum, *Heathen: Religion and Race in American
   History* (Cambridge, MA: Harvard University Press, 2022).

knowledge networks involved in reconstructing the Bible: people motivated by personal identities (national, professional, racial, gendered, religious) as well as by personal motives (greed, anger, love, ambition). Gospel Thrillers force us to confront the role of the personal in constructing, or dismantling, biblical truth and the vulnerability of the Bible to these personal identities and motives.

All of these political, theological, and personal tensions are produced and amplified by the way modern biblical studies has come to constitute the Bible as both a fixed yet continually revisable text. The role of biblical studies in generating and mediating these tensions is crucial to understanding the cultural work of Gospel Thrillers, and so I bookend my study with a look at the world of professional biblical studies: its emergence in an era of theological Bible Hunting (Chapter 1) and its attempts to grapple with real-world "shocking discoveries" in recent decades (Chapter 6). The production by professional biblical studies scholars of a constantly revised Bible, which produces its own paradoxes of fears and desires about biblical vulnerability, comes to a head in real-life narratives of gospel discovery that inform and reproduce the fictional narratives of the Gospel Thrillers.

This book is not a literary study of Gospel Thrillers, but rather uses their distinct (and exaggerated) themes and motifs to explore these fears and desires: the persistent "fantasy of 'the Bible,'" in Jill Hicks-Keeton's memorable phrase. My argument is not causal – Gospel Thrillers are inspired by real-world discoveries or biblical anxieties are shaped by Gospel Thrillers – but rather cultural: Gospel Thrillers give us a bright and bold technicolor expression of everyday, persistent, and ongoing hopes and concerns about the unending possibilities of biblical revision. Through them, we see the larger cultural landscape more vividly.[11]

While working on this project I have occasionally been asked why I focus on *gospels* and not *the Bible* as a whole: are there no Torah Thrillers or Prophets Thrillers? The short answer is: no. I can point to one or two novels that, like the Gospel Thrillers, imagine an archaeological or textual discovery related to the Hebrew Bible (the Christian Old Testament); but I have dozens of Gospel Thrillers. Part of this

---

[11] Jill Hicks-Keeton, "The Fantasy of 'the Bible' in the Museum of the Bible and Academic Biblical Studies," *Journal for Interdisciplinary Biblical Studies* 4.3 (2022): 1–18.

imbalance is archaeological realism: a text or even inscription from the time of Moses or David is possible but much less likely than the possibility of a full manuscript from the first century.[12]

But it is also the case that in the US cultural nexus in which *the Bible* emerges as an object of concern, that Bible is a Protestant Christian Bible: reconstructed by Protestant Christian scholarship, circulated by Protestant Christian presses, and normalized as an artifact of Protestant Christian worship. There are, of course, other Bibles: Jewish Bibles, Orthodox Bibles, Catholic Bibles, Mormon Bibles, and so on. The Protestant Christian Bible lying behind the Gospel Thrillers is the unmarked Bible – "the Bible" without qualifier. The comfort and familiarity of the unmarked Bible is temporarily disrupted by the possibility of a new find in the Gospel Thrillers but ultimately left safe. It is for this reason that the shocking secrets in these Gospel Thriller texts are, at the end of the day, rather banal and unlikely to change the world. Yet even when we recognize the ineffectiveness of these lost gospels' secrets, we remain compelled by biblical conspiracy and we keep telling the story of the Gospel Thriller.

---

[12] James Becker, *The Moses Stone* (Berkeley, CA: Onyx, 2009) is about a Hebrew Bible-related artifact and appears in a series featuring two other Gospel Thrillers (*The First Apostle* [2008] and *The Lost Testament* [2013]) as well as a novel about Jesus's body (James Becker, *The Messiah Secret* [Berkeley, CA: Onyx 2010]). Jerry Jenkins (co-author of the *Left Behind* series), *Dead Sea Rising* (Franklin, TN: Worthy Press, 2018) is an evangelical thriller about discovering proof of Abraham.

1 | The Bible Hunters

Two Bible Hunters

In the 1840s and 1850s, Constantin Tischendorf, a dashing and worldly expert on the Bible and ancient manuscripts, traveled from his home in Leipzig to the Greek Orthodox monastery of St. Catherine of Sinai, in Ottoman-controlled Egypt. His goal was to find ancient editions of the Bible to uphold his biblical Christian faith. Over three separate visits to this monastery, Tischendorf came across a complete version of the New Testament in Greek along with significant portions of the Christian Old Testament in a manuscript dating to the early fourth century. This manuscript was, to date, the oldest complete Greek New Testament ever uncovered; it allowed generations of scholars to affirm, correct, and amend the received text of the New Testament. Despite attempts by a noted Greek forger to claim credit for what became known as *Codex Sinaiticus*, Tischendorf's "discovery" remained a watershed moment in European biblical criticism.[1]

In the 1930s, a pious and thoroughly learned archaeologist named Sir William Braceridge arrived from London at the Greek Orthodox monastery of Mar Saba in Jerusalem, a territory under British control but subject to continuing strife from native Arab populations. Sir William was, like Tischendorf, on the hunt for ancient biblical manuscripts that would support his Christian faith. At Mar Saba he discovered, to his chagrin, a fragmentary text purportedly written by Nicodemus – to whom Christ had conveyed the need to be born again and who had assisted at Christ's burial (John 3 and John 19) – revealing that Christ had in fact not risen from the dead; the resurrection never happened and the lynchpin of Christian faith was a deceit and a lie. Fortunately, the local British constabulary in concert with a visiting American millionaire proved that the "Shred of

---

[1] Stanley E. Porter, *Constantine Tischendorf: The Life and Work of a 19th Century Bible Hunter* (London: Bloomsbury, 2015).

Nicodemus" was a forgery, perpetrated by a Greek expert under duress from Nazi plotters.

Tischendorf is historical; Braceridge is fictional, a secondary but crucial character in the 1940 novel *The Mystery of Mar Saba*. Together these two Bible Hunters highlight some of the key ideas about biblical discovery in the late nineteenth and early twentieth centuries, in the decades before the emergence of the conspiratorially minded Gospel Thrillers. Both Tischendorf and Sir William brave strange lands, wield European expertise, confront the possibility of forgery, and defend the biblical truth of their evangelical faiths. They bracket the age of the Bible Hunters.

In this chapter, I enter into the worlds of Tischendorf and Braceridge, a Bible Hunting era of Bible-based theology, textual criticism, colonial administration, and imperial adventure. These worlds offer key background and contrast to the conspiratorial era of the Gospel Thrillers. After tracing the rise of the narrative of the Bible Hunter in the period through World War I and some early fictional portrayals from this period, I turn to *The Mystery of Mar Saba*, which serves as an important prototype and transition to the narratives and themes of Gospel Thrillers. (*The Mystery of Mar Saba* will also undergo its own surprising resurrection in the twenty-first century as we shall see in Chapter 6.)

Major geopolitical shifts following World War II in the Middle East meant the establishment of new nation-states (ostensibly) free from European control. Two new major manuscript discoveries occur during this momentous political transition: the Nag Hammadi codices and the Dead Sea Scrolls. These new discoveries take up and transform the key themes of the Bible Hunter narrative, themes that will also be central to the Gospel Thrillers: imperialist uncertainties, academic pretensions, theological anxieties, and the West's desire for and fear of the biblical remains to be found in the dangerous and exotic East.

The Model of the Modern Bible Hunter

The nineteenth-century era of European imperialism was also the golden age of Euro-American Bible Hunters, who sought out biblical manuscripts along with other ancient testimonies from the apostolic age to bolster their faith. Their particular aims, methods, and political and cultural circumstances set them apart from earlier Christians who had sought out and incorporated new manuscript witnesses into their Bibles in hopes of improving the received text.

Origen, for instance, was a third-century theologian based first in Alexandria (Egypt) and later in Caesarea Maritima (Palestine). A devoted interpreter of the Christian Bible, Origen was dissatisfied with the received text of the Greek Old Testament, the Septuagint. He created a novel textual tool comprising six columns. In one column sat the Septuagint. The other columns contained the text in Hebrew; a transliterated version of the text, that is, the Hebrew words rendered in Greek letters; and three additional Greek translations executed in recent centuries. (Later Origen added two more recent Greek translations.) Origen's multivolume feat, known as the Hexapla (sixfold Bible) was encyclopedic and antiquarian, based on the work of those serious textual critics of his day who sought the best versions of classical texts like Plato and Homer. Medieval scriptoria and early modern scholars continued in Origen's antiquarian vein; the Renaissance saw a renewed burst of interest in producing improved versions of the Bible, now translated into vernacular languages like French, English, and Spanish.[2]

But if Bible Hunters like Tischendorf were not the first to attempt to improve the received text of the Bible, their ambitions took flight on a far grander scale. European powers in this second age of imperial expansion engaged vigorously with the vulnerable Islamic empires to their East and South. European colonial interests were not merely predatory but also grounded in the belief that deep wells of western patrimony lay waiting to be discovered in the "ruins" of the East. Early administrators of the British Raj in India encountered Sanskrit texts that they interpreted as key to understanding their (white) "Indo-European" roots. When Napoleon brought his army into Egypt in 1798, he was accompanied by historical, literary, and archaeological experts intent on finding the primitive roots of their own European (Christian) history. Napoleon's adventures in Egypt were short-lived,

---

[2] Anthony Grafton and Megan H. Williams, *Origen, Eusebius, and the Library of Caesarea* (Cambridge, MA: Harvard University Press, 2006); Wim François and August den Hollander (eds.), *Vernacular Bible and Religious Reform in the Middle Ages and the Early Modern Era*, Bibliotheca Ephemeridum Lovaniensium 287(Leuven: Peeters, 2017); Jonathan Sheehan, *The Enlightenment Bible: Translation, Scholarship, Culture* (Princeton, NJ: Princeton University Press, 2005), 1–25.

but the next Ottoman governor of Egypt sent as an offering to the imperial powers of England and France ancient Egyptian obelisks – "Cleopatra's needles," as they were dubbed – to be erected in European capitals as monuments to a masculinized Roman (that is, white) history extracted from the feminized sands of the Middle East.[3]

As antiquities flowed from the corners of the Ottoman Empire into European hands, so too Protestant missionaries went forth in their belief that all the peoples of the world would soon submit to Christian truth under the banner of empire. Encounters with these objects of Christian missionary zeal produced new ways of understanding "religion" that nonetheless reaffirmed the natural superiority of western (white) Christianity. Drawing on the reports of missionaries, academics began producing complex taxonomies and genealogies of world religions, creating yet more hierarchical connective tissue between the "primitive" East and the "civilized" West.[4]

Into this matrix of colonial-missionary fervor stepped the Bible Hunters of the nineteenth and twentieth centuries. These hunters were armed not only with philological expertise – that is, knowledge of the languages of the ancient world – but also with paleographic expertise – that is, knowledge of how to find, read, and translate ancient and medieval manuscripts out of their cloistered contexts. They began their searches in the libraries and repositories of European capitals, where earlier Renaissance scholars had collected medieval manuscripts. But very soon their targets were the monastic libraries of the lands to the East of Europe, where Christian treasures awaited. Among the most ambitious of these new Bible Hunters was Constantin Tischendorf.

---

[3] Bernard Cohn, *Colonialism and Its Forms of Knowledge: The British in India* (Princeton, NJ: Princeton University Press, 1996); Timothy Mitchell, *Colonising Egypt* (Berkeley, CA: University of California Press, 1991); Bob Brier, *Cleopatra's Needles: The Lost Obelisks of Egypt* (London: Bloomsbury, 2016), 93–155; Donald M. Reid, *Whose Pharaohs? Archaeology, Museums, and Egyptian National Identity from Napoleon to World War I* (Berkeley, CA: University of California Press, 2002).

[4] Tomoko Masuzawa, *The Invention of World Religions: Or, How European Universalism Was Preserved in the Language of Pluralism* (Chicago, IL: University of Chicago Press, 2005); David Chidester, *Empire of Religion: Imperialism and Comparative Religion* (Chicago, IL: University of Chicago Press, 2014).

Two Constantines

Tischendorf had reason to think precious finds awaited him in the East. Already in the eighteenth century, European adventurers had brought back Christian manuscripts among their various exotic souvenirs. In the 1760s, a wealthy and ambitious Scot named James Bruce headed to Africa to find the source of the Nile River. In addition to returning home with elaborate accounts of his exploratory successes, Bruce returned with early Christian manuscripts in Egyptian Coptic and Ethiopic Ge'ez, a tantalizing hint of the textual resources available outside the bounds of Europe. In the 1830s, a minor noble named Robert Curzon extended his Grand Tour from Europe to the Levant and Egypt; his collection of antiquities included manuscripts painstakingly acquired from eastern monasteries where, Curzon claimed, monks were either greedy in their unwillingness to part with ancient texts or so ignorant of their value that they could not imagine what he might use the pages for.[5]

No wonder, then, that young Tischendorf, having already done his best to examine the most reliable biblical manuscripts in the libraries of Europe, turned his sights eastward. Like Origen centuries earlier, Tischendorf was impelled by the desire to improve and correct the received versions of the Christian Bible in Greek. Unlike Origen, Tischendorf was also responding to a school of thought among some German theologians that questioned the historical reliability of the Bible. This new "Higher Criticism," as it was called, was pioneered in the first half of the nineteenth century by German scholars like Friedrich Schleiermacher and Wilhelm de Wette. Its approach to the Bible called for more rigorous attention to the ways that biblical texts came to be compiled, edited, and transmitted over time, ultimately questioning their historical (and theological) reliability. This rationalist stance to the biblical text allowed liberal theologian David Friedrich

---

[5] James Bruce recorded his explorations in five volumes: *Travels to Discover the Source of the Nile* (London: G.G.J. and J. Robinson, 1790); see Rebekah Mitsein, "'Come and Triumph with Your Don Quixote': or, How James Bruce Travelled to Discover the Nile but Found Scotland Instead," *Studies in Travel Writing* 18 (2014): 1–17. Curzon also published accounts of his travels: *Visits to the Monasteries of the Levant* (London: John Murray, 1849); see Ian Fraser, *The Heir of Parham: Robert Curzon, 14th Baron Zouche* (Norfolk: Paradigm Press, 1986).

Strauss, in 1833, to publish his blockbuster *Das Leben Jesu kritisch bearbeitet* (The Life of Jesus Critically Treated), in which he argued that the gospel accounts were largely mythological and self-evidently contradictory, an extreme argument that cost him a prestigious academic post.[6]

Against this rising tide of Higher Critical skepticism, Tischendorf sought refuge in the text, properly and rationally restored by recourse to more ancient and reliable textual witnesses. Tischendorf's approach was "scientific" (in German *wissenschaftliche*, a broader term than the English word), grounded in clear principles of textual criticism that would become the academic discipline of paleography. In his own account of his most famous discovery, *Codex Sinaiticus*, Tischendorf's scientific endeavor naturally leads him to the East. Here's how Tischendorf puts it in a popular account entitled *When Were Our Gospels Written?*, delivered in the 1860s and immediately translated and circulated widely:

The literary treasures which I have sought to explore have been drawn in most cases from the convents of the East, where, for ages, the pens of industrious monks have copied the sacred writings, and collected manuscripts of all kinds. It therefore occurred to me whether it was not probable that in some recess of Greek or Coptic, Syrian or Armenian monasteries, there might be some precious manuscripts slumbering for ages in dust and darkness? And would not every sheet of parchment so found, covered with writings of the fifth, sixth and seventh centuries, be a kind of literary treasure, and a valuable addition to our Christian literature? These considerations have, ever since the year 1842, fired me with a strong desire to visit the East.[7]

The passage is redolent with the Orientalist fantasies that would long animate Euro-American knowledge-making. The "treasures" that would add value to "our Christian literature" – and by "our" Tischendorf surely means his fellow Protestant European Christians, not their eastern Orthodox cousins – are merely "slumbering for ages

---

[6] Porter, *Constantine Tischendorf*, 81–89; Sheehan, *Enlightenment Bible*; John Rogerson, *Old Testament Criticism in the Nineteenth Century: England and Germany* (London: SPCK, 1984).

[7] Constantine [sic] Tischendorf, *When Were Our Gospels Written? An Argument by Constantine Tischendorf with a Narrative of the Discovery of the Sinaitic Manuscript*, 2nd ed. (London: Religious Tract Society, 1867), 20. Porter includes this translation with commentary in *Constantine Tischendorf*.

18 The Bible Hunters

in dust and darkness," unappreciated by their faceless monastic care-
takers. Tischendorf recounts how he discovered and rescued the Greek
Bible from the monastery of St. Catherine's over three separate trips,
literally saving the dismembered codex from being used for kindling by
the ignorant monks. (This trope of rescuing manuscripts from ignorant
eastern destruction persists throughout the modern period.)[8]

At some point during Tischendorf's attempts to find and copy this
precious manuscript, the monks of St. Catherine's become wise to the
value of their holdings. Delicate negotiations, eventually brokered by
the court of Czar Alexander II of Russia ("the natural protector of the
Greek Orthodox faith," Tischendorf reasons), allow Tischendorf to
borrow the remains of the fourth-century codex and transcribe and
reproduce it in his hometown of Leipzig. This Greek Bible he called
Codex Sinaiticus Petropolitanus, a Latin nomenclature that evoked the
scientific labeling current in the biological sciences. *Codex* refers to the
form of the manuscript: a set of leaves bound into a book (like our
modern book), as opposed to a scroll; *Sinaiticus* refers to its site of
"discovery," the monastery of St. Catherine's in Ottoman Egypt; and
Petropolitanus refers to St. Petersburg, the capital of Russia, from
which the Czar financed Tischendorf's work and where soon after
the codex was housed as the Czar's property. (After the Russian
Revolution, *Petropolitanus* was sold to the British Museum; other
portions of the full codex remain scattered across Europe.)[9]

---

[8] On Tischendorf's western disdain for the backward conditions of the "convents"
to which he traveled, see his *Travels in the East by a Pilgrim*. Trans. W. E.
Schukard (London: Longman, Brown, Green, and Longmans, 1851), 95–99, for
his description of St. Catherine's monastery. On the trope of peril – especially
burning – faced by manuscripts before their "rescue" by westerners, see Brent
Nongbri, *God's Library: The Archaeology of the Earliest Christian Manuscripts*
(New Haven, CT: Yale University Press, 2018), 313, n.1.

[9] Tischendorf, *When Were Our Gospels Written*, 25 on the monks who have
"learned the value of these sheets of parchment." Porter, *Constantine
Tischendorf*, 23–47, gives a lucid account of Tischendorf's travels and
codicological and paleographic work on *Sinaiticus*. On the scientizing influence
of Linnaeus and Darwin on biblical criticism – which, as she argues, is also
colonializing, racializing, and sexualizing – see Yii-Jan Lin, *The Erotic Life of
Manuscripts: New Testament Textual Criticism and the Biological Sciences* (New
York: Oxford University Press, 2016). An earlier portion of the codex retrieved
by Tischendorf and published as *Codex Friderico-Augustanus*, in honor of the
King of Saxony who sponsored Tischendorf's first trip east, remains in Leipzig;
other pieces remain in the possession of the Russian National Library and St.
Catherine's Monastery. The disparate sections have been virtually reunited on

This extraction and publication of a biblical treasure slumbering temporarily in the East affirmed the Bible as a piece of western, European patrimony, whose natural home was the scientifically (*wissenschaftliche*) rigorous library of the trained – and pious – text critic. This biblical witness upheld at once western imperial authority and true Christian piety. Theology and politics intertwined. In concluding his account of the Sinaitic discovery in *When Were Our Gospels Written?*, Tischendorf relays the following exchange on the occasion of his receiving honorary degrees from Cambridge and Oxford:

"I would rather," said an old man – himself of the highest distinction for learning – "I would rather have discovered this Sinaitic manuscript than the Koh-i-noor of the Queen of England."

Koh-i-noor, like *Codex Sinaiticus*, was a "treasure" extracted from the East, a massive diamond handed over to Queen Victoria upon her formal annexation of Punjab; it remains today part of the British royal family's Crown Jewels. So too, Tischendorf notes, is *Codex Sinaiticus* a crown jewel of pious Christian faith retrieved from the East:

Providence has given to our age, in which attacks on Christianity are so common, the Sinaitic Bible, to be to us a full and clear light as to what is the real text of God's Word written, and to assist us in defending the truth by establishing its authentic form.[10]

Tischendorf's crown jewel was not without its skeptics. Skepticism of new manuscript discoveries was perhaps to be expected: the prices paid by governments, universities, and museums to acquire rare ancient texts could be steep and created an atmosphere rife for exploitation by honest brokers and forgers alike. Tischendorf worked assiduously to demonstrate the authenticity and antiquity of *Sinaiticus*. It is a telling irony, then, that the most spectacular challenge to Tischendorf's textual triumph came from a notorious forger of manuscripts: Konstantinos Simonides.[11]

---

www.codexsinaiticus.org. See also David Parker, *Codex Sinaiticus: The Story of the World's Oldest Bible* (London: British Library, 2010).

[10] Tischendorf, *When Were the Gospels Written*, 36.

[11] On forgery and its relationship to early modern historical criticism, see Anthony Grafton, *Forgers and Critics: Creativity and Duplicity in Western Scholarship*, new ed. Foreword by Ann Bair (Princeton, NJ: Princeton University Press, 2019). On Simonides, see Andreas Müller, Lilia Diamantopoulou, Christian Gastgeber, and Athanasia Katsiakiori-Rankl (eds.), *Die getäuschte*

By the early 1860s, Simonides had already been involved in several scandalous manuscript forgeries across western Europe, even tangling with Tischendorf in Leipzig earlier in the 1850s. Indeed, it was the highly skilled forgeries passed off by people like Simonides that cast *all* such discoveries, including *Codex Sinaiticus*, under suspicion. How shocked Tischendorf must have been, then, when Simonides published a letter in the London *Guardian* claiming that, as a young man, *he* had written out the Greek biblical codex now erroneously called Sinaiticus.[12]

According to Simonides, the volume was produced as a gift for Czar Nicholas I by the monks of Mount Athos; young Simonides, whose uncle Benedict was the head of one of the monasteries on Athos, had taken over the task from the overworked calligrapher of the monastery, learning to form the ancient letters and consulting the best biblical texts. He was astounded, years later, to find his beautifully bound gift in "much altered" condition, artificially aged, its dedication to the Czar cut away along with his own signature. His attempts to warn learned colleagues – including, he hints, Tischendorf himself – went unheeded, so he thought it best to publicly proclaim that *Codex Sinaiticus* was, in reality, *Codex Simonideios*. (In addition to mocking the pseudoscientific Latin name devised by Tischendorf, Simonides also subtly dewesternized it by using a Greek adjective, *Simonideios*, in place of the Latin one, *Sinaiticus*.)[13]

Scholars now agree that Simonides was lying, but the controversy raged in the English press for almost a full year, with a back-and-forth between Simonides's opponents and supporters. Simonides went to a great deal of trouble to insist on his authorship of this Greek Bible from Sinai; at one point he even produced letters from a certain "Hieromonk Kallinikos" of Alexandria to support his story, letters almost certainly

Wissenschaft: Ein Genie betrügt Europa – Konstantinos Simonides (Vienna: Vienna University Press, 2017).

[12] On Simonides's career as a biblical forger, see Tommy Wasserman, "Simonides' New Testament Papyri: Their Production and Purported Provenance," *Marginalia: LA Review of Books* (July 6, 2018).

[13] Simonides's letter appeared in the September 13, 1862, issue of the *Guardian*; the voluminous press clippings following Simonides's charge are handily collected and commented upon by J. K. Elliott, *Codex Sinaiticus and the Simonides Affair*, Analecta Vlatadon 33 (Thessaloniki: Patriarchal Institute for Patristic Studies, 1982). See also Pasquale Massimo Pinto, "Simonides in England: A Forger's Progress," in *Getäuschte Wissenschaft*, eds., Müller et al., 109–26.

forged by Simonides. His opponents, in turn, solicited British agents abroad to hunt down Kallinikos to prove Simonides's ongoing malfeasance. When the dust finally settled Simonides left England, perhaps for Egypt, and was little heard from again. (In an 1864 book he did, however, include *Codex Sinaiticus-Petropolitanus* as being among his previous publications.) His disruptive intervention into Tischendorf's biblical triumph was short-lived but brings vividly to life many of the underlying political, personal, and theological anxieties that accompanied the endeavors of the Bible Hunters.[14]

Tischendorf framed his "discovery" of *Codex Sinaiticus* as an expert extraction of Christian biblical wisdom from the East; Simonides's bold claim to be *Codex Sinaiticus*'s composer dismantled Tischendorf's triumph on two levels. At the individual level, it suggested the German paleographer's lack of expertise, unable to tell the difference between ancient and modern writing. This little piece of revenge against Tischendorf, whose expertise had been used against Simonides, was no doubt one of Simonides's principal aims.

In a larger sense, however, Simonides called into question the entire enterprise of European Bible Hunting. Bible Hunters relied on the East being a relatively passive and stable treasury of riches available for scholarly examination. While it is true that they might be subject to benign neglect or the occasional ignorant fire, ancient texts were slumbering until awakened by the European paleographer's kiss. Simonides painted a very different picture: active monks, composing new texts in ancient handwriting, reusing premodern codices, masters of their own libraries. Out of these industrious and creative locales, how could any European be certain what he was looking at?

Simonides positioned himself and other native brokers of newly found antiquities as the only safeguards against the kind of whopper of which he accused Tischendorf. Simonides overturned the intellectual

---

[14] Simonides lists Tischendorf's finds as his own compositions, in the front matter of *The Periplus of Hannon, King of the Karchedonians* (London: Trübner & Co., 1864). Lilia Diamantopoulou, "Konstantinos Simonides: Leben und Werk. Ein tabellarischer Überblick," in *Getäuschte Wissenschaft*, eds. Müller et al., 305–25, notes reports of Simonides's death in 1867, 1868, and 1890. The 1867 notice records Simonides dying of leprosy in Alexandria; Anna Mykoniati, "Biographische Bemerkungen zu Konstantinos Simonides," in *Getäuschte Wissenschaft*, eds. Müller et al., 87–106, remarks with skepticism that this was a "somewhat Romantic cause of death (*eine etwas romanhafte Todesursache*)" and that forgeries by him continued to circulate through the 1870s (105, n.55).

and economic system within which Bible Hunters like Tischendorf operated. If they wanted to find ancient authorities to support their biblical text, they would have to rely on eastern expertise *and* pay a sufficient price. Of course, they could never *really* know what they were getting: an ancient manuscript and a clever forgery looked identical. Simonides revealed the East to be an inherently unreliable site for western biblical discovery and recovery, a claim that would land with pointed irony coming from a notorious foreign forger.

In the end, of course, Simonides's gambit failed: Constantin Tischendorf is remembered as the Bible Hunter *extraordinaire* and Konstantinos Simonides as the disgraced forger. Bible Hunters from Europe would continue their hunts throughout the nineteenth and into the twentieth century, taking advantage of the rising might of industrialized Europe and the slow dissolution of Ottoman control over the Middle East. But the subtle anxieties represented by Simonides persisted throughout this Bible Hunting age: that discovery could be revealed as forgery, that western knowledge and power could meet resistance, that the treasure chest of the East could prove an unstable mirage.

Forgers, Converts, and Women among the Bible Hunters

The confrontation between Simonides and Tischendorf also revealed the necessary link between the institutional imperatives of the Bible Hunter and his personal character. Tightly connected institutional sites of knowledge and power made the Bible Hunt possible: empire, university, and church. Imperial money supported the growing prestige of academic expertise which, for these Bible Hunters, was always in service of upholding correct biblical theology. The discovery of biblical antiquities in the East was a boon to all three institutions, enriching and ennobling academics (Tischendorf gained the aristocratic "von" before his surname), enhancing the piety of Europe's rulers, and securing the faith of believers.

The character of individuals was as important as the power of institutions in this enterprise. Biblical knowledge had to be sought and verified through perilous adventure in the East, requiring the upstanding personal character of the Bible Hunter to embody the values of empire, university, and church. Part of Tischendorf's triumph over Simonides, then, was an assertion of personal superiority by the western scholar over the eastern "native": he was the better (whiter) man. Simonides's marked foreignness in many ways made the outcome a foregone conclusion. Yet other more marginal and less straightforward characters from Bible Hunting narratives in the later nineteenth century served as limit cases, testing the image of the pious, noble, learned Bible Hunter.

Moses Wilhelm Shapira was a Christian convert from Judaism who found success as an antiquities dealer in Jerusalem, specializing in biblical antiquities. In 1883, he brought to London what he claimed were almost 3000-year-old fragments of Deuteronomy discovered by Arabs in a cave in the desert. Shapira offered the strips of ancient text to the British Museum (later press accounts said he asked for the staggering amount of £1 million; 50 years later the Museum would purchase *Codex Sinaiticus* for £100,000). Shapira had a decades-long relationship with the British Museum as a supplier of antiquities; he had also been involved ten years earlier in the sale of fraudulent Moabite artifacts to the Old Museum in Berlin. Christian David Ginsburg, a Semiticist consulting with the British Museum, spent a month studying the Deuteronomy fragments; he even published a series of articles on them. At the end of the month, however, Ginsburg proclaimed the fragments forgeries; Shapira fled to the Continent and committed suicide in Amsterdam the following summer, purportedly in shame at his exposure.[15]

The story as told is shot through with the familiar tensions of the Bible Hunting plot: the desire for new ancient texts, the mistrust of the eastern sources of western biblical knowledge, the sure hand of the upright scholar aligned with the institutions responsible for producing knowledge. For decades after Shapira presented his leathery manuscripts for inspection, the story as told continued to pit the shifty easterner against the stalwart European expert, a kind of replay of

---

[15] Fred N. Reiner, "C. D. Ginsburg and the Shapira Affair: A Nineteenth-Century Dead Sea Scroll Controversy," *The British Library Journal* 21 (1995): 109–27; Michael Press, "The Career of Moses Shapira, Bookseller and Antiquarian," *Palestine Exploration Quarterly* (forthcoming, 2023); Chanan Tigay, *The Lost Book of Moses: The Hunt for the World's Oldest Bible* (New York: Harper, 2016). On the role of the British Museum in gatekeeping the white, Christian, imperial framework of the Bible through collection and curation, see Gregory Lee Cuéllar, *Empire, the British Museum, and the Making of the Biblical Scholar in the Nineteenth Century: Archival Fever* (Cham: Palgrave Macmillan, 2019).

Tischendorf and Simonides (including the tragic death of the thwarted forger).

As more recent studies show, the details of the case may not necessarily be so straightforward. Ginsburg, for instance, seemed poised during his month of study to endorse the finds as authentic. He would then have been claiming the mantle of successful Bible Hunter ably assisted by the "native" informant with whom he had worked in the past. Under pressure from various outside experts, however, particularly the French scholar Charles Clermont-Ganneau, Ginsburg chose another narrative path; he preserved his own institutional credentials, as well as his personal bona fides, by portraying Shapira as a foreign fraud.[16]

Yet even this framing of the story obscures important nuance. It is easy, in the imaginary world of the Bible Hunters, to posit Ginsburg as the western authority and Shapira as the eastern informant (or fraud). In fact, both men were Christian converts from Judaism who had emigrated from different areas of Russia-controlled Poland. Both had converted to Christianity before relocating to new territories to pursue careers as experts in the world of biblical antiquities. (Shapira had even published studies of his antiquities in the same literary journal, *The Athenaeum*, in which Ginsburg published his first tentative pieces on Shapira's Deuteronomy fragments.) To portray Ginsburg and Shapira as similar doesn't fit the Bible Hunter story, in which western expertise grapples with eastern chicanery and ignorance. A nakedly anti-Semitic *Punch* cartoon of the time casually portrayed Ginsburg as the white, bespectacled British manuscript detective apprehending the swarthy, hook-nosed "Sharp-*eye*-ra." Only by recasting Shapira as ethnically distinct – non-white – can he become the foreign villain who upholds the familiar image of the Bible Hunter.[17]

Shapira threatened to disrupt the ethnic ideal of the European Bible Hunter. In the final decades of the nineteenth century, two Scottish

---

[16] See Reiner, "C.D. Ginsburg"; Clermont-Ganneau had tangled with Shapira a decade earlier over the faked Moabite statues.

[17] The *Punch* cartoon appeared in the September 8, 1883, issue as *Punch's Fancy Portraits. – No. 152.* (p. 118). Recently scholars have argued for the authenticity of Shapira's scrolls: Shlomo Guil, "The Shapira Scroll Was an Authentic Dead Sea Scroll," *Palestine Exploration Quarterly* 149 (2017): 6–27; Idan Dershowitz, *The Valediction of Moses: A Proto-Biblical Book* (Tübingen: Mohr-Siebeck, 2021).

widows briefly challenged the Bible Hunter's manliness. Twin sisters Agnes Lewis and Margaret Gibson (nées Agnes and Margaret Smith), after decades of intense language study and foreign travels, followed Tischendorf's footsteps to Sinai. There they "discovered" more ancient texts, most spectacularly palimpsests, or reused, overwritten manuscripts, which contained very early version of the canonical gospels written in Syriac (a late form of Aramaic, the language of Jesus). The sisters hunted for the Bible outside of the intertwined institutions of empire, university, and church. Independently wealthy, Lewis and Gibson required no royal patrons to finance their journey. Although highly educated, as women the sisters were excluded from the academic halls of Cambridge, where they had made their home. And while certainly driven by Presbyterian piety to seek out the oldest biblical texts, the sisters, perhaps due to their own socially marginal status, were great friends and supporters of intellectuals well outside their religious circles.[18]

Lewis and Gibson, due primarily to their enormous wealth, were ultimately successful in "discovering" gospel texts, along with other ancient sources, and publishing them back in Great Britain. But they tangled constantly with the institutional forces, primarily at Cambridge, who often sought to transmit the sisters' discoveries through more official (that is, male) university channels. Newspaper accounts of their discovery of the Syriac gospels emphasized their male manuscript "instructor," Cambridge paleographer J. Rendel Harris, and almost always included the picturesque detail that the "lady Orientalists" steamed open the dried pages of the Syriac codex "with their tea-kettle." It is unclear whether their texts would even have been published without the (sometimes reluctant) support of

---

[18] Janet Soskice, *The Sisters of Sinai: How Two Lady Adventurers Discovered the Hidden Gospels* (New York: Vintage Books, 2009). Among their close friends were the Semiticist William Robertson Smith, who narrowly escaped charges of heresy in the 1870s before moving to Cambridge, and Solomon Schechter, a specialist in rabbinics at Cambridge who later became President of the Jewish Theological Seminary in New York: see Stefan C. Reif, "Giblews, Jews and Genizah Views," *Journal of Jewish Studies* 55 (2004): 332–46 and Rebecca J. W. Jefferson, *The Cairo Genizah and the Age of Discovery in Egypt* (London: I. B. Tauris, 2022), 103: "The Schechters also gained friends outside of the university, like Agnes Lewis and Margaret Dunlop Gibson, who, thanks to their gender or religion or both, were excluded from mainstream university life."

University-affiliated colleagues such as Harris, Robert Lubbock Bensly, and Francis Crawford Burkitt.[19]

It is beyond question that Lewis and Gibson had the necessary experience, means, and expertise to engage in the adventures of Bible Hunting. Run-of-the-mill sexism certainly played a role in their snubbing by Cambridge dons and their marginalization in press accounts. But this particular instance of sexism highlights the stubborn image of the Bible Hunting enterprise: it took the institutional surety of men and kings to secure the perilous finds from the East into safe, western hands. This was *adventuring*, after all. Lewis and Gibson, with their independent means, knowledge of modern Greek and Arabic, and their handy tea-kettle, became an exception that proved the rule. Just as Shapira's moral and literal darkening affirmed the upright white character of the Bible Hunter, so Lewis and Gibson's marginalization affirmed his rigorous manliness. These limit cases reinforced the personal character of the Bible Hunter, who must be pious, learned, brave, white, Christian, and male, embodying in his person the virtues of church, university, and empire.[20]

Bible Hunters reproduced certain "truths" about the personal, political, and religious relationship between the West and the East. While it is certainly true that these Bible Hunters enjoyed warm and collaborative relationships with their eastern hosts and assistants, their work was first and foremost the deployment of material and social capital in the service of extracting Christian knowledge from East to West, from the "slumbering" cells of monks to the "scientific" collections of university libraries and museums.

The Bible Hunters enjoyed forms of privilege, indicated by institutional and personal superiority, to transfer these precious textual resources (back) to their supposed proper home, in the West. At the same time, the machinations of a tricky operator like Simonides demonstrated that those precious texts could never shake their foreign roots; they would always bear some remainder of their time in the East

[19] Soskice, *Sisters of Sinai*, 143–213. On the subordination of the women to Harris and the "tea-kettle" see the anonymous early account (printed in multiple venues): "A Syrian Text of the Gospels," *London Echo* (April 13, 1893): 2.

[20] On the very different, multireligious trajectories of the so-called Cairo Genizah in the nineteenth century, see Rebecca J. W. Jefferson, "Deconstructing the 'Cairo Genizah': A Fresh Look at Manuscript Discoveries in Cairo before 1897," *Jewish Quarterly Review* 108 (2018): 422–48 and *Cairo Genizah*.

(as, quite literally, the palimpsests "discovered" by Smith and Gibson retained traces of their overwritten secondary texts). Pious knowledge "recovered" from the shifting sands of the East could never be totally trustworthy; behind every *Codex Sinaiticus* loomed the threat of a *Codex Simonideios*.

Tales of Adventure

The hope for and fear of a biblical text that appears out of the mists of time moved easily from the accounts of public lectures and magazines into the pages of US and British fiction. In a late Sherlock Holmes story, the great detective encounters a sad-sack old professor in a country house; the professor's young assistant has been killed in a failed robbery, and the professor laments the interruption of his work:

"Yes, sir, it is a crushing blow," said the old man. "That is my *magnum opus* – the pile of papers on the side table yonder. It is my analysis of the documents found in the Coptic monasteries of Syria and Egypt, a work which will cut deep at the very foundation of revealed religion."[21]

The unsympathetic professor is a comical and sinister foil to the academic adventurers of previous centuries like Tischendorf or Lewis and Gibson. He is a sickly invalid, unable to adventure on his own to the East. He is also theologically suspect: he doesn't want to uphold biblical truth but rather subvert "revealed religion," probably due to his Russian, Bolshevik roots. Little surprise that Holmes will deduce his complicity in his assistant's death.

In 1924, a US attorney and writer named Arthur Cheney Train, known primarily for his courtroom dramas, published a story in *The Saturday Evening Post* called "The Lost Gospel." While the Holmes story conjures the dark shadow of the nineteenth-century Bible Hunter, Train's "Lost Gospel" updates him for a new age. Here readers encounter the intrepid, upper-class archaeologist digging up secrets in Near Eastern sands now fully liberated from Ottoman rule. After World War I, the aristocratic archaeologist and collector of antiquities became a favorite of mystery writers like Agatha Christie and Dorothy Sayers. The dashing, rich, and well-educated Briton or American with

---

[21] Arthur Conan Doyle, "The Adventure of the Golden Pince-Nez," in *The Return of Sherlock Holmes* (New York: McClure, Philips, and Co., 1905), 260–90, at 277–78.

his glass of sherry and his lucky spade embodied a new set of imperial fantasies. Having survived the fires and gas of a tragic war, what might this adventurer with his wit, wisdom, and will to recover and rebuild the world discover of himself in the exotic sands of the East? Further: What secrets had the sands of the East been concealing for untold centuries?[22]

Train's novella begins among a smart set of British, US, and European travelers, along with an Oxford-educated Egyptian nobleman, on a pleasure cruise down the Nile in 1924. (The echoes of other boats playing recent popular hits on their phonographs create a dissonant sonic backdrop.) A mysteriously recovered letter sends the most intrepid of the group, a stalwart and apparently very wealthy young American man named Calthrop, on the trail of a vanished archaeological expedition from 1914, before the War. That expedition had been led by a pair of archaeologists, one from the United States and one from Germany. Calthrop finds that they had, in fact, discovered not only an Egyptian pyramid (named by the German after their imperial German sponsor, "Wilhelm der Zweite") and a bejeweled Roman sword but the lost gospel itself: a journal written by a traveling Roman aristocrat to the Emperor Tiberius, containing firsthand accounts of Christ's last words and deeds. The German and American fall out over the gospel's apparently pacifist message: the German, enraged, kills his US comrade with the Roman sword and is in turn killed by their fearful Arab guides. The gospel is lost to fire; only the blood-stained sword and a tantalizing Latin fragment remain.

We can recognize key elements from the nonfictional accounts of an earlier era of Bible Hunters: religious discovery intersects with personal character and political interests, all against the dangerous yet alluringly exotic backdrop of the East. What is new, of course, is the fictional gospel, inspired by but very different from the biblical manuscripts brought West by Tischendorf and Gibson and Lewis. Here it's not a

---

[22] Arthur Cheney Train, "The Lost Gospel," *The Saturday Evening Post* 196.49 (June 7, 1924): 3–5, 216–18, 220–22; published the next year by Scribner's. Robert Price, *Secret Scrolls: Revelations from the Lost Gospel Novels* (Eugene, OR: Wipf & Stock, 2011), 14–18 credits Train with creating "a new sub-genre of mystery-adventure." The figure of the swashbuckling archaeologist in the post-War period also appears in early film and endures, of course, in figures like Indiana Jones in the *Raiders of the Lost Ark* franchise: see Jerome de Groot, *Consuming History: Historians and Heritage in Popular Culture* (London: Routledge, 2008), 51.

question of restoring verses or securing a new translation. Train's "Lost Gospel," readers are told, "might have changed the whole history of civilization!" Imagining a new gospel ramps up the personal, theological, and political stakes of the "discoveries" emanating from the East. The atmosphere in these new fictions is still one of adventure, however; characters in these Bible Adventure tales inhabit a world burnt and scarred by World War I, but a world whose order is being restored. "The Lost Gospel" is still a story about western privilege and theological and political triumph over danger.

The Mystery of Mar Saba and the End of Bible Hunting

An evangelical adventure novel published in Canada in 1940 sits at the cusp of the Bible adventures inspired by the Bible Hunters and the new genre of Gospel Thriller that will arise during the Cold War. As we have already seen, James Hunter's *The Mystery of Mar Saba* featured Sir William Bracedridge, a character who evoked the Bible Hunters of the previous century. Sir William is a secondary character, however; the main protagonists are adventuresome imperial agents figuring out how to manage the wily and disruptive East in the wake of the first World War and the fall of the Ottoman Empire.

James Hunter, the author, was an émigré from Scotland who edited the Toronto-based *Evangelical Christian*, a magazine founded to support missionary endeavors abroad. *The Mystery of Mar Saba* was his first novel, followed in 1947 by its sequel *Banners of Blood*; both were published by the same evangelical press that printed his magazine. Hunter wrote other adventure novels, winning awards for his writing from evangelical Zondervan Publishers in the United States. All of Hunter's fiction is rooted in a Bible-focused, global missionary zeal.[23]

The Mystery of Mar Saba's themes and structure replicate Hunter's white, missionary, evangelical, Protestant worldview, mapped onto the military and political divisions of the 1930s. The story revolves around a Nazi plot to cripple the British Empire through acts of terrorism and

---

[23] On Hunter's life and career see my fuller account in "'This Piece of Parchment Will Shake the World': *The Mystery of Mar Saba* and the Evangelical Prototype of a Secular Fiction Genre," *Christianity & Literature* 69 (2020): 91–106 at 91–92; for more analysis of his first two novels, see Reeva S. Simon, *The Middle East in Crime Fiction: Mysteries, Spies, Novels, and Thrillers From 1916 to the 1980s* (New York: Lilian Barber Press, 1989), 116–17.

espionage in British-controlled Palestine. The villain of the novel almost cartoonishly captures the intersection of political, theological, and personal dispositions:

He had the square head that is associated with the typical German, thick lips, a heavy chin and a high forehead. The eyes were small, blue and piercing. In his face there was no pity, humor or kindness. It was that of a man in whom the soul had died, and from whom the spirit had departed leaving only a fleshly automaton to carry out the evil devices of the heart. Such was Professor Heimworth, noted German Higher Critic and archaeologist. (p. 11)[24]

Within a few pages of his sinister entrance Professor Heine Heimworth proclaims the triumph of the unconquerable Fuehrer and the imminent demise of the British Empire. His unwitting archaeologist colleague, Peter Yphantis, piously resists Heimworth's nefarious plans. Yphantis links Heimworth's Nazism, impiety, and biblical criticism explicitly:

"No truer word was ever spoken than that of Queen Victoria when she said that the secret of British greatness was in the Word of God. That faith has been weakened as you, Herr Professor, know, through the permeation of her colleges with the destructive teaching of Higher Criticism, and the use of your text-books in particular. But so many of your 'assured results' are being overthrown today, that you will never succeed that way." (p. 15)[25]

We have already seen how opposition to Higher Criticism's skeptical attitude toward biblical truth animated Tischendorf and the other Bible Hunters of the nineteenth century. In Hunter's novel, Higher Criticism has metastasized into the insidious tool of German academic atheists, disseminated through British universities to weaken faith and empire with its "assured results."[26]

---

[24] On links between German "barbarism," militarism, and Higher Criticism in US evangelical thinking beginning during World War I, see George M. Marsden, *Fundamentalism and American Cultures*, 2nd ed. (Oxford: Oxford University Press, 2006), 141–83.

[25] Victoria's apocryphal bon mot is repeated later in the novel (p. 317), and was immortalized in Thomas Jones Barker's 1863 painting *The Secret of England's Greatness*: see Lynda Nead, "The Secret of England's Greatness," *Journal of Victorian Culture* 19 (2014): 161–82; Jan Marsh, "Icon of the Age: Victoria and *The Secret of England's Greatness*," in *Black Victorians: Black People and British Art*, ed. Jan Marsh (Manchester Art Gallery: Manchester, 2005), 57–67.

[26] Opponents of Higher Criticism referred scornfully to its "assured results" (see Harriet Harris, "Fundamentalist Readings of the Bible," in *The New Cambridge*

Heimworth's Higher Criticism has, however, proved insufficient for Germany's attempts to undermine the British Empire. Heimworth has devised a new plan, only hinted at in this opening chapter but unveiled in the course of the novel: the forgery of a first-century testimony that will prove the resurrection of Christ never happened. One of Heimworth's co-conspirators acknowledges with awe, "'You will not only destroy the British Empire. You will change the history of the world'" (p. 19), a claim repeated throughout the novel. Heimworth blackmails Yphantis, "the greatest living authority on ancient manuscripts," the Protestant child of a Greek father and a German Jewess, into executing the forgery, holding Peter's sister Natalie hostage. Heimworth later attempts to force Natalie to marry him by threatening Peter's life.

Heimworth plants the forgery in the titular monastery of Mar Saba, outside of Jerusalem "in the heart of the Wilderness of Judea" (p. 181). As I described at the beginning of this chapter, it is discovered there by Sir William Braceridge, "one of the greatest living authorities on ancient manuscripts" (after Yphantis, one presumes), on a tour of "several monasteries in search for more Biblical documents" (p. 166). Sir William makes the discovery, which he calls the "Shred of Nicodemus"; the pious Bible Hunter is devastated to be the potential instrument of Christianity's demise. Far from being a destructive critic, Sir William seeks to bolster the biblical text through new discoveries, modeled explicitly on the example of Tischendorf (pp. 166–67, 281, 293).

Sir William presents his findings to the Governors of the British Museum back home and, after the Prime Minister ("a Unitarian" [p. 298]) refuses to intervene, the "Shred of Nicodemus" is published: "the bomb burst on an unsuspecting world" (p. 299). "THE DOWN-FALL OF CHRISTIANITY," screams one headline (p. 301). The godless defenders of "rational Christianity" rejoice while more faithful heads strive to prove the document a forgery. Riots devastate US cities, Indian nationalists call for the expulsion of "all Christian missionaries," and "Communism was increasing" (pp. 306–8, 314).

History of the Bible. Vol. 4: From 1750 to the Present, ed. John Riches [Cambridge: Cambridge University Press, 2015], 328–43, at 331); protagonist Colonel Alderson also ponders how "the Tel Amarna tablets . . . had sadly damaged some of the 'assured results' of Higher Criticism" (p. 22).

Eventually the plot is uncovered and overthrown by the heroes of the tale – Colonel Alderson, the evangelical British head of the Palestine Police, and square-jawed, blue-eyed, US millionaire George Anthony "Tony" Medhurst, whose description contrasts notably with Heimworth's:

Life seemed to have cast all her gifts in his lap. Wealth, a fair measure of good looks and health and strength were his. He stood six feet one in his socks and weighed 195 pounds. His eye was blue and his jaw was square, a little too set perhaps. (p. 31)

Medhurst, a well-educated religious skeptic at the novel's outset, falls in love with Natalie Yphantis and undergoes a dramatic conversion experience in Jerusalem. Working with Alderson and with Dennis, his faithful Methodist retainer, Medhurst saves Natalie, proves the Shred a forgery, and defeats the local band of Arab terrorists – "the Hooded Ones" – who have been organized by Heimworth and his Nazi compatriots. "CHRIST IS RISEN," rejoices the headline in the *Times* of London; biblical faith is restored and Hitler's sinister machinations are delayed, if only for a few years (pp. 407, 410). Tony and Natalie, united in their faith, plan a wedding in the Garden of the Resurrection in Jerusalem.[27]

Much of the novel follows Medhurst's dashing heroics in Palestine, interspersed with strong doses of evangelical Zionism. Britain's imperialist interests and her Christian commitments are intertwined in Palestine. At one point Colonel Alderson notes: "'I believe it is of divine ordination that Britain has the mandate for the Holy Land'" (p. 68). The Jews settling the holy land are praised as a sign of God's providence; Jewish settler displacement of the local Arabs is even at one point compared positively to the displacement of North American "Indians" by European settlers (p. 123). The defeat of the Higher Critic is also the defeat of the Nazi threat and the beating back of the anticolonial resistance of the native Arabs of Palestine. (By the time of his second novel, in 1947, Hunter had grown leery of Jewish settlers,

---

[27] The Garden Tomb was established by the evangelical Palestine Exploration Fund in the late nineteenth century as the authentic site of the Resurrection, far removed from the gaudy inauthenticity of the Church of the Holy Sepulchre (noted by Hunter, *Mystery of Mar Saba*, 266–67): see Annabel Jane Wharton, *Selling Jerusalem: Relics, Replicas, Theme Parks* (Chicago, IL: University of Chicago Press, 2006), 197–206.

whose quest for an independent Jewish state no longer jibed with his apocalyptic Zionism.)[28]

Hunter further maps this intertwining of the political and theological onto ethnicity and gender through his conflict between the handsome, Christian American and the grotesque, faithless Nazi. The contested love interest of both, Natalie Yphantis, the beautiful evangelical daughter of a Greek father and a Jewess, is an unsubtle metaphor for the Christian Bible itself, the merging of Jew and Greek, beloved by the faithful and despoiled by the wicked. It's no wonder her brother Peter can so convincingly forge a false gospel. The triumph of the United States and Britain over Nazi Germany is also the triumph of (evangelical) piety over (higher critical) impiety as well as the triumph of pious manhood – "muscular Christianity" (p. 151) – over impious weakness.

The novel presents us with the same worldview that shaped the Bible Hunters of the previous century: the political, the theological, and the personal united to defend the vulnerable Bible in the dangerous territory of the East. But as the world drifts away from the false sense of hope that followed the first World War into the global conflict of World War II, *danger* looms larger and the hope for triumph feels less secure. Hunter's imperial, missionary, masculinist biblical triumphalism teeters precariously, as Heimworth's careful forgery very nearly *did* bring down the British Empire and pave the way for Nazi victory. The Bible, it seems, is more vulnerable than before.

The "wilderness" of the Middle East had, since before Tischendorf, been an unsettling and unsettled site for the recovery of pious biblical truth, a danger zone only lightly controlled by a secure western hand. *The Mystery of Mar Saba* asks us to imagine that danger coming not only from the hot zone of the East, but from political, theological, and personal divisions in the West. The "native" resistance of Konstantinos Simonides is one thing; what if the pious Bible Hunters also had to contend with shadowy forces in the West colluding to obscure the

---

[28] On evangelical Zionism, see Yaakov Ariel, *An Unusual Relationship: Evangelical Christians and Jews* (New York: NYU Press, 2013) and Robert O. Smith, *More Desired Than Our Owne Salvation: The Roots of Christian Zionism* (Oxford: Oxford University Press, 2013). On *The Mystery of Mar Saba* as "an 'apocalyptic' spy novel," see Reeva S. Simon, *Spies and Holy Wars: The Middle East in 20th-Century Crime Fiction* (Austin, TX: University of Texas Press, 2010), 119; at one point Colonel Alderson proclaims: "I think we are living at the climax of history" (p. 67).

biblical truth? Hunter's novel came out while the Second World War was still raging; Heimworth's defeat was not the final blow against this global enemy of truth and faith. Readers are left to imagine the next round of conflict, as perhaps another new forgery or – perhaps even worse – an authentic *new gospel* comes to light, threatening to change the history of the world.

The political climate in the West and Middle East following World War II, as one age of empires came to a close and a neocolonial age of eastern and western blocs took hold, transformed the imaginary world of biblical discovery. The post-War political reality shaped how two new astounding manuscript finds unfolded in the 1940s and 1950s, and how the story of Bible Hunting adventurers would give way to the conspiracy-minded Gospel Thrillers.

New Discoveries, New Dangers, New Stories

In November of 1953, the *New York Times* on its front page (below the fold) reported an announcement by the Jung Institute for Analytical Psychology in Zurich, Switzerland, of the "preservation of a book of early Christian writings, some of which date from about 150 A.D." The book, the article explains, was one of "thirteen volumes of Gnostic manuscripts containing forty-eight texts or Gospels found in 1945 by Egyptian peasants at a place called Nag Hammadi on the Upper Nile." The other twelve volumes had been, over time, recovered and were held in the "Coptic library in Cairo" where they were "not being made readily available to Western scholars." How this "Jung Codex" (so-called because it was presented as a gift to famous psychoanalyst Carl Jung) had reached Switzerland "the institute ... either does not know or will not reveal."[29]

This is the first major headline in a US newspaper about the finding of various gnostic codices in Egypt in 1945, books which provided new, seemingly first-hand evidence for varieties of gnostic or heretical Christianity from its early centuries, now commonly referred to as the Nag Hammadi codices. That this headline appears a half-decade after the discovery and is about the single volume held outside of Egypt in a

---

[29] Michael L. Hoffman, "Gnostic Gospels of 150 A.D. Found: Throw Light on Early Christianity," *New York Times* (November 16, 1953): 1; see James M. Robinson, *The Nag Hammadi Story*, Nag Hammadi and Manichaean Studies 86 (Leiden: Brill, 2014), 351–485.

European collection hints at some of the new political realities surrounding eastern biblical "discoveries" in the period following World
War II. First, we note the lack of any western Bible Hunter: the books
were "found ... by Egyptian peasants." The texts emerge, unbidden,
from the desert. (I return to the particular Orientalist fantasies contained in this discovery account in Chapter 4.) We also note the
reticence to claim western patrimony over these ancient Christian
books, a reticence notably lacking among the eighteenth- and
nineteenth-century Bible Hunters. The one volume held by Europeans
had arrived in the West by means unknown (or untold). The remaining
books were being maintained as patrimony of the new Republic of
Egypt, not "readily available to Western scholars."

The post-World War II reconfiguration of the Middle East made
Bible Hunting practically and politically difficult. While the British and
French had held direct or indirect control over large swaths of the
Middle East in the decades between World War I and World War II,
their grip loosened dramatically following 1945. In 1952, the year
before the announcement of a gnostic book in Switzerland, a military
coup had toppled the King of Egypt and driven the last British troops
from Suez; in the same year the Egyptian Antiquities Service passed
from French to local control. In 1948, the State of Israel was founded,
which also signaled the formal end of British control of Palestine.
Suddenly the hunting grounds of biblical antiquities were no longer
the sleepy, exotic sands of colonial holdings, but independent nation-
states with volatile and shifting relationships with the West. Instead of
precious texts retrieved by western adventurers we encounter native
finds, like the Nag Hammadi books, haltingly and sporadically made
available to Western scholars.[30]

In his enormously detailed chronicle of the history of scholarship on
the Nag Hammadi books, James Robinson outlines the prolonged
diplomatic efforts undertaken by European and US scholars who
wanted to study, translate, and disseminate the texts found in the

---

[30] On the rise and fall of European control over Egyptian antiquities, see Reid,
Whose Pharaohs and *Contesting Antiquity in Egypt: Archaeologies, Museums,
and the Struggle for Identities from World War I to Nasser* (Cairo: American
University in Cairo Press, 2015), esp. 329–54 on the decolonization of the 1940s
and 1950s. The Nag Hammadi find lies outside Reid's chronological
parameters, but he includes a brief discussion of the find on pp. 223–25 in the
larger context of the Coptic Museum's history.

1940s. (Eventually the return of the Jung Codex, henceforth "Codex I," to Egypt became a precondition for full international access to the remaining volumes.) From 1952 the books were kept in the Coptic Museum (not, as the *New York Times* reported, the "Coptic library in Cairo") as part of Egypt's national patrimony.[31]

Reading through the voluminous correspondence collected by Robinson from the 1950s and 1960s one can sense the impatience of western scholars engaged with the Egyptian authorities and the tussles between rival European academics for access to the ancient texts: "I hope," wrote one French scholar to another while waiting for word about such access, "to have by then some further information that will permit me to see a bit more clearly into a situation that seems to me singularly complicated and difficult."[32]

From the perspective of these European scholars, as long as the texts remained unseen by western eyes they remained in a sort of stasis, reminiscent of Tischendorf's manuscripts "slumbering" in monasteries or – even worse – subject to "mutilation" at the hands of purportedly inexpert Egyptian conservators working without western "consultants." The colonial sense of privilege enjoyed by earlier Bible Hunters diminished, but by no means disappeared. Scholars were eager to participate in an international committee dedicated to the study and publication of the Nag Hammadi texts, but at the same time bristled at the perceived lack of rigor or fairness under Egyptian leadership. Eventually, European scholars managed to form a team under the international auspices of UNESCO, a neocolonial concession that allowed the West to act as partners with the East rather than outright dominators.[33]

The other major discovery of the 1940s, the Dead Sea Scrolls, reveals even more starkly the post- and neocolonial shifts in biblical "discoveries" following World War II. In 1946 or 1947, within a year or so of the appearance of the Nag Hammadi texts, a cache of ancient documents in Hebrew and Aramaic began filtering into the antiquities market. Early documents included the oldest Hebrew versions of biblical books; soon biblical interpretations and sectarian literature

[31] Robinson, *Nag Hammadi Story*, 123, 487–88.

[32] From a letter from C.-H. Puech to Jean Doresse in 1956, translated and cited by Robinson, *Nag Hammadi Story*, 697.

[33] Robinson, *Nag Hammadi Story*, 342–43 on "mutilation" of the codices; pp. 948–1038 on the orchestrated takeover by UNESCO.

emerged, as well. The first English-language press announcements
from 1948 reported that the Scrolls were found "in the library of the
Syrian Orthodox monastery of St. Mark in Jerusalem." These echoes
of that familiar Bible Hunting era narrative – including at one point
accusations of forgery – soon gave way to a story a lot like the one
surrounding the Nag Hammadi books: a serendipitous discovery by
unsuspecting locals, the true magnitude of which could only be
affirmed by some exertion of western expertise. (I return to the particular Orientalist fantasies of *this* discovery account in Chapter 3.)[34]

In 1955, US writer and literary critic Edmund Wilson wrote an
extended piece for the *New Yorker* magazine, laying out the contexts,
debates, and ramifications of the discovery of millennia-old Hebrew
and Aramaic scrolls recovered from caves near the Dead Sea. Much of
the standard popular and scholarly narratives surrounding the Scrolls
takes shape in Wilson's account: the find by Muhammed "the Wolf";
the attempts by the Syrian Orthodox bishop of St. Mark's, Metropolitan
Samuel, to raise money from the Scrolls; parallel attempts by scholars
from multiple faiths and national backgrounds to secure the Scrolls; the
Scrolls' relation to an ancient "monastic" Jewish sect and to the origins
of Jesus's movement. All of these strands continue to be unspooled in
historical and historiographic accounts of the Dead Sea Scrolls today.
What remains more vivid in Wilson's 1955 account are the post-World
War II politics that shaped the early life of the Scrolls, politics which
have receded in more recent accounts.[35]

[34] The announcement came from the public relations office of Yale University,
where Millar Burrows, director of the American Schools of Oriental Research in
Jerusalem, was on faculty. The announcement is reproduced in John J. Collins,
The Dead Sea Scrolls: A Biography, Lives of Great Religious Books (Princeton,
NJ: Princeton University Press, 2013), 1–2 and 146. When Burrows published
photographs of the scrolls found by Metropolitan Samuel, he titled the two-
volume set *The Dead Sea Scrolls of St. Mark's Monastery* (New Haven, CT:
American Schools of Oriental Research, 1950–1951), acknowledging the
monastery's ownership of the Scrolls but still evoking earlier Bible Hunting
narratives. Accusations of forgery were lodged by historian Solomon Zeitlin: see
my discussion in Chapter 3.

[35] Edmund Wilson, "A Reporter at Large: The Scrolls from the Dead Sea," *New
Yorker* (May 14, 1955): 45–131, lightly expanded as *The Scrolls from the Dead
Sea* (New York: Oxford University Press, 1955) and expanded further as *The
Dead Sea Scrolls: 1947–1969* (New York: Farrar, Straus, Giroux, 1969). On the
persistent narratives in Dead Sea Scrolls studies, see Edna Ullmann-Margalit,
Out of the Cave: A Philosophical Inquiry into the Dead Sea Scrolls Research
(Cambridge, MA: Harvard University Press, 2006). Geza Vermes, *The Story of*

The early months after the first Scrolls appeared on the antiquities market were busy ones. Metropolitan Samuel was trying to verify the worth of the Scrolls; Eleazar Sukenik, the lead archaeologist from the Zionist Hebrew University, was seeking to acquire his own scrolls directly from the Bedouin; and scholars from the Palestine Archaeological Museum and the École Biblique, led by French Dominican priest Roland de Vaux, were exploring the caves where the first Scrolls were found, eventually uncovering thousands more fragments and remains. These first years of Dead Sea Scrolls exploration and recovery were also embedded in political turmoil, as the British prepared to withdraw from Palestine in spring of 1948 and the United Nations announced a partition of the territory between Zionist Jews and the surrounding Arab states.

Wilson paints a picture of constant violence and danger. On the first page he describes the Jewish "terrorist groups which had been murdering British soldiers." When Sukenik successfully returned from Bedouin territory with his own scrolls and called an exhilarated press conference, Wilson describes him as "quite unperturbed by the flashing and banging" of bombs around him. (By contrast, a US journalist who tried to attend the press conference "fainted in the street on the way, and had to be carried in by his colleagues.") When the British formally withdrew in 1948, "leaving the Jews and the Arabs already at one another's throats," the Monastery of St. Mark from which Metropolitan Samuel hailed was nearly destroyed in the shelling of the Old City of Jerusalem.

While the Egyptian Revolution of the early 1950s established total control over the sovereign nation and its antiquities, including the Nag Hammadi codices, the Dead Sea Scrolls were split by the international lines established in the wake of the wars following the establishment of the State of Israel in May 1948. The armistice of 1949 left the Scrolls divided: Metropolitan Samuel had fled with his Scrolls to the United States, where he hoped to sell them and rebuild his monastery; Sukenik and Hebrew University's Scrolls were in the new State of Israel; the Dead Sea caves and the Scrolls recovered from them by the École

the Scrolls (New York: Penguin, 2010), 22–23, briefly acknowledges the fraught political context. Weston W. Fields, *The Dead Sea Scrolls: A Full History.* *Vol. 1: 1947–1960* (Leiden: Brill, 2009) is the most detailed account of the first decade of Scrolls scholarship.

Biblique and the Palestine Archaeological Museum were now subject to Jordan's Department of Antiquities.

By the time he wrote his extended piece in the early 1950s, Wilson was observing an academic landscape of Dead Sea Scrolls studies shaped by and reproducing the violent geopolitical and religious contexts of their discovery. Israeli Jews did not cross into Jordan, nor did the international team of predominantly Christian scholars under Father de Vaux attend lectures at Hebrew University. The religious and political boundary functioned as a scholarly barricade:

> The people at [Hebrew] University know nothing of de Vaux's discoveries, except what they learn at long intervals from the reports in the *Revue Biblique* (a quarterly journal published in Paris but edited by de Vaux from Jerusalem) . . . At the same time, till the very recent publication of the Hebrew University texts, the Christian scholars had no access to them . . . Thus the enmity between Jew and Arab is contributing to the obstacles and touchiness of this curious situation, which has also been a little affected by the rivalry between Jews and Christians.[36]

Until 1967, when the Israeli military reunited Jerusalem, the Scrolls remained divided between two scholarly centers with nebulous connections to the West. The international scholars under de Vaux's leadership were obviously linked to western scholarship but also remained under non-western control: Wilson notes that de Vaux's *Revue Biblique* emerges simultaneously from Paris and Jerusalem. The pale aura of Vatican authority behind the Catholic scholars of the École Biblique would, over time, engender even more suspicion and confusion.[37]

Meanwhile the first generation of Jewish scholars at the Hebrew University had one foot in the European university, after which their own institution was modeled and from which most of them had received their training; at the same time, their academic project was grounded in a "return" to Zion predicated on their native "middle easternness." Sukenik's son, Yigael, followed in his father's footsteps after serving in the new Israeli Defense Force in the first years of the new nation; he wrote a dissertation on Hebrew University's Dead Sea

---

[36] Wilson, "Scrolls from the Dead Sea," 106.
[37] On the École Biblique and De Vaux, see Collins, *Dead Sea Scrolls*, 10, 16–20 and Vermes, *Story of the Scrolls*, 24–51, 66–67 and my further discussion in Chapter 3.

Scrolls and managed to purchase the Scrolls Metropolitan Samuel had put up for sale in the United States. By the time Yigael Sukenik was established as the premier archaeologist of Dead Sea antiquities he had begun to go by a Hebrew surname acquired during his time in the military: *Yigael Yadin*. The one-generation path from immigrant Eleazar Sukenik to native Yigael Yadin conveys the similar transformation of Zionist European Jewry into something more ambiguously non-European: the "native" Israeli, the *Sabra*.[38]

The discovery and dissemination of the Dead Sea Scrolls caught public imagination more quickly and flamboyantly than the study of the Nag Hammadi texts taking place at the same time. There are several reasons for this difference. The biblical and parabiblical contents of the Dead Sea Scrolls made them more familiar to western audiences, akin to the manuscript "discoveries" of the earlier, Bible Hunting era. Their context, too, was more evocative: near in space and time to the life of Jesus, always carrying the hope and promise of illuminating something from Christ's life. Finally, the complex networks in which the Scrolls were embedded immediately and continuously generated controversy across multiple political and religious lines. The new State of Israel embodied in a new way the ambiguous role of the Middle East as a site of western discovery, founded primarily by European and US immigrants, but quickly calling into question the rather recent whiteness acquired by Jews in the West.[39]

Both archives, however, represent critical transformations in the imaginary world from which new fictional gospels would emerge beginning in the 1960s. To be sure, key elements of the "discovery" narrative from the earlier Bible Hunting era remained: religious discovery intersected with personal character and political interests, all

---

[38] On Yadin, see Neil Asher Silberman, *A Prophet from Amongst You: The Life of Yigael Yadin: Soldier, Scholar, and Mythmaker of Modern Israel* (Reading: Addison-Wesley, 1993); on the complications of European/white identity in Israel, see Raz Yosef, *Beyond Flesh: Queer Masculinities and Nationalism in Israeli Cinema* (New Brunswick, NJ: Rutgers University Press, 2004), 31–47 and my further discussion in Chapter 3.

[39] On the precarious and recent whiteness of (especially US) Jews see Karen Brodkin, *How Jews Became White and What That Says About Race in America* (New Brunswick, NJ: Rutgers University Press, 1998); Eric Goldstein, *The Price of Whiteness: Jews, Race, and American Identity* (Princeton, NJ: Princeton University Press, 2006); Cynthia Levine-Rasky, *Whiteness Fractured* (New York: Routledge, 2013), 133–41.

against the dangerous yet alluringly exotic backdrop of the East. But the depth and proportion of these themes changed. The East could no longer be imagined as a site of western privilege, the locale from which knowledgeable European and US hunters could extract new biblical truths, unstable but timeless, like the pyramids. These were now sovereign states, requiring negotiation and asserting their own rights to control and produce biblical knowledge. They sat at a crossroads of new geopolitical rivalries, able to ally themselves with political blocs. As if to reinforce this independent East, the texts were no longer "discovered" by western adventurers but were brought forth and brokered directly by the inhabitants. Any sense of control that men like Tischendorf might have asserted a century earlier was now even more tenuous.

The unsettling contents of the Nag Hammadi books and the Dead Sea Scrolls only reinforced this sense of loss of control. Tischendorf and Lewis and Gibson found in the East biblical manuscripts that might obligingly shore up their theologically sound Bibles; these new texts were more apt to disrupt than affirm the Protestant, Christian Bible. The earliest Dead Sea Scrolls to be made public were reassuringly biblical; early headlines usually trumpeted the discovery of the "Oldest Copy of the Book of Isaiah." Later Scrolls were more florid and esoteric, remains of a Jewish sectarian group whose strange rules and customs could paint a very different picture of Jesus's milieu. While the Nag Hammadi texts were later, they were also evidence of decidedly unorthodox forms of earliest Christianity.

As I explain in the Chapter 2, US anxieties about the Bible as well as the new, Cold War genre of *thriller* quickly incorporated these new, disruptive possibilities of biblical discoveries. When the first authors of Gospel Thrillers in the 1960s sat down to imagine what might emerge from the sands of history, and how the West would deal with them, their stories were transformed and mutated versions of Cheney's and Hunter's tales of Bible Hunting adventure and triumph. Gospel Thrillers would imagine a vulnerable Bible in a world disturbed and overturned by new discoveries, new politics, and new possibilities.

2 | *Birth of a Genre*

Two Meetings

The early 1980s: two professors and a graduate student from different US universities are summoned to a hotel room in Geneva by an anonymous antiquities dealer, "an Egyptian," to examine three ancient books for sale. Two are in Greek and one is in Coptic, the language of the Nag Hammadi codices. No photographs are allowed, only a brief time for the three men to inspect the books. Unable to come to terms with the Egyptian dealer – the academics can muster up about $200,000; he is asking $3 million – the two professors, the graduate student, the dealer, and his translator retire to an amiable lunch. During lunch, the graduate student sneaks to the bathroom to makes notes on the Coptic text he has seen; it includes a mysterious dialogue between Jesus and his apostles, particularly Judas. The men part ways, and this Gospel of Judas vanishes before pieces of it turn up in a safe deposit box in New York twenty years later.

Also the early 1980s: a US journalist taking a Mediterranean cruise is approached while touring ancient sites in Ephesus by a man posing as a US vice-consul. The "vice-consul" wants to introduce the journalist to a local retired archaeologist with an amazing tale about a discovery made decades earlier: a secret gospel written by the apostle John with stories told to him by Jesus's mother Mary. The meeting takes place in the journalist's state room where the old man unfolds an incredible tale about a gospel whose contents will shock the world. Before the journalist can see photographic proof of this astounding find, the old man is murdered and all traces of these lost "Ephesus scrolls" vanish before its missing pages finally turn up in a monastery in Greece.

The first meeting actually happened and the second is fictional. The first has been recounted in many contexts by the graduate student in question, Stephen Emmel (now a senior professor in Germany), following the reemergence in 2006 of the Coptic codex containing the Gospel of Judas. (I discuss this Gospel and its attendant publicity in

Chapter 6.) The second meeting comes from a novel, *The Keepers of the Secret*, published in 1983 and coauthored by a flamboyant US writer and Greek media impresario. These two meetings give us an entry point the origins, characteristics, and scope of the Gospel Thrillers as a genre. Both meetings envelop a newfound gospel in secrecy and deception. Unnamed dealers, false identities, and international intrigue transmute the heroic tales of Bible Hunting adventure into the shadowy realms of the Gospel Thrillers. Constantin Tischendorf retrieving manuscripts "slumbering" in eastern monasteries makes way for the US graduate student making surreptitious notes in a café bathroom to avoid detection.

Bible Hunters inhabited a world of colonial adventuring; Gospel Thrillers imagine a world of conspiratorial danger, at the center of which lies the Bible. In this chapter, I enter into this new imaginative world by exploring these twin themes of conspiracy and the Bible in US politics and culture as they developed during the Cold War era. I dive into the shadowlands of conspiracy, the controversies over "the Bible" in the United States, and then turn to the first published Gospel Thriller from a US press, *The Q Document*, to break down the anatomy of this new genre.

Conspiracy Theory: Politics and Aesthetics

It may feel like our present moment is particularly rich in conspiracy theories. We live in the age of "fake news": 9/11 Truthers, birthers, Q-anon, and countless other conspiracy theories that promise to expose the sinister truth behind the veneer of the visible. In May 2020, *The Atlantic* magazine published an online project called "Shadowland," a cluster of essays and articles on the current prevalence of conspiracy theories in the United States. In his brief introduction, *The Atlantic* editor-in-chief Jeffrey Goldberg expressed dismay that the President of the United States at the time displayed the same "weakness for conspiratorial thinking" as 9/11 deniers or mendacious talk radio hosts. Goldberg analogized conspiracy theories to a disease against which "healthy societies develop antibodies." The suggestion is that the United States right now is sick.[1]

---

[1] "Shadowland": www.theatlantic.com/shadowland. Of these essays only Adrienne LaFrance's on Q-anon appeared in the subsequent print issue: "Nothing Can Stop What Is Coming," *The Atlantic* (June 2020): 27–38. Jeffrey Goldberg, "The Conspiracy Theorists Are Winning," online at www.theatlantic

The hook of "Shadowland" is the boom in conspiracy theories at the time of publication; the special threat of Trump and Trumpism is a thread weaving together all of these essays. Yet the series also acknowledges how deeply embedded conspiratorial thinking has been in US history: "America owes its existence, at least in part," the introductory splash page announces, "to conspiracy thinking." One essay even dives into the nineteenth-century archives of *The Atlantic* itself to trace the conspiratorial atmosphere during and after the US Civil War. Undeniably, conspiracy theories in the twenty-first century are more visible, thanks mainly to social media's amplification effects. They have also taken on a particular shape in US politics and culture since the latter half of the twentieth century.[2]

It was during the Cold War that theorizing about conspiracy theory became its own sort of US pastime. The doyen of conspiracy theory was Pulitzer-prize winning historian Richard Hofstadter. In a lecture delivered at Oxford on November 21, 1963 – the eve of the assassination of US President John F. Kennedy – Hofstadter offered his first diagnosis of what he called the "paranoid style" of US politics. (Hofstadter clarified that his use of the term "paranoia" – which has persisted as a term of art in studies of conspiracy theory – was meant analogically, not "in a clinical sense.") In 1964 he published an abbreviated version of the speech as an essay in *Harper's Magazine*; in 1965 an expanded version formed the core essay of a book with the same title. In this essay Hofstadter posits that conspiracy theories are an irrational response to perceived democratic disenfranchisement.[3]

Like *The Atlantic* authors writing almost sixty years later, Hofstadter acknowledges the deep roots of conspiracy in US history:

.com/ideas/archive/2020/05/shadowland-introduction/610840. See also Jesse Walker, *The United States of Paranoia: A Conspiracy Theory* (New York: Harper Perennial, 2013).
[2] Annika Neklason, "The Conspiracy Theories That Fueled the Civil War," *The Atlantic* (May 29, 2020), online at www.theatlantic.com/politics/archive/2020/05/conspiracy-theories-civil-war/612283; see also Gordon Wood, "Conspiracy and the Paranoid Style: Causality and Deceit in the Eighteenth Century," *William and Mary Quarterly* 39 (1982): 401–41.
[3] Richard Hofstadter, "The Paranoid Style in American Politics," *Harpers Magazine* (November 1964): 77–86. I cite from the latest version of the expanded essay in *The Paranoid Style in American Politics*, intro. Sean Wilentz (New York: Vintage Books, 2008), 3–40. For Hofstadter's professional and political context, see Mark Fenster, *Conspiracy Theories: Secrecy and Power in American Culture*, rev. ed. (Minneapolis, MN: University of Minnesota Press, 2008), 23–42.

from fear of the Illuminati in the eighteenth century to anti-Masonic and anti-Jesuit conspiracies in the nineteenth century. Also like *The Atlantic* writers, Hofstadter suggests something is different now: "mass media" has amplified the message of "Radical Right" conspiracists (the primary targets of Hofstadter's analysis); they exist on a "vast theater" of international politics first opened up by World War II but reinforced by the Korean War and the Cold War; they perceive a deeply embedded (Communist) infiltration into the US government that must be rooted out by other, more faithful agents in that same government.[4]

For Hofstadter, the modern conspiracist is distinguished by his "paranoid style" of viewing the world: "History *is* conspiracy, set in motion by demonic forces of almost transcendent power, and what is felt to be needed to defeat it is not the usual methods of political give-and-take, but an all-out crusade" (emphasis in original). While engaged in this urgent, "apocalyptic" thinking, this paranoid style is also obsessively fact-based, collecting as much information as possible on the shadowy forces at work to appear "if not wholly rational, at least intensely rationalistic." Hofstadter repeats throughout his essay that the "paranoid style" is not a "normal" (that is, "rational") way of doing politics in the United States, that is, not "the normal political processes of bargain and compromise." The suggestion, like Goldberg's in *The Atlantic*, is that the rise of conspiratorial thinking in US politics is anomalous (if persistent) and therefore can be overcome, or at least tamped down, by a return to rational political consensus-building.[5]

Hofstadter's pathological framing of conspiracy theory has been challenged from other political vantage points that are less optimistic about the "normal political processes of bargain and compromise" in the United States. Critical theorist Frederic Jameson in a long essay entitled "Totality as Conspiracy" analyzed US films from the 1970s and 1980s, such as *Videodrome*, *The Parallax View*, and *Three Days of the Condor*. These films grapple with the new form of conspiracy theory "on the scale of the globe itself": "a narrative structure capable of reuniting the minimal basic components: a potentially infinite network, along with a plausible explanation of its invisibility." In a world in which the hidden mechanics of global capitalism move the levers of everyday existence through the faceless workings of bureaucracy,

---

[4] Hofstadter, *Paranoid Style*, 24–26.   [5] Hofstadter, *Paranoid Style*, 29, 36.

conspiracy narratives "promise a deeper inside view" of the otherwise ungraspable political and economic forces that control our lives. The idea that a protagonist who has stumbled onto the conspiracy might actually expose and dethrone the plot is, Jameson admits, "Utopian" and ultimately bound to fail; the hope is nevertheless a reasonable response to the immensity of life under late capitalism.[6]

More recently Mark Fenster has argued that conspiracy theory is marginal but is "an integral aspect of American ... life," a populist element endemic to the peculiar democratic/technocratic paradoxes of US politics. "Conspiracy theory," he writes, "as a populist theory of power ... is an ideological misrecognition of power relations, calling believers and audiences together and into being as 'the people' opposed to a relatively secret, elite 'power bloc.'" Conspiracy theory, he suggests, is a democratic fantasy that makes perfect sense in a political system that is idealistically "by the people" but is realistically controlled by a very few elites.[7]

While Fenster rejects Hoftstadter's view of conspiracists as marginal or pathological, he happily adopts the notion that conspiracy has a particular *style*, a specific kind of interpretive engagement. Conspiracy theory in the twentieth and twenty-first centuries, he states, is a form of "hyperactive semiosis in which history and politics serve as reservoirs of signs that demand (over)interpretation, and that signify, for the interpreter, far more than their conventional meaning." This chain of overinterpretation is functionally endless: "Each new detail leads to the need for more details." Conspiracy's style is kaleidoscopic and somewhat dizzying in its attempts to seek out and find new pieces of an everexpanding puzzle.[8]

Paranoia American Style: From the Cold War to Q-anon

The particular style of conspiracy theory at issue is also distinctly "American": an aesthetics of time, place, culture, and politics grounded in ideas and ideals about the United States. The Cold War that followed World War II was shaped by and reproduced this "paranoid style." By definition the Cold War was conducted not with

---

[6] Frederic Jameson, *The Geopolitical Aesthetic* (Bloomington, IN: Indiana University Press, 1992), 9–86.
[7] Fenster, *Conspiracy Theories*, 89.   [8] Fenster, *Conspiracy Theories*, 95, 107.

open conflict and armies but with espionage and secret information. When Senator Joseph McCarthy warned in 1950 that "the State Department ... is thoroughly infested with Communists" and held up a sheet of paper supposedly listing fifty-seven such infiltrators, he gave voice to the paradoxical paranoia of the age. The "cold war" that McCarthy described was global and operated on a "vast theater" (to use Hofstadter's phrase): "All the world is split into two vast, increasingly hostile armed camps ... You can see it, feel it, and hear it all the way from the hills of Indochina, from the shores of Formosa, right over into the very heart of Europe itself." Naturally one could not "see, feel, and hear" these far-off places from the Wheeling, West Virginia, Republican women's meeting where McCarthy delivered these remarks or from the floor of the Senate where he read them into the *Congressional Record* a few weeks later. For McCarthy, the danger emanating from this "vast" and unseen conflict came from those inside the United States who sympathized with "their" ideology, of whom the fifty-seven infiltrators were the tip of a conspiratorial iceberg.[9]

The pervasiveness and invisibility of the "enemy" required constant vigilance. The Cold War as it took shape in the 1950s was the age of the double-cross: the enemy who was at once diametrically opposed to "our" values (McCarthy states it baldly: "communistic atheism" versus "Christianity") yet could pass among "us" unseen. The political realm was the site of danger, vulnerable to attack; yet it was also the scene of hope and resistance where heroic patriots like McCarthy worked to root out the infiltrators. The same oppressive bureaucratic tools that proliferated throughout postwar society could be transformed into the tools of salvation. McCarthy's specificity about numbers of names on sheets of paper makes the growing paper-pushing bureaucracy a crucial source for the truth-seekers to unmask their hidden enemies. The musty archive allowed the enemy to move in the shadows but also allowed the hero to discover and expose them.[10]

The idea that the US state was being furtively divided against its own interests and ideals was not, of course, the sole purview of

---

[9] For the Senate version of McCarthy's speech, see *Congressional Record* 96.2 (February 20, 1950): 1954–56, online at www.govinfo.gov/content/pkg/GPO-CRECB-1950-pt2/pdf/GPO-CRECB-1950-pt2-12-1.pdf.

[10] On the conspiratorial fears about rising bureaucracy during following World War II, see Timothy Melley, *Empire of Conspiracy: The Culture of Paranoia in Postwar America* (Ithaca, NY: Cornell University Press, 2000), 47–79.

anti-Communist right-wing politics. The growing entanglement of the United States in military incursions abroad (McCarthy's "hills of Indochina"), culminating in the disastrous war in Vietnam, propelled an anti-war movement positioned against the shadowy and vast "military industrial complex." Opponents of war in Asia assumed that the motives of the hawks were disingenuous, propelled by love of either power or money or both. The publication of the so-called Pentagon Papers by the *New York Times* in 1971 provided fodder for left-wing accusations of conspiracy. In this case, too, a principled former government worker, Daniel Ellsberg, turned the State Department's archive of secrecy against itself.[11]

Behind the shadowy cat-and-mouse Cold War games of Communist sympathizers, war-hungry hawks, and government loyalists lay fears of a nuclear "hot" war. Already in 1950 McCarthy was warning of "armaments," and the rise of atomic bomb testing in the early 1950s made clear the devastating impact a nuclear war would have. The fear was real, driven home by specific scares in the 1960s (such as the Cuban Missile Crisis in 1962) as well as the pervasive presence of nuclear preparedness (shelters, air raid drills) and sensational media (movies as well as the new medium of television).[12]

Hofstadter had noted the "apocalyptic" tenor of right-wing paranoia; in his study of conspiracy theory, Fenster considers Christian apocalyptic conspiracies fueling right-wing militia movements in the 1970s and 1980s. Fenster links them to a broader undercurrent of "popular eschatology" emerging out of fundamentalist Christianity. Perhaps this popular eschatology fueled the nuclear panic that, in turn, gave such urgency to Cold War fears of conspiracy and infiltration. Or perhaps the reverse is true and Christian apocalyptic conspiracies drew their energy from earlier nuclear fears. Whether the secular nuclear egg preceded the Christian apocalyptic chicken may be less important than

---

[11] Peter Dale Scott, *The War Conspiracy: The Secret Road to the Second Indochina War* (Indianapolis, IN: Bobbs-Merrill, 1972); Daniel Ellsberg, *Secrets: A Memoir of Vietnam and the Pentagon Papers* (New York: Penguin, 2003).

[12] Sean M. Maloney, *Deconstructing* Dr. Strangelove: *The Secret History of Nuclear War Films* (Lincoln, NE: Potomac Books, 2020); Kenneth Rose, *One Nation Underground: The Fallout Shelter in American Culture* (New York: NYU Press, 2001), with discussion of a famous *Twilight Zone* episode "The Shelter" on pp. 110–11; Erik Mortenson, "A Journey into the Shadows: *The Twilight Zone*'s Visual Critique of the Cold War," *Science Fiction Film and Television* 7 (2014): 55–76, with discussion of the same episode on pp. 70–73.

the fact of conspiracy's global sense of urgency: at their most dire the sinister plots might lead to the end of the world. Even if the world does survive, the logic of conspiracy demands that its consequences be momentous, even if not world-ending: why else would the secret be kept and why would it be so dangerous to uncover?[13]

This aesthetics of conspiracy, in which the US state apparatus is the stage of both the bad guy infiltrators and the good guy saviors, has outlived the East/West polarities of the Cold War and sprawled across multiple cultural and political spaces. The almost incomprehensible tangle of the "Q-anon" conspiracy in recent years has substituted Communist double-agents with a global ring of pedophiles who pervert the organs of the state for their own twisted ends. The mysterious and anonymous "Q" is supposedly a "good guy" operating within a thicket of governmental evildoers (the "deep state"); he is slowly revealing their maleficence on social media through complex series of hints and codes. ("Q" refers to a high level of government security access, "Q clearance," including access to national security and nuclear information.)[14]

As Adrienne LaFrance detailed in her *Atlantic* contribution to "Shadowland," Q first appeared online in 2017 but their conspiratorial plot builds on existing right-wing fantasies about a conflict between the "deep state," entrenched government bureaucrats pursuing their secret nefarious agenda in collusion with "globalist" plutocrats, and the virtuous new agent of redemption in the government, President Trump (who may or may not be "Q" himself). Q-anon has also incorporated Christian evangelical language, giving this newest US conspiracy movement its own apocalyptic fervor. One of Q's rallying cries is "Enjoy the show," as LaFrance remarks: "a phrase that his disciples regard as a reference to a coming apocalypse: When the world as we know it comes to an end, everyone's a spectator." In Q-anon we see elements of the same style traced by Hofstadter, Jameson, and

---

[13] Fenster, *Conspiracy Theories*, 199–200; A. J. Weigert, "Christian Eschatological Identities and the Nuclear Context," *Journal for the Scientific Study of Religion* 27 (1988): 175–91.

[14] LaFrance, "Nothing Can Stop"; LaFrance's article was the cover story of the June 2020 issue of *The Atlantic*; the online version that appeared as part of the "Shadowland" package was headlined "The Prophecies of Q," www.theatlantic .com/magazine/archive/2020/06/qanon-nothing-can-stop-what-is-coming/ 610567.

Fenster: voracious appetite for signs and knowledge; simultaneous mistrust of and absolute faith in the US state apparatus; projection of a moral and political rot within onto a ruthless international network; a certainty that the stakes are as high as the end of the world. These same aesthetic elements will flesh out fears and desires about the Bible in Gospel Thrillers.[15]

Thrillers: The Conspiracy Genre

Conspiracy is, above all, a narrative. It is the story of an individual (whom Jameson calls the "social detective" to distinguish him from his official police counterpart) stumbling upon "the plot" and risking his life to find the truth. It is the story of rival communities: the "good guys," with whom the protagonist must ally himself, and the "bad guys," against whom they struggle (although frequently the distinction between the two is hazy at best). It is also the story of the plot itself, a body of secret knowledge that can only dimly be reconstructed by the accumulation of clues and evidence. These three elements – individual, community, and truth – are held in tension: Can the protagonist trust his newfound allies? How do we know who is secretly working for "them"? How will we know when we have uncovered the whole truth? These narratives twists and turns are often pleasurable, even for true believers deeply invested in them, as LaFrance's dive into the world of Q-anon demonstrates.

Part of the pleasure of the conspiracy narrative, as well as its frustration, lies in its open-endedness, "a longing for closure and resolution that its formal resources cannot satisfy" (to quote Fenster). The conspiracy narrative lionizes individual agency, embodied in the "social detective" on the hunt for the truth. But the very fact that the protagonist had to stumble onto a plot of which he was previously unaware proves the pervasiveness and success of the plot. He is a lone seeker for truth, eventually accompanied by a few others whom he has convinced or who, also uniquely awakened to the truth, embarked on the path soon before him (or double-agents sent to stop

---

[15] LaFrance, "Nothing Can Stop," 31. Russell Muirhead and Nancy
   L. Rosenblum, *A Lot of People Are Saying: The New Conspiracism and the Assault on Democracy* (Princeton, NJ: Princeton University Press, 2019) argue for the ideological emptiness of Trump-era conspiracy theory.

him). Everyone else in the society around him, however, remains in thrall to the conspiracy: How can one man (or five, or a dozen) hope to bring it down?[16]

In his literary study of "paranoia in postwar America," Timothy Melley labels this tension between the individual protagonist and the perennially duped populace "agency panic": "intense anxiety about an apparent loss of autonomy or self-control, the conviction that one's actions are being controlled by someone else, that one has been 'constructed' by powerful external agents." For Melley, agency panic is a crucial part of the social imaginary during the Cold War period, an attempt to come to terms with a growing feeling that the deeply "American" value of individualism was under threat from outside and from within. As the agency of individuals shrank, the agency of hidden systems grew more powerful. By spinning tales of the lone protagonist hot on the trail of the secret truth, conspiracy narratives reinforce that desire for an individual agency always at risk.[17]

The line between historical and fictional conspiracies has been thin since the Cold War. In *Conspiracy Theories*, Fenster looks at both history and fiction, as well as fiction that claims the mantle of "historical" and "factual," such as Oliver Stone's *JFK* and Dan Brown's *The Da Vinci Code*, which has "FACTS" emblazoned on its opening page. Fictional stories of conspiracy rely on the same "hypersemiosis" that characterizes conspiracy theory more generally, the same kaleidoscopic aesthetic of overinterpretation that promises more answers always just out of reach. For decades the thriller has been the classic narrative outlet for conspiratorial fictions across multiple media: prose, cinema, television, video games.

In his 1999 exploration of the thrillers, primarily through US cinema, Martin Rubin notes that the "'thriller' falls somewhere between a genre proper and a descriptive quality that is attached to other, more clearly defined genres." "Thriller" becomes a stylistic qualifier for other types of genre fiction: spy thrillers, horror thrillers, technothrillers, and so on. Like conspiracy narratives more generally, then, we do better to speak of the thriller as a *style* of narrative, in which all the elements of the conspiracy play out in certain formulaic modes: the secret truth, the protagonist trying to find it, the assertion

---

[16] Fenster, *Conspiracy Theories*, 122.   [17] Melley, *Empire of Conspiracy*, 7–16.

of individual agency repeatedly thwarted by the invisible powers desperate to hide the truth.[18]

Literary critic Anne Longmuir posits key features of the thriller that show its resonance with the conspiracy plot:

> Thrillers are generally tightly plotted, using suspense and the lure of a final denouement or resolution to keep the reader's attention ... The thriller's simplistic prose ensures a quick and easy read, essential to fulfill the genre's promise of fast-paced entertainment ... [An] ideology of extreme individualism underpins this genre. Characteristically, the thriller presents "one sensibility (that of the agent or detective) pitted against a conspiracy of the whole (involving police, politicians, the underworld, the 'other side')." ... The thriller is also, usually, a masculine genre.[19]

The pace and tone of the thriller translates into narrative style the pitch and urgency of the modern conspiracy theory; the simplicity of prose strips away artifice in the same way the protagonist will translate complex codes and ciphers into self-evident truth; and the "individual" going up against "a conspiracy of the whole" reproduces the agency panic Melley sees as so central to the paranoid culture of US conspiracy theory.

The narrative form of the fictional thriller also grants two possibilities lacking in the conspiracy theory as found in the wild: manageability and closure. As Fenster, Jameson, and other conspiracy theory theorists note, the interpretive struggle of the conspiracy theory is endless: "Each new detail leads to the need for more details." I am writing in the early 2020s about Q-anon as if it were condensable into a few tidy paragraphs when in fact at this moment countless YouTube videos, blog posts, and other social media transmissions are generating ever more "data" for the followers of Q to analyze and circulate in further videos, blog posts, and other social media. It is literally impossible to comprehend all of it.

---

[18] Martin Rubin, *Thrillers* (Cambridge: Cambridge University Press, 1999), 4. Literary critics have adapted Hofstadter's "paranoia" language for thrillers: Paul Cobley, "The Semiotics of Paranoia: The Thriller, Abduction, and the Self," *Semiotica* 148 (2004): 317–36; Christopher K. Coffman, "Taming Paranoia: Underground Cinema and the Domestication of the Thriller in McElroy, DeLillo, Wallace, and Danielewski," *Genre* 42 (2009): 119–43.

[19] Anne Longmuir, "Genre and Gender in Don DeLillo's *Players* and *Running Dog*," *Journal of Narrative Theory* 37 (2007): 128–45, at 130, citing (in quotation marks) Patrick O'Donnell, "Obvious Paranoia: The Politics of Don DeLillo's *Running Dog*," *Centennial Review* 34 (1990): 56–72, at 64; see also Coffman, "Taming Paranoia," 120.

The thriller contained between two covers (or between the opening and closing credits of a feature-length film) at least suggests the possibility of comprehension, insofar as *this* chapter of the plot featuring *these* characters has a beginning and an end. More often than not, the thriller ends on a note of uncertainty: a stray clue remains undeciphered, a key agent of "the plot" has escaped, hints of wheels within wheels suggest further chapters of the plot unfolding. (Indeed, thrillers are often serialized.) But this episode, at least, has come to a close, providing some insight into the hidden truth. What may be unmanageably complex and open-ended in the real world is, in fictional form, made temporarily digestible. At the same time, of course, the consumer of the thriller is aware that it is precisely a scaled down version of something that – in the wild – would be that much more complex and unwieldy.

The Bible (as) Plot: Translation and Trial

So far I have been speaking of conspiracy and its narrative embodiment in the thriller primarily as a political narrative or, in a broader sense, a story about American cultural values and anxieties. How does the Bible fit into this? That is, how does a specific form of the thriller, the Gospel Thriller, emerge during this Cold War period and how does it engage in the paranoid style of the conspiratorial thriller: the protagonist, the quest for the truth, the shadowy forces that may or may not succeed in duping the world?

Much like the US state apparatus in political conspiracy theories, the Bible in US culture has been viewed as an instrument of both salvation and danger. For staunch defenders of "the American Way," the Bible has been a powerful totem of white Christian nationhood under threat from outsiders and agitators wielding new textual discoveries and historical methods. For progressive seekers of change, the Bible has been part of the insidious machinery of institutional control that could be exposed and dethroned from the center of national consciousness. One side fears the vulnerability of the Bible; the other hopes for it. The Bible has needed to be defended, or defended against, and it has been all too easy to imagine the shadowy forces at work on all sides.[20]

---

[20] On the racialization of the Bible in the nineteenth century, see Elizabeth L. Jemison, *Christian Citizens: Reading the Bible in Black and White in the Postemancipation South* (Chapel Hill, NC: University of North Carolina Press, 2020) and Kathryn Gin Lum, *Heathen: Religion and Race in American History*

While the Bible as political artifact and intertext has been present to varying degrees since the founding era of the United States, in the 1960s and 1970s – the teeth of the Cold War – the Bible became an object of speculation, consternation, and even conspiratorial thinking in US politics and culture. Much like conspiracy itself, then, the Bible both occupies the background of much of US political and cultural history and takes on new significance in the second half of the twentieth century. We can see this new anxiety around the Bible, to take one example, in the mid-century publication of a new translation of the Christian Bible.

In September 1952, the National Council of the Churches of Christ in the USA published a new translation of the Christian Old and New Testaments which they called the Revised Standard Version (RSV). An interdenominational committee of US scholars had been at work on the new version for almost fifteen years and had already published the RSV of the New Testament on its own in 1946. In anticipation of the new version's full publication, the journal *Religious Education* (the official publication of the interfaith Religious Education Association) published a symposium on the RSV. It began with a preview of the preface to the new version.[21]

In this preface, the Committee responsible for the RSV was at pains to highlight its deep continuity with the tradition of English Bible translation: "The Revised Standard Version of the Bible is an authorized version of the American Standard Version published in 1901, which was a revision of the King James Version, published in 1611," it begins. As historians of Bible publication will quickly note, this statement is true in only the most basic sense: to be sure the translators

(Cambridge, MA: Harvard University Press, 2022). On the production of "the Bible" as a totem of white, Protestant, US identity see Jill Hicks-Keeton and Cavan Concannon, *Does Scripture Speak for Itself? The Museum of the Bible and the Politics of Interpretation* (Cambridge: Cambridge University Press, 2022). On the broader contexts, see Kristin K. Du Mez, *Jesus and John Wayne: How White Evangelicals Corrupted a Faith and Fractured a Nation* (New York: Liveright, 2020) and Anthea Butler, *White Evangelical Racism: The Politics of Morality in America* (Chapel Hill, NC: University of North Carolina Press, 2021).

21 "The Revised Standard Version of the Bible: A Symposium," *Religious Education* 47 (1951): 243–77. On the background of the project, the team, and their aims see Peter J. Thuesen, *In Discordance with the Scriptures: American Protestant Battles over Translating the Bible* (New York: Oxford University Press, 1999), 68–91.

of the RSV took into consideration the ubiquitous "King James Version" (how could they not?) and began their task with the more recent work of the so-called American Standard Version which was itself a US rendition of the Revised Version published in Great Britain in 1881. But the RSV, far from being a mere revision, was an entirely new translation which adopted new styles and norms for expressing the scriptural text. It was conceived in a period of biblical conservatism in the United States; by the time it appeared it would end up highlighting the fissures and suspicions developing around the mid-century US reception of the Bible.[22]

The same fear of Higher Criticism that had propelled Tischendorf to "explore" the monasteries of the East had also catalyzed dramatic changes in Bible translation and publication in the late nineteenth and early twentieth centuries. Fundamentalist presses were founded in the US Midwest dedicated to circulating God's Word to true believers as widely as possible. The American Standard Version, which in some ways modernized the beloved and archaic King James Version, was also meant to be a tool for those clinging tightly to the biblical word: "For much of the twentieth century," writes US Bible historian Paul Gutjahr, "the ASV . . . was considered the gold standard for those who were serious about the original languages of the scriptures and sought out a word-for-word translation for their biblical studies."[23]

The impulse for a "Revised Standard Version" came from similar desires to make the "original" Bible more accessible to modern Protestant readers of all denominations. (During the same period the papal decree *Divino afflante Spiritu* [1943] allowed Roman Catholics to translate Scriptures from their original languages, rather than from the Latin Vulgate; the eventual result was the New American Bible that began appearing in the 1960s.) The International Committee on Religious Education (later merged into the larger but more modestly named National Council of Churches) rented out their copyright on the ASV to Bible publisher Thomas Nelson in order to fund the work of a Standard Committee of mostly elite academic theologians and biblical scholars led by Luther Weigle, dean of Yale Divinity School.

---

[22] Paul C. Gutjahr, "Protestant English-Language Bible Publishing and Translation," in *The Oxford Handbook of the Bible in America*, ed. Paul C. Gutjahr (New York: Oxford University Press, 2018), 3–18, at 9–12.

[23] Gutjahr, "Protestant English-Language Bible Publishing," 10.

Some new Greek texts were incorporated into the New Testament translation, as well as new scholarly insights into the vernacular nature of the *koine* ("common") Greek in which most texts were written. The Old Testament subcommittee controversially added a single Jewish member (Harry Orlinsky of the Hebrew Union College) but made little use of the recent discoveries near the Dead Sea. When the New Testament was published alone in 1946 it was met with tentative approval by Protestants of mainline and evangelical stripe (most of whom still read the King James Version in Sunday schools and churches). But when the full version was published in 1952 with great fanfare and ceremony reaction was more volatile.[24]

Many Christians objected to what they saw as the deemphasis on Christ's divinity in the Old Testament translation, most famously and controversially in changing Isaiah 7:14 from "behold a virgin shall conceive" to the more accurate "behold a young woman shall conceive." Far from ascribing these changes to philological or even honest theological disagreement, critics conjured up shadowy conspiratorial motives. They pointed to the Protestant conglomerate responsible for the new translation which supposedly smacked of attempts to construct a "super-church" that would force theological conformity (critics pointed to the RSV's claim to be "authorized": by and for whom?). Behind this accusation lay a deep-seated US anti-Catholicism that pitted Protestant individualism, derived from a personal relationship with Scriptures, against "Romish" submission to clerical authority.[25]

Very quickly this contrast between individual piety and sinister groupthink was plotted along political axes as well; the RSV was portrayed as part of a Communist conspiracy to tear at the foundation of good (US, white) Protestants' connection to God through Scriptures. A US Air Force Reserve manual written in 1960 warned reservists that "Communists and Communist fellow-travelers have successfully infiltrated our churches" and used the RSV as a signal example of this attempt at infiltration, decrying that "of the 95 persons who served on

---

[24] Thuesen, *In Discordance*, 94–119. The subcommittee on the Old Testament downplayed the use of Dead Sea Scrolls, but see Weston W. Fields, *The Dead Sea Scrolls: A Full History. Vol. 1: 1947–1960* (Leiden: Brill, 2009), 80.

[25] Maura Jane Farrelly, *Anti-Catholicism in America, 1620–1860* (Cambridge: Cambridge University Press, 2018); Mark Massa, *Anti-Catholicism in America: The Last Acceptable Prejudice* (New York: Crossroad, 2003).

this project, 30 have been affiliated with pro-Communist fronts, projects, and publications." Upon objection from the National Council of Churches, the Air Force withdrew the pamphlet from circulation.[26]

The Bible had always been a flashpoint of cultural tension in the United States, particularly at moments of demographic and political change. In the nineteenth century, disagreement between Catholics and Protestants over the appropriate Bible to read to schoolchildren led to conflict in Philadelphia (1844, where real violence broke out) and Cincinnati (1869–73, where the "war" was a series of legal battles). These earlier conflicts took the importance of "the Bible" for granted and centered around specifics, such as which translation to use (the Protestant King James Version or the Roman Catholic Douay-Rheims). By the time the RSV came out, there was a new sense that the Bible itself was under attack: from "modernists," "secularists," and, above all, "Communists." While part of this sense of biblical vulnerability was due to shifting US religious demographics following waves of non-Christian immigration during the late nineteenth and early twentieth centuries, it also followed from a growing sense that the Bible was vulnerable to shifting norms. The flashpoints mid-century came in US schools and courts.[27]

In 1958, a young man at Abington High School in Pennsylvania refused to participate in his school's daily recitation of ten Bible verses followed by the Lord's Prayer. Ellory Schempp (who as an adult spelled his name "Ellery") was a progressive Unitarian who believed the legally required recitation of Bible verses, on the books in Pennsylvania since 1913, violated the Establishment Clause of the First Amendment. Throughout the 1940s the US Supreme Court issued a series of decisions that "incorporated" the Bill of Rights at all levels of US government. These rulings meant that the freedoms enunciated in these amendments to the US Constitution bound not only federal but state and local governments as well. Ellory believed the law requiring the reading of Bible verses in Pennsylvania schools violated his Constitutional rights and, with support from the local chapter of the

---

[26] The citations from the manual appeared (among a barrage of press) on the front page of the *Washington Post* (February 17, 1960) under the headline: "Churches Flay AF Manual Linking Them with Reds" (continued on p. A14). See also Thuesen, *In Discordance*, 104 and William Martin, *With God on Our Side: The Rise of the Religious Right in America* (New York: Broadway Books, 1996), 37.

[27] Farrelly, *Anti-Catholicism*, 146–51, 184.

American Civil Liberties Union (ACLU), he and his family filed a
federal lawsuit against his school district.[28]

Cases challenging local school funding and hosting of religious
education classes and Bible study had worked their way to the US
Supreme Court in the 1940s and early 1950s, but no definitive ruling
had emerged. That a case involving mandatory Bible reading should be
elevated and framed as the key test of the public role of religion in the
United States shows us clearly how the Bible by this period had become
framed as simultaneously central to US identity and vulnerable to
attack from within. The Schempp case was heard at the high court
alongside another suit brought by Baltimore resident Madalyn Murray
on behalf of her son against the Baltimore schools; there the Lord's
Prayer was specified as a requirement that Murray, an atheist, ardently
opposed. Although Murray's case reached the high court first, much of
the testimony and eventual ruling focused on the Schempps and the
question of the Bible in the public-school classroom.

Defenders of the Pennsylvania statute described the Bible reading as
"nonsectarian," an attempt to instill "values" into students. They
pointed out that the verses were read (following the law) "without
commentary," meaning no religious perspective was forced on the
students. (This clause originated in attempts to prevent one
Protestant view from being favored over others.) This defense, of
course, only makes sense if the Bible is already taken as central to
"American" values. The Schempps and their attorneys argued that the
reading was by definition "devotional": Why else would you read the
Bible instead of some other "moral" text? In doing so they were
operating from a different set of assumptions which divided the scho-
lastic formation of US citizens in public schools from the religious
content of the Bible. In one sense this separation of the Bible from
pedagogical formation had been coming slowly down the pike for
more than a century. But the 1963 US Supreme Court decision in favor
of the Schempps against the Abington school district nevertheless hit
the public like a shock wave.

---

[28] Stephen D. Solomon, *Ellery's Protest: How One Young Man Defied Tradition
and Sparked the Battle Over School Prayer*, rev. ed. (Ann Arbor, MI: University
of Michigan Press, 2010); Mark Chancey, "The Bible and American Public
Schools," in *The Oxford Handbook of Religion and American Education*, eds.
Michael D. Waggoner and Nathan C. Walker (New York: Oxford University
Press, 2018), 271–82.

The ruling made front-page headlines throughout the United States. The *Boston Globe*, like many other papers, ran a series of analyses and responses, including a scathing editorial that was slated to appear later that week in *The Pilot*, the newspaper of Boston's Catholic diocese. The *Chicago Tribune* ran the screaming headline BANS RELIGION IN SCHOOLS, with a jump headline on p. 2 that read ATHEISTS, UNITARIANS WIN BAN ON PRAYERS (an accurate if slightly inflammatory description of the plaintiffs). The *Washington Post* and *New York Times* also ran with the story on their front page and printed the complete ruling and lone dissent (from Justice Potter Stewart) inside the paper.

The hometown papers of the Murrays and Schempps, of course, had sustained interest in the cases. The *Baltimore Sun* on June 18 declared CHURCH LEADERS DIVIDED AS SUPREME COURT BARS REQUIRED BIBLE READING AND PRAYERS IN SCHOOLS. The *Philadelphia Inquirer* ran a photo of the Schempp family (without Ellory, who by then had graduated college and was traveling on his honeymoon when the decision came down) under the banner headline: COURT OUTLAWS BIBLE READING IN SCHOOLS. Most stories noted the distressed response of clergy (although not all) and congressional leaders (many of whom began introducing Constitutional amendments on prayer and Bible-reading).

This landmark case is sometimes remembered as being about school prayer (as in the *Chicago Tribune* headline); attorney and journalist Stephen Solomon's detailed account of the case is even subtitled: "How One Young Man Defied Tradition and Sparked the Battle over School Prayer." But through the case the Bible stood at the center of the controversy, both in the law Ellory Schempp opposed and in public consciousness. The Bible was so long associated with "US values" that a legal ruling relegating it solely to the private realm of religion struck opponents as un-American. Much like the translators of the RSV, the Schempps and Murrays were accused of being Communists for their perceived attempts to remove religion, embodied in the Bible, from the public square. The Bible for some was an instrument of enforced conformity by the state; for others it was a totem of US identity under attack from nefarious networks.

Promoting the Public Bible

Since 1963, attempts have continued to reintroduce the Bible into public classrooms not just as a literary or historical artifact but as a source of distinctly US moral values. Mark Chancey, a professor of biblical studies at Southern Methodist University, began studying various twentieth-century public school Bible curricula when the Texas Freedom Network asked him to evaluate a curriculum promoted and sold by the North Carolina-based National Council on Bible Curriculum in Public Schools (NCBCPS). Chancey was not impressed: "Though some components were unobjectionable, much of it was riddled with factual errors, idiosyncratic claims, and explicitly sectarian statements. In addition, it suggested that the Declaration of Independence and Constitution were inspired by the Bible and that the Bible should be the center of American civic life."[29]

This link between core US values (embodied in the founding documents), Protestant Christianity, and the Bible has been central to right-wing religious rhetoric since the 1950s. Haunted by the Cold War specter of Communist atheism and spurred by the Supreme Court's efforts at religious disestablishment, white conservative Christians engaged in large-scale political activism. In the early twentieth century, Higher Criticism led some evangelical Christians to mobilize to defend biblical truth against scientific secularism (the context for the so-called Scopes Monkey Trial). By mid-century, they united to defend the biblical core of US culture and politics against the incursions of Communists, secularists, atheists, and modernists (which all became synonyms). As evangelical radio and later TV preacher Billy James Hargis wrote in his self-published manifesto *Communist America – Must it Be?* in 1960: "America is a Christian country. The men and women who braved an uncharted wilderness to carve out this Republic, were rich in faith. With a Bible under one arm, and a musket under the other, they were willing to fight for their faith and their freedom."[30]

While the fall of Soviet Communism in the 1990s took some of the wind out of the religious Right's sails (eventually replaced, in part, by the "war on terror"), other cultural issues, particularly surrounding sexual identity and reproductive justice, have continued to motivate

---

[29] Mark Chancey, "Bible Bills, Bible Curricula, and Controversies of Biblical Proportions: Legislative Efforts to Promote Bible Courses in Public Schools," *Religion and Education* 34 (2007): 28–47, at 31.

[30] Billy James Hargis, *Communist America – Must It Be?* (Tulsa, OK: Christian Crusade, 1960), 31, cited by Daniel Williams, *God's Own Party: The Making of the Christian Right* (New York: Oxford University Press, 2010), 41. See also Martin, *With God on Our Side,* 33–39, 75–78.

white evangelical Christians to promote the Bible as the necessary pillar of US identity. Attempts to assert the centrality of biblical Christianity in the public square are often framed as a battle against invisible forces determined to disenfranchise that biblical Christianity. Much like Cold War fears of Red infiltrators, these biblical conspiracy theories often frame the state as both the enemy and the site of redemption.[31]

This conspiratorial thinking has materialized most effectively in the nation's capital. In *Saving History*, a study of Christian heritage tours of Washington, DC, Lauren Kerby explores the symbolic and embodied practices of white evangelical Christians trying to uncover the traces of Christian values – most notably references to the Bible and "biblical values" – they believe are being effaced. These tours promote a conspiratorial view of US religious politics in which a nation founded in the Bible has been hoodwinked into secularism; clues, however, remain dotted in the landscape. As Kerby points out, the tours' efforts are somewhat paradoxical: they are claiming the role of the United States's founders but also see themselves as martyrs on the pyre of US impiety. Their language is couched in the familiar style of US conspiracy theory: the quest for clues, the disclosure of the hidden truths, the realization of the vastness of the forces arrayed against them, the belief that the state can be ultimately redeemed from within. Kerby explains:

Their experience of D.C. is not a vacation but an initiation. They join the ranks of those who know the real story and who have seen the evidence for themselves. Armed with this knowledge, they are called to take action, usually in the form of becoming politically involved themselves and supporting efforts to promote Christianity in the American public square.[32]

As one of the tour guides Kerby observed puts it plainly: "Someone has stolen from you the truths you need to know."[33]

---

[31] Williams, *God's Own Party*, 245–76. According to sociological surveys, the Bible remains a central facet of life for many inhabitants of the United States, despite its seeming displacement: see the essays in Philip Goff, Arthur Farnsley, and Peter Thuesen (eds.), *The Bible in American Life* (New York: Oxford University Press, 2017).

[32] Lauren R. Kerby, *Saving History: How White Evangelicals Tour the Nation's Capital and Redeem a Christian America* (Chapel Hill, NC: University of North Carolina Press, 2020), 108.

[33] Kerby, *Saving History*, 60. In the wake of rioters storming the US Capitol on January 6, 2021, Kerby published a piece connecting the Christian white

Much like the political conspiracy of Q-anon, the energy of this brand of white evangelical suspicion and hope coalesced around President Trump, assisted by Trump's own self-framing as the fearless leader out to "drain the swamp" and upend the "deep state." In an interview with CBN (Christian Broadcast Network) News, Franklin Graham, the son of famous evangelical mega-preacher Billy Graham, brought the victimization of white evangelical Christians to an apocalyptic pitch in language that echoed Q-anon: "I think God brought [Trump] here for this season ... I believe the storm is coming. You're going to see Christians attacked; you're going to see churches close; you're going to see a real hatred expressed toward people of faith. That's coming."[34]

The video of Graham's interview shows a clear, panoramic view of Washington, DC, including a view of the Washington Monument (described by one of the tour guides Kerby observed as "one of the most important sites if you want to understand 'our Christian history'"). In fact, Graham gave this interview from inside the gleaming new Museum of the Bible which sits just down the Mall from the Washington Monument. The Museum of the Bible is a private museum, funded by the Green family, the billionaire owners of the craft chain Hobby Lobby, but is walking distance from the public museums of the Smithsonian in Washington, DC.[35]

As Candida Moss and Joel Baden detail in their book *Bible Nation*, the Museum of the Bible is the culmination of decades of work by one white evangelical family to restore the Bible to a central place in US culture and politics through private collection, education, and even litigation (in 2014 the Green family successfully argued before the US Supreme Court that the Affordable Care Act's inclusion of contraception as part of guaranteed health care violated their family business's

---

nationalism of many of the rioters with these heritage tours: "White Nationalists Want More Than Just Political Power," *The Atlantic* (January 15, 2021), online at www.theatlantic.com/ideas/archive/2021/01/white-evangelicals-fixation-on-washington-dc/617690.

[34] David Brody, "EXCLUSIVE: Franklin Graham Tells CBN News He Thinks Democratic Party is 'Opposed to Faith,'" *CBNNews.com* (August 28, 2020), online at www1.cbn.com/cbnnews/2020/august/exclusive-franklin-graham-tells-news-he-thinks-democrats-are-opposed-to-faith. My thanks to Cavan Concannon for pointing out this interview and its location. Kerby, *Saving History*, 145–46.

[35] Kerby, *Saving History*, 53.

religious freedoms). The public-facing rationale for the Museum of the Bible has shifted over the years since its construction began in 2015 and its doors opened in 2017. Moss and Baden argue cogently that the new museum is of a piece with the family's promotion of the Bible as the bedrock of US values and idea; the Green family elsewhere is explicit about the links between biblical faith and national pride.[36]

The presence of the massive red-brick building with golden doors etched with pages from Gutenberg's Bible is a paradoxical presence near the Mall, to be sure. On the one hand, surely it speaks to the (literally) oversized presence of the Bible in the US public square; it has enjoyed robust attendance since opening and is among the more popular private museums in a town full of free, government-subsidized museums. Yet that exclusion from the collection of government-sponsored museums so close by stands as a kind of silent rebuke: much like the Christian heritage tours, the subtext is that the Museum of the Bible must promote biblical values precisely because the (lamentably) secular federal government will not. For this reason, surely, Franklin Graham gave his apocalyptic interview to CBN News from the Museum's gleaming sixth floor exhibit hall. Somewhere between a "museum and a monument," the Museum of the Bible serves as a refuge for the faithful and a (hopeful) signal to the wavering.[37]

Predictably the Museum of the Bible enacts the white evangelical values of its founders, intertwined throughout with a focus on the Bible as an anchor of US identity (part of its permanent exhibit addresses "The Impact of the Bible in America"). The vast accumulation of artifacts, carefully curated into "historical" and "cultural" exhibits, seek to bring into the twenty-first century older ideas about the western (indeed, particularly US) Bible that has been "recovered" from the slumbering East. The organization of exhibits presses the need for US publics to recognize the centrality of the Bible to "American" values

---

[36] Candida R. Moss and Joel S. Baden, *Bible Nation: The United States of Hobby Lobby* (Princeton, NJ: Princeton University Press, 2017). On the Green family's biblical nationalism see Jackie and Steve Green, *This Dangerous Book: How the Bible Has Shaped Our World and Why It Matters Today* (Grand Rapids, MI: Zondervan, 2017).

[37] See Hicks-Keeton and Concannon, *Speak for Itself?* and Jill Hicks-Keeton and Cavan Concannon (eds.), *The Museum of the Bible: A Critical Introduction* (London: Rowan & Littlefield, 2019); Gregory Lee Cuéllar, *Empire, the British Museum, and the Making of the Biblical Scholar in the Nineteenth Century: Archival Fever* (Cham: Palgrave Macmillan, 2019), 177–83.

(such as abolition, and freedom more generally). Its appropriation of Biblical archaeology to locate the Bible in Near Eastern history promotes a brand of Christian Zionism alongside a supersessionist narrative in which Christian truth overwrites a Jewish past.

The Museum of the Bible does not, in its exhibits or educational materials, overtly participate in the kind of conspiratorial style underlying other right-wing Christian discourses (although its insistence on past "persecutions" alongside its central location in the nation's capital are pointed). In fact, it has provoked some irritation from more secular-minded US publics who remain suspicious of the role of the Bible in public life. Kerby, in a moving passage in the concluding pages of *Saving History*, reports her feeling of annoyance at the way the Museum of the Bible cloaks its specific brand of white evangelical Protestantism under the exclusionary binary of "religious versus secular." This annoyance has manifested elsewhere in reactions against public biblicism that, much like their evangelical counterparts, become occasionally cloaked in a conspiratorial style.[38]

Resisting the Public Bible

In autumn 1966, a provocative ad began appearing across US newspapers that read: IN ANOTHER AGE, THE AUTHOR OF THIS BOOK WOULD HAVE BEEN BURNED AT THE STAKE. The book being advertised, *The Passover Plot*, had been published the year before in the UK and within weeks of its US release hit the *New York Times* nonfiction bestseller list (October 16, 1966) where it remained for almost two months. The ad featured the book's cover art (a drawing of a man's arm being nailed into a cross) and the tagline "A Daring New Interpretation of the Life and Death of Jesus"; it also tells us that the author, Dr. Hugh G. Schonfield, previously wrote "*Secrets of the Dead Sea Scrolls.*" The invocation of public censure ("burned at the stake"), new finds that might call the received biblical truth into question (*Secrets of the Dead Sea Scrolls*), and a "daring new" narrative encapsulate in one mass-produced image the flipside of conspiratorial thinking about the Bible emerging alongside the white evangelical panic: that the Bible is not an instrument of freedom, truth, and US values, but an oppressive tool of censorship that must be resisted.

[38] Kerby, *Saving History*, 130–34.

Schonfield's book posits that Jesus, in an effort to prove his messiahship, engaged in a complicated plot to fake his own death and resurrection. Foiled by the unexpected – a Roman spear at his crucifixion – Jesus's "plot" eventually had to be carried out by his followers, who staged the empty tomb and began to tell tales of miracles. To arrive at his "daring" interpretation Schonfield presses on Jesus's Jewish context (bolstered in part by the "secrets" found in the Dead Sea Scrolls) and a rereading of the gospel texts. Schonfield's rationalist reading of the historical Jesus hearkens back to the Higher Critics opposed by Tischendorf and friends. The insistence on Jesus's Jewish context was more novel but of a piece with scholarship in the 1960s and 1970s.[39]

If Schonfield's book emerges from existing scholarship, why do ads invoke the Inquisitor's stake? The marketing of the book conjures up a US cultural scene in which the Bible has become prone to conspiratorial thinking. For conservative white Christians, the Bible is the object of conspiracy: under attack from atheists, Communists, or secularists, even, at times, from the very government for which it served as a key source of moral authority. For a different audience the Bible is the perpetrator of a conspiracy, covering up hidden truths that only the intrepid dare to uncover through careful sifting of esoteric clues, often at their peril. For conservative Christians, the legal cases brought by the Schempps and others in the 1950s and 1960s were part of an attempts to dislodge (Christian) religion from its rightful place at the moral center of US public life. Yet others were more sympathetic to this separation, mistrustful of the influence of institutional religion, and eager to envision a secular public sphere free of theological and biblical influence.

In April 1966, a few months before *The Passover Plot* ad hit newspapers, *Time* magazine ran one of its most famous cover stories: IS GOD DEAD? The wide-ranging article covered a lot of ground: philosophical nihilism, postwar exhaustion, radical (Christian theology), and the embrace of scientific progressivism. While noting that religion still seemed central to life in the United States – "a country where public faith in God seems to be as secure as it was in medieval France" – the article goes on to distinguish routine church-going from

---

[39] Hugh G. Schonfield, *The Passover Plot* (New York: Random House, 1965). I discuss the rise of the "Jewish Jesus" in Chapter 3.

sincere trust in institutional religion, even quoting one "anguished teenager" as crying out: "I love God but I hate the church."[40]

As the Religious Right grew to prominence in the 1970s and 1980s and wielded the authority of the Bible as part of their political message, a counterpolitics portrayed the Bible as inimical to the progressive future of US life. When feminist historian Gerda Lerner published the first volume of her "Woman and History" series, *The Creation of Patriarchy*, in 1982, she granted the Bible – which, after all, starts with the stories of "the patriarchs" – a key role in the imposition of a modern social structure that devalued women. Lerner's historicization of the patriarchal narratives of the Bible suggested that modern societies adhering to such "biblical" understandings of sex and gender were moored in a primitive past. Other feminist thinkers were already pushing back against the perceived patriarchal sexism of the Bible: Judith Plaskow in 1972 published her famous feminist midrash "The Coming of Lilith," which centered on the sexual and personal liberation of Adam's (noncanonical) first wife, Lilith. Later in the 1970s, *Lilith* was founded as a Jewish, feminist, US magazine (still in print). In both Lerner's history and Plaskow's theology, the Bible as it exists in mainstream US culture is a premodern anachronism inimical to progressive thought.[41]

Neither Plaskow nor Lerner, writing from a perspective of feminist liberation, claimed that the US Bible was the instrument of a vast and unseen conspiracy so much as an outdated tool of run-of-the-mill patriarchy. But during the same period new discoveries and new attitudes toward institutional religion did prompt some to wonder: What was the Bible hiding and who was behind it? In Chapters 3 and 4, I discuss how the Dead Sea Scrolls and Nag Hammadi texts

---

[40] John Elson, "Toward a Hidden God," *Time* 87.14 (April 8, 1966): 82–87. See more generally Robert Fuller, *Spiritual, But Not Religious: Understanding Unchurched America* (New York: Oxford University Press, 2001).

[41] Gerda Lerner, *The Creation of Patriarchy* (New York: Oxford University Press, 1986); Judith Plaksow, "The Coming of Lilith," in *Religion and Sexism: Images of Women in the Jewish and Christian Traditions*, ed. Rosemary Radford Ruether (New York: Simon & Schuster, 1974), 341–43 and republished with an extended introduction in Judith Plaskow, *The Coming of Lilith: Essays on Feminism, Judaism, and Sexual Ethics, 1972–2003*, ed. with Donna Berman (Boston, MA: Beacon Press, 2005), 23–33. For broader contexts, see *The Bible and Feminism: Remapping the Field*, ed. Yvonne Sherwood with Anna Fisk (New York: Oxford University Press, 2017).

dramatically buried in antiquity and unearthed in modernity came to be seen as evidence for biblical suppression and cover-up that continue into the present. The ongoing circulation of evidence for "alternative" Christianities fueled both religious and political dissatisfaction with the centrality of the Christian Bible. On the one hand, these new texts were seen to offer up the possibility of a more progressive, spiritual form of Christianity than the (perceived) repressive church of orthodoxy (sometimes resulting in the publication of "other Bibles" and the establishment of "neo-Gnostic" churches). On the other hand, the very fact that these more progressive or spiritual gospels had been suppressed by an authoritarian church showed the patriarchal machinations of that repressive orthodox church.[42]

This ongoing appeal of lost gospels and the suspicion that they were suppressed by "the Church" was so commonplace by the early 2000s that it prompted two popular responses. The first was a work of nonfiction by conservative Christian historian Philip Jenkins. In *Hidden Gospels: How the Search for Jesus Lost Its Way*, Jenkins bemoaned the repetitive cycle, since the 1960s, in which scholars push "new" gospels into the public sphere, which stokes a desire for other "new gospels," none of which (according to Jenkins) are any better or more authentic than the canonical gospels:

The lay public has a strong predisposition to accept that additional information is (or should be) available about Jesus, that the truth is out there, and this gives a definite advantage to those scholars who make claims about supposed new sources, new gospels … In fact, successive claims gain strength by a kind of cumulative process, as each new theory evokes popular expectations based upon memories of earlier discoveries … Ideas and fantasies concerning hidden gospels will continue to flourish as long as people are interested in the figure of Jesus and as long as they wish to root their beliefs in some acceptable scripture.[43]

---

[42] I discuss the rising popularity of alternative Christianities in Chapter 4. On the emergence of neo-Gnostic churches out of earlier Theosophist and esoteric movements, see Olav Hammer, "The Jungian Gnosticism of the Ecclesia Gnostica," *International Journal for the Study of New Religions* 9 (2018): 33–56. On "other bibles" see the often reprinted work of poet and scholar Willis Barnstone, *The Other Bible: Jewish Pseudepigrapha, Christian Apocrypha, Gnostic Scriptures, Kabbalah, Dead Sea Scrolls* (San Francisco, CA: HarperSanFrancisco, 1984).

[43] Philip Jenkins, *Hidden Gospels: How the Search for Jesus Lost Its Way* (New York: Oxford University Press, 2001), 214–15.

Jenkins, in *Hidden Gospels*, seeks to demystify this process and so break what he sees as an unhelpful cycle; in the end he's not hopeful. The suspicion of "hidden gospels" and longing for "the truth out there" (an allusion to the conspiratorial television series *The X-Files*) is too strong.

As if to drive home Jenkins's point about the insatiable desire to find "the truth out there" about Jesus, two years later *The Da Vinci Code* exploded onto the scene. The "big secret" at the heart of *The Da Vinci Code* is recycled from an earlier nonfiction conspiracy thriller, *The Holy Blood and the Holy Grail* by Michael Baigent, Richard Leigh, and Henry Lincoln (the first and second surnames are combined in the name of the novel's antagonist, Leigh Teabing). Lincoln, Leigh, and Baigent claimed to have run down a centuries-long conspiracy of the "Prieuré de Sion" which had safeguarded the bloodline of Jesus and Mary Magdalene through the ages. In Dan Brown's fictional reworking, the Christian Bible is the instrument of conspiratorial attempts to erase all knowledge of this bloodline and the truth about Jesus.[44]

During a long section of exposition, Teabing explains to the novel's protagonist, Robert Langdon, that of the "'more than *eighty* gospels ... considered for the New Testament'" (emphasis in original) only four were chosen by the "pagan" emperor Constantine to emphasize Christ's divinity and deemphasize his humanity:

"Fortunately for historians," Teabing said, "some of the gospels that Constantine attempted to eradicate managed to survive. The Dead Sea Scrolls were found in the 1950s hidden in a cave near Qumran in the Judean desert. And, of course, the Coptic Scrolls in 1945 at Nag Hammadi. In addition to telling the true Grail story, these documents speak of Christ's ministry in very human terms. Of course, the Vatican ... tried very hard to suppress the release of these scrolls."[45]

To prove his point, Teabing hauls down from his shelves "a huge book ... poster-sized, like a huge atlas" whose cover read "*The Gnostic Gospels*": "'These are photocopies of the Nag Hammadi

---

[44] Dan Brown, *The Da Vinci Code* (New York: Doubleday, 2003); Michael Baigent, Richard Leigh, and Henry Lincoln, *The Holy Blood and the Holy Grail* (London: Jonathan Cape, 1982). Of the many analyses, rebuttals, and refutations of the historical content of *The Da Vinci Code*, I recommend Bart D. Ehrman, *Truth and Fiction in The Da Vinci Code* (New York: Oxford University Press, 2004).

[45] Brown, *Da Vinci Code*, 234.

and Dead Sea Scrolls, which I mentioned earlier,' Teabing said. 'The earliest Christian records.'" Teabing reads passages from the Gospel of Philip and the Gospel of Mary that support his contention about the marriage of Jesus and Mary Magdalene.[46]

Literature professor Christopher Douglas pinpoints the centrality of the Bible to Brown's novel and to its success in a US culture still reeling from the religious and biblical culture wars of the Cold War era:

> Beneath the anti-Catholic veneer of *The Da Vinci Code* lay a deeper attack on Protestantism ... What seems to be the anti-Catholic content of the novel's shadowy European plot and exposition is better understood as an attack on the biblical theology characteristic of the Protestantism at the core of the conservative Christian resurgence.

Brown takes up the core suppositions of the academic study of the Bible (the Higher Criticism that so irked Tischendorf and Hunter) and amplifies them into a method for revealing conspiratorial forces aligned (even if subtextually) with conservative Christian US politics. Douglas briefly notes the evangelical backlash against the novel, which was swift and emphatic. Indeed, we might even view the Museum of the Bible, a defiant monument to evangelical biblical truth in the US capital, as one more response to the conspiratorial thinking of *The Da Vinci Code*: dueling biblical conspiracy theories.[47]

When Dan Brown set out to exploit what Jenkins diagnosed as "fantasies concerning hidden gospels" he did so, notably, using existing historical material, narratively bound together in Teabing's huge *Gnostic Gospels* tome. Teabing does at one point make reference to "'the legendary 'Q' Document – a manuscript that even the Vatican admits they believe exists ... a book of Jesus' teachings written in His own hand.'" He imagines it to be hidden among the "'thousands of unaltered, pre-Constantine documents, written by the early followers of Jesus'" along with a "'complete genealogy of the early descendants of Christ.'" These "lost gospels" are not the animating focus of *The Da*

---

[46] Brown, *Da Vinci Code*, 245–48. Many details here are incorrect (presumably mistakes made by Brown and not deliberate misstatements put in the mouth of his character, Teabing): the Nag Hammadi books are not scrolls, there is no Christian material in the Dead Sea Scrolls, and the Gospel of Mary was discovered in the 1870s, not at Nag Hammadi.

[47] Christopher Douglas, *If God Meant to Interfere: American Literature and the Rise of the Christian Right* (Ithaca, NY: Cornell University Press, 2016), 245–79, at 248.

Vinci Code, however; instead it is "the grail," the venerated remains of Jesus's wife Mary Magdalene. For Brown, the truth was already hidden in plain sight in the "gnostic gospels" available to all, much like Leonardo's "Last Supper."[48]

By assuming that the conspiratorial truth could be puzzled out from existing documents, Brown was following in the footsteps of Schonfield and *The Passover Plot*. But Brown also hints at another narrative that was already emerging by the 1970s: the ongoing suppression of "explosive" proof about Jesus and Christian origins. In 1972, Australian journalist Donovan Joyce published a thin but dramatic piece of nonfiction entitled *The Jesus Scroll*. The cover of one US paperback version promised "shocking documentary evidence that goes beyond *The Passover Plot*." In *The Jesus Scroll*, Joyce recounts a visit to Israel in 1964 when an unscrupulous archaeologist sought his help in smuggling an ancient scroll out of Israel. The scroll, purportedly discovered at Masada during Yigael Yadin's excavations, was the autobiography of Jesus, an heir to the Hasmonean throne of Israel, who survived the crucifixion, got married (to Mary Magdalene, of course), had children, and died an old man, still royally venerated, at the siege of Masada decades later. His remains, then, would have been reinterred with others discovered in 1964.[49]

The scroll, Joyce reports, vanished along with the unscrupulous archaeologist, possibly to be sold to the Soviets (a suspicion Joyce believes confirmed by the sudden thaw in relations between the USSR and the Vatican in 1967). Although the scroll has vanished, Joyce describes it as a "time bomb" (a phrase which also appeared in the form of a question on some paperback versions: "A TIME BOMB FOR CHRISTIANITY?"). Dan Brown in his novel had offhandedly referred to lost documents from Jesus's time, but they did not form the center of his conspiracy. In Joyce's "nonfiction" book, a scroll has been found; it contains shocking secrets; it has emerged from and vanished in the

---

[48] Brown, *Da Vinci Code*, 256; see Douglas, *If God Meant to Interfere*, 275–76.

[49] Donovan Joyce, *The Jesus Scroll* (Sydney: Angus and Robertson, 1972), published in 1973 in the UK (London: Angus and Robertson) and the United States (New York: Dial Press). The "shocking documentary" tagline appears on the 1973 paperback version. The Zionist mythologizing of Masada began even before the founding of Israel but was magnified into international consciousness by Yadin's excavations and publications: see Jodi Magness, *Masada: From Jewish Revolt to Modern Myth* (Princeton, NJ: Princeton University Press, 2019), 198–200.

mists of shifty geopolitical borderlands; it is waiting to be found again, and for that bomb to explode. It is a clever narrative spun out of the conspiratorial biblical politics of the 1970s. It is also the plot of the Gospel Thrillers, the first of which had already appeared several years earlier.[50]

The Q Document: Anatomy of a Genre

The Q Document by James Hall Roberts came out in 1964. (By 1966 "Roberts" was unmasked in a *Los Angeles Times* profile as television screenwriter Robert L. Duncan.) In many ways it is typical of the line of Gospel Thrillers that will follow it, although I've found no evidence that any other author in this genre knew of or self-consciously adapted Roberts's formula. As I noted in Chapter 1, "lost gospel" stories had appeared decades earlier; what we see for the first time in *The Q Document*, and what will persist in the genre to the present day, are the ways that the earlier themes of the gospel adventure tales are transformed to fit a new era: the Cold War and its aftermath, the age of conspiracy and thrillers.[51]

Marketed as a suspense novel, *The Q Document* contains all the ingredients of the thriller: the lone protagonist, the unfolding clues, the sinister forces behind the scenes, a dangerous race against time, the tentative but ultimately provisional resolution. Exotic settings, casual sex, lurid crime, and vast sums of money flowing outside legal channels round out the usual accoutrements of the genre. What sets *The Q Document* apart from other 1960s thrillers is the object of intrigue at its center: not atomic weapons or state secrets but the Bible and Christian origins. An ad in the *New York Times* captures neatly how conspiratorial thinking about the Bible could be narrated as a thriller:

How long has it been since you stayed up all night reading a book? Why did Red China want The Q Document? Why did the Vatican send someone to buy it? Why did the Nazis believe it even though its discoverer was a Jew?

---

[50] While *The Jesus Scroll* was published in the United States and the UK, it doesn't seem to have made much of splash, receiving some tepid reviews but never cracking bestseller lists.

[51] Full publication information for all the Gospel Thrillers can be found in this book's Appendix. On Duncan's background, see William R. Melton, Jr., "Duncan's Pen Mightier than His Typewriter," *Los Angeles Times* (June 19, 1966): B18.

Why did a Catholic priest contemplate murder because of it? What did The Q Document reveal?[52]

For *New York Times* readers who might not associate "The Q Document" with the Bible, the copy below clarifies: "It tells what happens when a 2000-year-old scroll that casts substantial doubt upon the divinity of Christ is discovered."

This description is not entirely accurate with respect to the novel's contents, but it captures well the themes that make Gospel Thrillers appealing: political conspiracy (Nazis and Red China), religious cover-up (the Vatican and a murderous Catholic priest), theological deviance (a Jew), and the promise of thrills and suspense. When the *New York Times* ran its review two days later, the reviewer praised the novel's conceit by noting the disappointment the (presumably Christian) public had with the Dead Sea Scrolls: "When the discovery of the Dead Sea scrolls became known a few years ago many people were vaguely disappointed. All right, they thought, so it's a contribution to scholarship ... If the Dead Sea scrolls were insufficiently exciting, Mr. Roberts could imagine documents that would be."[53]

The protagonist of *The Q Document* is George Cooper, a disaffected US historian with expertise in ancient manuscripts living abroad in Japan. To support himself, Cooper translates and evaluates ancient manuscripts for an unsavory importer (of objects and, it turns out, humans), Victor Hawkins. Hawkins provides Cooper with a cache of documents that belonged to Martin Baum-Brenner, a German Jewish scholar who had converted and become a Nazi working for Hitler's regime. The documents were smuggled out of Red China by a Roman Catholic priest and acquired by Hawkins. Along with some of Baum-Brenner's correspondence are ancient texts in Latin, Greek, Hebrew, and Aramaic from the first century. These texts tell a "shocking" story of Jesus and his movement, the story of a "mad warrior Messiah" (p. 255) convinced he would rise from the dead whose body was hidden in a cover-up when the resurrection didn't happen. The texts also reveal the condemnation of the apostle Paul, who murdered a disillusioned follower of Jesus in order to perpetuate the cover-up. Eventually, using clues left behind by Baum-Brenner, Cooper realizes that the documents

---

[52] *New York Times* (June 3, 1964): 41.

[53] Orville Prescott, "Ingenious Plot Makes Implausible Tale," *New York Times* (June 5, 1964): 29.

are all forgeries, executed by the brilliant Baum-Brenner for the Nazi regime in an attempt to demoralize and defeat the Allied powers.

Much of this sounds like James Hunter's war-time adventure story, *The Mystery of Mar Saba*, which I discussed in Chapter 1. The differences, however, are key, particularly in how *The Q Document* treats the three themes: the political, the theological, and the personal. Like *The Mystery of Mar Saba*, *The Q Document* concerns an urgent attempt to prove that the shocking documents are Nazi forgeries; the geopolitical context, however, is not the burgeoning armed conflict between European powers but the Cold War battle of ideologies. The action takes place in the early 1960s, amid covertly operating foreign powers and underground knowledge brokers. The Japanese setting was chosen because of the author's own experience there after World War II but also because it provides a venue that is both exotic for US readers and a crossroads for all the novel's various global actors to converge.[54]

The Nazi threat of the 1940s stands in tenuous continuity with the new Communist antagonists of the Cold War. Cooper learns that Hawkins is offering to sell the documents back to "the Red Chinese government" (p. 85), which is willing to pay enormous sums for them, presumably because their atheist leaders want to demoralize the Christian West. The climax of the novel is not, as in *The Mystery of Mar Saba*, a series of shoot-outs and armed stand-offs, but a secret auction conducted by Hawkins between the Chinese representative, Dr. Lu Hsiao-p'ing, a Marxist historian who favors the "abolition" of Chinese Christianity (p. 235), and Dr. H. B. Vacelli "from the Vatican Library" (p. 219). The villainous Hawkins practically licks his lips in anticipation:

"I had considered having Dr. Lu and Dr. Vacelli submit written bids and so forth, but that would be much too slow a process. And it excites me, dear boy, to consider the prospects of a face-to-face confrontation, East against West, atheist against Christian, with so very much resting on the outcome, a whole way of life, so to speak." (p. 225)

Unfortunately for Hawkins, it is during this live auction that Cooper realizes that the documents are forged and demonstrates the forgery to all assembled.

[54] The convoluted route these documents took from Nazi Germany to 1960s Japan highlights the transformed circuits of global exchange: Hawkins posits they were stolen by members of the Japanese embassy in Berlin and sold on after the war, making their way to Red China (p. 10).

The bifurcation of the anti-Biblical villains – Nazis in the past, Chinese communists in the present – makes sense from a US Christian perspective (they are both enemies of the freedom-loving West) but also highlights the distance readers have traveled since the 1940s and *The Mystery of Mar Saba*. While the stakes are still enormous – "to release these documents would crucify Christ again," Cooper thinks to himself (p. 212, a point reiterated throughout the novel) – the combatants are no longer opposing sides in a military conflict but depersonalized ideologies, "East against West," for whom Lu and Vacelli are more or less ciphers. The conflict and resolution all take place in secret, unlike the explosive and public revelations and retractions in *The Mystery of Mar Saba*. This particular geopolitical conflict is resolved but readers are left to imagine other equally fraught exchanges of shadowy secrets taking place in other hidden rooms.[55]

The shifting politics also add nuance to the theological distress these new documents will supposedly unleash upon the world (assuming, as several characters do in the novel, that the Chinese intend to make them public). As in *The Mystery of Mar Saba*, the Baum-Brenner documents "prove" that the resurrection never happened; this shocking secret appears in many later Gospel Thrillers. But the context for this hidden secret is very different: a "Jewish nationalist" rebellion dedicated to "the overthrow of the oppressive Roman legions in Judea" (p. 123). The most valuable document, written in "neo-Aramaic," "'was written by Jesus himself,'" Hawkins explains to Willa Cummings, a US journalist and Cooper's lover, "'in his own hand, a record of his sayings and some of the precepts of the heavenly kingdom he intended to establish with the overthrow of Rome'" (p. 138). (This is the "Q document" of the title, a reference to a hypothetical source document used by the canonical gospel writers [p. 33]; I return to Q in Chapter 6). The Latin and Greek documents attest to Paul's conviction by Roman authorities of murder. The shadow of a Jewish people struggling for freedom against tyranny would have very specific resonances in the decades after World War II.

---

[55] A similar temporal splitting of global threats, Nazis in the 1930s and global terror organizations in the 1970s, appears in Ludlum's 1989 multigenerational Gospel Thriller, *The Gemini Contenders*.

The state of Israel does not play much of a role in the novel, except in one scene when Willa Cummings tries to find information on Martin Baum-Brenner:

She went to the Israeli Legation in Shibuya to see if they could provide her with any information on Baum-Brenner only to find that they too were confused by his apparent political schizophrenia ... As Martin Baum, he typified the rabbinical resistance to Hitler and had become something of a folk hero for his bravery in those terrible days in Warsaw. On the other hand, as Martin Brenner, he had betrayed his people, ostensibly to insure his own safety and comfort. (p. 73)

We might compare Baum-Brenner to Peter Yphantis in *The Mystery of Mar Saba*, another scholar of Jewish descent forced to produce anti-Christian forgeries under Nazi duress. Yphantis, however, was a pious evangelical Christian, opposed to Higher Criticism. That is, his Jewishness was past tense, a suitable metaphor for the absorption of Jewish Scriptures into a Christian Bible. This brief scene at the Israeli Legation asks readers to view Baum-Brenner not through the lens of Christian supersessionism but as a casualty along the path leading from the Holocaust to the Jewish nation-state. As I explore in more detail in Chapter 3, the Jewishness of Jesus and the tangled relationship of the United States and Israel provide fertile ground for Gospel Thrillers to explore intersecting political and theological anxieties.

Often in Gospel Thrillers the theological anxiety about a Jewish Jesus appears inscribed in the main characters of the novels, protagonists with nebulous Jewish backgrounds. In *The Q Document* Martin Baum-Brenner is long dead and the novel finds other ways to interlace the personal into its political and theological themes. Cooper spends much of *The Q Document* in a kind of moral haze, caused by the traumatic death of a wife and child back in the United States, which led him to abandon his academic career and native country. His work for Hawkins and his affair with Willa are both conducted with cold detachment. Yet Cooper's detached stance is not only a product of personal trauma; it's also part of his professional demeanor: "It was up to him to translate, examine, and assess in the cold light of educated reason, to determine the 'how' instead of the 'why'" (p. 39). *The Q Document* levels an early critique of the ways biblical knowledge is assessed and evaluated; we see this abiding fascination with biblical knowledge brokers of all sorts develop into a key feature of Gospel Thrillers.

This icy professional detachment begins to thaw in the course of the novel, impelled first by his rescue of a young Japanese girl from Hawkins's sinister clutches and then by Cooper's dawning realization that his work on the Baum-Brenner documents might actually matter in more than an abstract academic sense. By the time he meets with Baum-Brenner's daughter, who is also living in Japan, he has decided he cannot abide the consequences of his own historical work:

"If I can't find a way to disprove the Baum-Brenner papers, then I'll destroy the Q document."

"Destroy it?" she said, startled. "Mind telling me why?"

"I'm not sure in my own mind," he said. "I've always prided myself on being a cold, objective, impersonal man when it comes to my work. When I've published anything, it's represented a conservative point of view, all very defensible. I know this doesn't seem like an answer, but there's such a thing as being too rational, too impressed with the demonstrable things of the world. Do you see what I'm getting at?"

"No," she said, "I don't."

"I try to tell myself that if the Baum-Brenner papers can't be disproved, then they should be published. I try to tell myself that as far as most people are concerned it won't make a bit of difference. The people who have faith are going to continue to believe and the people without faith won't be affected one way or another. But I know it isn't true. The world isn't like that. If Dr. Lu is successful and the collection goes to Red China they'll kill Christianity once and for all." (p. 196)

The personal arc of *The Mystery of Mar Saba* was religious: Medhurst progresses in the novel from quietist atheism to heroic piety. Cooper's personal arc is about the stakes in biblical knowledge production. Both narratives make claims about the personal stakes of biblical knowledge, discovered in the nexus of political intrigue and biblical theology. Cooper's encounter with Nazi forgeries takes him from academic disinterest to warm-hearted compassion. Cooper is stirred by Baum-Brenner's sacrifice for his family, shocked out of his complacency at the theological threat posed by the Q document, and ultimately moved out of his self-imposed exile at the political crossroads. At the end of the novel he returns to the United States, although it's not clear if he is returning to academia. What he has acquired through his brief encounter with these gospel conspiracies is, it seems, a moral center that makes him fit for life back in the United States.

By contrast Hawkins, the rapacious smuggler of objects and persons, remains unredeemed. He, too, originally came from the United States but in his itinerant life has become fully unmoored from the country: "an American by birth" who now passed himself off as a "bogus Englishman" after living in London, France, and New York, leaving the United States once more after "a scandal ... sufficiently heinous in a town sated with common sexual scandal to propel him to Japan" (p. 57). Hawkins is the true conspiratorial mastermind of the novel, manipulating people and profiting from the instabilities of a Cold War world from the shadows. He is also fat and effeminate, physically and morally monstrous (pp. 30–31). Cooper's slow move back toward the moral gravity of his Christian US upbringing – the son, it turns out, of a Presbyterian minister (p. 56) – is precisely mirrored by the static villainy of Hawkins. Only one man can return home to the United States at the end.

In *The Q Document*, human decency triumphs over amoral greed – for the moment. A decades-old plot to dethrone Christianity goes up like a puff of smoke and the protagonist goes home. What is left in place, however, is the entire infrastructure that allowed this threat to resurface: a subterranean network of manuscripts, smugglers, international money, and biblical intrigue. As students of conspiracy theory tell us, conspiracy theories are by nature unending; even as one chapter ends, others begin to unfold. *The Q Document* was merely the first novel to place the Bible squarely at the center of this tide of conspiratorial thinking, giving fictional life to anxieties which the Bible was generating in US culture and politics. More would follow in its wake.

The Q Document seems to have been a success for its author; it inaugurated an entire subgenre of novels, seemingly unaware of or at least uninterested in the others' existence. But their central concerns remain remarkably consistent over the decades. Many aspects of this first foray into the Gospel Thrillers genre are unique (the setting in Japan, for instance); some will be repeated (the threat of forgery, the shadow of Nazis); others will become routine (the presence of the Vatican, the mistrust of academic expertise). Not all of them were written by US authors, although all were published in the United States and speak directly to US concerns about conspiracy and the Bible. All of the novels, from the 1960s to the present, share a similar anatomy: they probe, explore, and fantasize about the possibilities of biblical vulnerability and conspiracy, contained neatly within the pages of a novel. They all shine new light on the political, theological, and personal stakes fears and desires surrounding the US Bible, an object of conspiratorial thinking always at risk from a new biblical "discovery."

3 | *Shifting Sands*

Two Discoveries: The Goatherd and the Semiticist

The story of the first discovery has been told many times over the years, with more and less elaboration. Here I quote the opening paragraph of Edmund Wilson's foundational account from his extended 1955 essay in the *New Yorker*, which I discussed in Chapter 1:

At some point rather early in the spring of 1947, a Bedouin boy called Muhammed the Wolf was minding some goats near a cliff on the western shore of the Dead Sea. Climbing up after one that had strayed, he noticed a cave that he had not seen before, and he idly threw a stone into it. There was an unfamiliar sound of breakage. The boy was frightened and ran away. But later he came back with another boy, and together they explored the cave. Inside were several tall clay jars, among fragments of other jars. They took off the bowl-like lids; a very bad smell arose; this turned out to arise from dark, oblong lumps which were found in all the jars. When they got the lumps out of the cave, they saw they were wrapped up in lengths of linen and coated with a black layer of what seemed to be pitch or wax. They unrolled them and found long, manuscripts, inscribed in parallel columns on thin sheets that had been sewn together.[1]

The two boys continued to Bethlehem "to sell their stuff on the black market" (Wilson now notes they were part of a "party of contrabanders") and made contact with a "Syrian" merchant who alerted the Syrian Metropolitan (ecclesiastical leader), who eventually acquired some of the manuscripts.[2]

---

[1] Edmund Wilson, "A Reporter at Large: The Scrolls from the Dead Sea," *New Yorker* (May 14, 1955): 45–131, at 45.

[2] On this story see John J. Collins, *The Dead Sea Scrolls: A Biography* (Princeton, NJ: Princeton University Press, 2013), 1–21. For an exhaustive account based on interviews and archival work, see Weston W. Fields, *The Dead Sea Scrolls: A Full History. Vol. 1: 1947–1960* (Leiden: Brill, 2009), 23–89.

In the 1972 novel *Judas!* (published in the United States as *The Judas Gospel*, from which version I cite), British author Peter van Greenaway spun out a violent and fantastic version of a scroll discovered in a cave. The serendipitous find is made by Geoffrey Mallory, a weaselly British lecturer in Semitics who had been convinced against his better judgment to go on a search for lost scrolls by valiant archaeologist Sir Max Lonsdale. Mere days into their search near the supposed site of "the Wolf's" discovery, their expedition was attacked by local terrorists. Everyone but Mallory was killed; the Semiticist had wandered off from the camp to urinate and now, facing masked gunmen, ran for his life into a nearby cave. Having crawled into a hole and dropped six feet into a hidden cave, he paused for breath:

The sudden shock displaced his sense of precarious well-being. Shock that men were hunting him, Geoffrey Mallory, lecturer in Semitic languages, hunting him as other men hunt animals. An outflow of adrenalin pumped new life into his fears and for a moment he felt he would faint. It passed ... Mallory's fingers closed over something hard and recoiled at the unexpected. He frowned in near darkness at the introduction of a new element into the game. His tactile sense was sufficiently developed to distinguish between a familiar and unfamiliar object ... Carefully he picked up the object and carried it to the better light of the cave's mouth. Not excited so much as puzzled he saw that he was holding what appeared to be a scroll.

Unlike the Bedouin boys who couldn't recognize or read the script on their scrolls, Mallory could clearly make out the faint writing visible in ancient Hebrew: "The Testament of Judas" (pp. 55–56).

At first blush these two accounts, the journalistic and the novelistic, seem very different: a bucolic moment of quiet goatherding (in the course of some light smuggling) broken by the sound of a rock hitting ceramic versus the hail of gunfire, the adrenaline-fueled flight, the discovery made in terror for one's life. Our agents of discovery are different as well: a native boy and a foreigner, the first not knowing what he's found and the second already on the search for a lost text. Yet the commonalities of these two stories reveal a great deal about biblical thinking emanating from the terrain of the Dead Sea.

In this chapter, I look at how some Gospel Thrillers reflect and refract the conspiratorial aura of the Dead Sea Scrolls and Israel in the US biblical imaginary. I begin by looking at this narrative pattern of "the find" and how it shapes the particular imaginative terrain of these novels: a terrain rich in discovery and danger. After outlining the particular nexus of secrecy, revelation, and conspiracy surrounding the Scrolls I think with the novels about the new Bible that might emerge from the land of Israel, what it might say about a Jewish Jesus, and how it might resonate with deeper anxieties about "biblical" identity.

The Find

Central to these stories is, of course, the discovery of a precious lost manuscript, often in a cave. This narrative is so well-known that, in modern times, it has ironically become evidence for skeptics that a find has been faked and a discovery forged. When the story of the Dead Sea Scrolls became public, for some it recalled almost too precisely the find story peddled by Moses Shapira (whom we met in Chapter 1) to authenticate the early Deuteronomy text he was offering for sale to the British Museum: Bedouin (this time, like our fictional Semiticist, hiding from military attack) supposedly took refuge in a cave and stumbled upon "strips of leather" which turned out, according to Shapira, to be worth a fortune. When the strips were declared a forgery, Shapira's discovery account was also discredited.[3]

Biblical scholar Eva Mroczek has traced the many iterations of the "cave find" from the premodern past to the Dead Sea Scrolls. These find tales, she points out, are not just means of authenticating lost old texts; their very stereotypical format is as likely to raise suspicion as allay fears. Instead Mroczek argues that we should read these repetitive stories as "a literary genre, part of a narrative tradition" doing particular ideological work. In the stories Mroczek examines, including the story of "the Wolf" and his goats, that work is theological: "concealment and memory work to join the scriptural past to the present." The mythic hiddenness of a vital text, emerging at just the right moment, asserts the persistence and providence of divine revelation: "how the sacred past is threatened, lost, hidden, and – perhaps, but always precariously – recoverable."[4]

---

[3] Chanan Tigay, *The Lost Book of Moses: The Hunt for the World's Oldest Bible* (New York: Harper, 2016) and now Idan Dershowitz, *The Valediction of Moses: A Proto-Biblical Book* (Tübingen: Mohr Siebeck, 2021), as well as my discussion in Chapter 1.

[4] Eva Mroczek, "Truth and Doubt in Discovery Narratives," in *Rethinking "Authority" in Late Antiquity: Authorship, Law, and Transmission in Jewish*

Let's turn back to our first two stories, the "historical" and the fictional, the goatherd and the Semiticist. Certainly, in both of our stories the serendipity of the cave producing its precious secrets evokes the precarious persistence of the sacred past. Other ideological themes also emerge that make this land into a distinctive kind of textual territory. That is, the find inscribes that sacred past into a specific kind of landscape: the uninhabited desert of Judea, the slumbering wilderness adjacent to the setting of Jesus's ministry and death. Archaeology at Qumran in the 1950s revealed that there were settlements near the finds in that cave; nonetheless, the assumption remains that the scrolls ended up in caves because they were hidden there, safe from unworthy eyes. The cave is a container fixed in a biblical landscape frozen in time, offering up its secrets to the unsuspecting passerby, whether wandering goatherd or cowering Semiticist. Even Mallory, on a mission to *find* such a text in such a location, is caught unawares by his discovery. Unlike the prey of the Bible Hunters, the scrolls emerging from this wilderness are not hunted but mined.

This wilderness may be slumbering but it is not safe. It's a no-man's land rife with lawlessness and violence. Muhammed "the Wolf" is no pastoral shepherd; already in the 1950s Wilson had identified him as a smuggler (including of goats). Van Greenaway hints at the violence of these Bedouin smugglers in his fictional account. Mallory learns from the Israeli soldiers who rescue him that his group was attacked by "Ta'mireh tribesmen," that is, members of the same Bedouin tribe to which Muhammed "the Wolf" belonged (p. 60). The very presence of the Israeli military further highlights the perils of the biblical desert.

These two stories also center the monetary value of these discoveries. Muhammed and his companions do not go to religious leaders with their discovery, but to merchants. Mallory, even while still huddling in the cave with his newly found scroll, hatches a scheme to make money: "He would smuggle his discovery out of the country, get it to England. And let them howl. It had happened before, with devious Syrians, dollar-struck Bedouin, priests, patriarchs, and God knew what others in a mixed and none too clean ragbag of jostling opportunists" (pp. 57–58). The "ragbag of jostling opportunists" listed here are

and Christian Tradition, Routledge Monographs in Classical Studies, ed. A. J. Berkovitz and Mark Letteney (London: Routledge, 2018), 139–60, at 139, 143, and 148. See also Eva Mroczek, "True Stories and the Poetics of Textual Discovery," *Bulletin for the Study of Religion* 45.2 (2016): 21–31.

meant to recall, in all likelihood, the various claimants to the original Dead Sea Scrolls: the Syrian Metropolitan who brought them to the United States to sell, the Catholic priests working with the Jordanian government to excavate at Qumran, even Muhammed and his friends, "dollar-struck Bedouin." These desert treasures are literally worth their weight in gold.[5]

Other Gospel Thrillers centered on lost gospels emerging from the Israeli wilderness deploy various "find" narratives to reinforce these key themes: the manuscripted landscape, the treacherous terrain, the promise of precious secrets. Notably, unlike *The Q Document*, almost none of these novels center on forgeries. (The one exception, which I discuss below, is Warren Kiefer's 1976 novel *The Pontius Pilate Papers*). The documents offered up from these shifting sands are authentic accounts of Jesus and his ministry from Jesus's own day (or even his own hand). They participate in a kind of Dead Sea Scrolls optimism that has characterized the scholarly and public attitude to finds from this region for the past half-century. New finds, or newly revealed finds, are greeted with relatively little skepticism. This lack of Dead Sea Scrolls skepticism promotes a view of the barren wilderness of Judea as continually generative, even though Dead Sea Scrolls forgeries are actually common. Furthermore, because these novels imagine authentic, long-lost accounts of Jesus they encourage readers to understand the canonical Bible, as it exists in the West, as the perpetrator of a conspiracy, an age-old instrument of deception awaiting the blistering truth to emerge at last.[6]

That readers bear witness to the find narrative in many of these novels bolsters the authenticity of the discovery but also sets up the larger themes around biblical conspiracy emerging from the

---

[5] Fields, *Dead Sea Scrolls*, 107–09 and 561–65, discusses and transcribes the "Scrolls Ledger" kept by the Palestinian Archaeological Museum, an itemized list of payments for information, artifacts, and ancient texts made out to local merchants and Bedouin.

[6] Michael Greshko, "'Dead Sea Scrolls' at the Museum of the Bible Are All Forgeries," *National Geographic Magazine* (March 13, 2020), online at www.nationalgeographic.com/history/article/museum-of-the-bible-dead-sea-scrolls-forgeries. See also Eibert Tigchelaar, "A Provisional List of Unprovenanced, Twenty-First Century, Dead Sea Scroll-Like Fragments," *Dead Sea Discoveries* 24 (2017): 173–88 and Årstein Justnes's blog "The Lying Pen of Scribes: Manuscript Forgeries and Counterfeiting Scripture in the Twenty-First Century," http://lyingpen.com.

dangerous, lucrative, uncanny sands of the Judean desert. Some novels, like van Greenaway's, imagine scrolls still undiscovered decades after "the Wolf" lost his goat, reinforcing the idea of biblical lands capable of endlessly producing new and dangerous secrets. Elizabeth Peters's 1970 novel *The Dead Sea Cipher* hinges upon a new cache of Aramaic scrolls discovered by an obsessive English archaeologist in the 1960s. Unlike the dashing Sir Max Lonsdale, though, the disgraced alcoholic Hank Layard dies after his "Big Find," killed in a dispute with his Arab partner. (Among the scrolls in Layard's "Big Find" are Aramaic originals of the canonical gospels in addition to a "Life of the Virgin" and a "Life of Jesus.") Roland Cutler's 2008 *The Secret Scroll* has its hero, preternaturally gifted US archaeologist Josh Cohan, find a jar with a gospel inside it while driving alone through the Judean desert. Cohan, like Lonsdale in *The Judas Gospel*, is impelled by a strong sense of fate and intuition: the desert finds call out to their western liberators. In Glenn Meade's 2011 *The Second Messiah*, two shocking scrolls that tell the same story about Jesus and an impostor messiah are discovered decades apart (in the 1990s and the 2010s), not far from the site of that original Qumran cave.

Other find narratives push outside the narrow bounds of the Dead Sea region. In the 1994 novel *The Negev Project* by Larry Witham, fragments of Aramaic texts with new sayings of Jesus are found by Bedouin in the Negev (the specifics are fuzzy) and traded across the border to members of the Muslim Brotherhood in Jordan. These fragments, desirable for both their monetary and theological value, bounce along the routes of Middle Eastern conflict (the novel begins with bombing in Jerusalem during the first Gulf War) amid quixotic hopes for regional peace (the titular "project" of the novel). In *The Masada Scroll*, from 2007, authors Paul Block and Robert Vaughan leverage the site of Israel's founding myth of military independence to weave a tale of global terrorists, local freedom fighters, and western expertise. The "scroll" hidden at Masada during the first-century revolt against Rome and miraculously uncovered in the twenty-first century is a polyglot Gospel of Dismas (the son of one of the thieves crucified with Christ) that conveys Jesus's true teaching of religious universalism in Greek and Hebrew.

The push for finds outside of the Dead Sea is, in some senses, pragmatic: how many texts might remain to be found after so much searching? (Although, as I noted above, "new Dead Sea Scrolls" have been making headlines routinely since the 1950s: while some end up proven forgeries, others may be authentically first century or older.) But they also serve to expand outward themes of danger and promise into other territories implicated in the militarized past and present of the Middle East.[7]

If these find narratives set in the present day serve to reinscribe the bountiful dangers of biblical texts long-buried, other novels plot the secrets of the Dead Sea along winding routes of global history and conspiracy. In these novels, the lost gospel has been extracted from the caves at some point in the past, long before "the Wolf" cast his stone. Complex chains of custody in turn generate networks of conspirators hiding, or seeking, the truth at all costs. In Alan Gold's 1994 *The Lost Testament*, a "Testament of Christ" was originally hidden near Qumran but later smuggled out of Judea by a second-century Christian. Its only trace in Israel is a line on a "treasure list" found by modern explorers in one of the Qumran caves. Gold's protagonists embark on a race around the world that maps the fault lines of global Jewry, from Masada to Ethiopia. *The 13th Apostle*, published in 2007 by Richard and Rachael Heller, reveals that a second copper scroll was given by Muslims to a Christian traveler during the crusades and concealed back in the crusader's seaside English monastery. Unlike the famous copper scroll found in the 1950s, which purportedly gave the location of a buried treasure, this scroll tells the true story of Jesus as recounted by Micah, the thirteenth apostle. The Hellers's novel, like Gold's, places biblical discovery in the context of the complicated relationship of a global diaspora of Jews to the Jewish nation-state.

Perhaps the most convoluted find narrative is in Daniel Easterman's *The Judas Testament*. In this 1994 novel, a scroll had made its way at some point in the unknown past from the Judean caves to a *genizah* (a Jewish storehouse for sacred texts) in Poland; there it had been found by Nazis, seized by Soviets, and ended up in the hands of our hero Jack Gould, who smuggles it into the United Kingdom. Jack narrowly defeats the antisemitic global conspirators seeking this firsthand account of Jesus's life. At the end of *The Judas Testament*, Jack then

---

[7] Isabel Kershner, "Israeli Researchers Show Dead Sea Scrolls Artifacts," *New York Times* (March 16, 2021): A9; Rosella Tercatin, "Are the Newest Dead Sea Scrolls Just the Beginning?" *The Jerusalem Post* (March 18, 2021), online at www.jpost.com/archaeology/dead-sea-scrolls-many-caves-left-more-biblical-texts-may-emerge-662327.

smuggles the "Jesus scroll" back *into* Israel, hides it in a cave at near Qumran, and plans to return in "a year or two, when it seemed the time was ready," to make his official discovery with a proper archaeological team. This inversion of the find story – bringing the secret scroll back *into* Israel and depositing it in a cave – destabilizes the entire narrative upon which Dead Sea Scrolls fantasies rest.[8]

Easterman inverts the find narrative; Luis M. Rocha blows it up entirely in *The Pope's Assassin*. This 2011 novel written in Portuguese is the only Gospel Thriller I am treating in this book not originally composed in English (although, unlike Rocha's earlier novels, it was simultaneously published in Portuguese and in English translation). While Rocha, a journalist who died young, composed all his novels in Portuguese, he had most of his success through their translations in English and publication in the United States and the UK. In *The Pope's Assassin*, the third novel in a quintet of Vatican-based thrillers, we learn that the entire narrative of Muhammed "the Wolf" was invented by an Israeli archaeologist named Ben Isaac, clandestinely working along the Dead Sea in the 1940s and 1950s. The "public" scrolls are only a fraction of what Isaac uncovered; the most explosive finds include a gospel written by Jesus in his old age in the city of Rome. Isaac keeps these finds hidden in his London mansion as part of a compact he entered into with the Vatican, confirming (as I explore later in this chapter) some of the darkest conspiracy theories surrounding the Dead Sea Scrolls.[9]

All of these find stories replicate the basic themes we saw in both the "historical" account of the Dead Sea Scrolls and the early fictional remix of *The Judas Gospel*: the dangerous, precious, serendipitous new secret that can only emerge from the biblical sands of Israel. They also evoke the broader themes that play out in the Dead Sea Scrolls Gospel Thrillers, themes which give voice to various fears and desires in the United States concerning the Bible and its problematic place of origin: the conspiratorial fears of biblical secrets and revelations; the geopolitical uncertainty of the westernized space of the new state of Israel; the

---

[8] "Daniel Easterman" is the *nom de plume* of Irish Islamicist Denis MacEoin who left academia in the 1980s and became a successful author of thrillers and ghost stories.

[9] The novel was simultaneously published in the original Portuguese as *A Mentira Sagrada* (Porto: Porto Editora, 2011), although the copyright in the English language version refers to the Portuguese as *Assassino do Papa*.

new, and anxious, theological attention from the 1960s onward to the Jewishness of Jesus; and the framing of protagonists and antagonists in the quest for biblical truth in the Middle East.

Secrecy and Revelation

From the beginning, the Dead Sea Scrolls were ripe for conspiratorial thinking. While most of the scholarly community and popular press excitedly embraced the authenticity of the Scrolls, some voices in the academy voiced their strident rejection of the Scrolls as authentically ancient. No voice was more strident than that of Solomon Zeitlin, a professor at Dropsie College (now the Katz Center for Advanced Judaic Studies at the University of Pennsylvania) and editor of the *Jewish Quarterly Review*.

Zeitlin's initial objections to the authenticity of "the Hebrew Scrolls" (it would be years before Zeitlin would deign to call them "Dead Sea Scrolls") were grounded in their rumored contents. The more he learned about the Scrolls, the more he protested. Over a decade, over hundreds of pages in the *Jewish Quarterly Review*, in articles with titles calling the Scrolls a "hoax," "fiction," "falsification," and "travesty," Zeitlin pointed out the inconsistency of the find narrative(s), the unlikeliness of scrolls remaining concealed in caves for centuries, and the credulity and inexperience of the western scholars hyping their significance. These scrolls, he maintained for the rest of his career, were poorly written medieval documents taken from a *genizah*, passed off as ancient by locals seeking financial gain, and accepted by poorly trained biblical studies scholars eager for "pre-Christian" Jewish texts that would give them insight into the Jesus movement.[10]

Zeitlin's prolix refusal to accept the antiquity of the Scrolls was not only an unwillingness to change his opinion of what Jews were doing, writing, and believing in the first centuries BCE and CE; it was also an unwillingness to view the land of Israel as an ongoing source for

---

[10] From 1948 to 1958, Zeitlin published articles on the Scrolls in most issues of the *Jewish Quarterly Review*. For summaries of his accumulating arguments, see esp. "The Hebrew Scrolls: Once More and Finally," *Jewish Quarterly Review* 41 (1950): 1–58 and "The Propaganda of the Hebrew Scrolls and the Falsification of History," *Jewish Quarterly Review* 46 (1955): 1–39, 116–80; 46 (1956): 209–58. On the desire to see the Scrolls as "pre-Christian" in order to learn more about Christian origins, see esp. "Propaganda, part III," 209–17.

Christian biblical discovery. To be sure, as Zeitlin pointed out ad nauseam, the find story had been inconsistent from the beginning, and almost every detail – who, what, when, where, and how – had been revised and reconsidered. As he pointed out in a three-part, 175-page essay spread out over three issues of the *Jewish Quarterly Review* in 1955 and 1956: "The entire discovery is shrouded in mystery." No one but Zeitlin, it seemed, cared. By the 1950s and 1960s, the authenticity of the Scrolls, and the belief that the sands of the desert were bountiful in their treasures was, as Zeitlin lamented, orthodoxy.[11]

It was precisely *because* these Scrolls were viewed as authentic that suspicious minds could spin out elaborate theories of hidden scrolls, secret discoveries, and shocking secrets being suppressed. The aura of institutional secrecy that soon surrounded the Scrolls fueled (and continues to fuel) conspiratorial speculation. The secrecy stemmed in part from the way the Scrolls were released for academic and public consumption. The seven scrolls purportedly discovered by Muhammed "the Wolf" in 1947 were photographed and quickly published in the 1950s. The vastly more numerous additional scrolls and fragments uncovered by archaeological teams working under the Jordan Department of Antiquities, however, were much more tightly controlled. Father Roland de Vaux, head of the École Biblique in Jerusalem, assembled an international team of experts who had the painstaking task of piecing together and translating thousands of fragments discovered in different caves. They worked alone, only rarely allowing outsiders to view the texts.[12]

That Roman Catholics were in charge of these ancient Jewish texts easily inflamed casual anti-Catholic sentiment among a suspicious public in the 1950s and 1960s. (In *The Lost Testament*, Gold introduces a highly exaggerated version of de Vaux, Père Romain de la Tour, a virulently anti-Semitic French Dominican still in charge of the Scrolls project in the 1990s; de Vaux died in 1971.) When Israel took over East Jerusalem following the 1967 military conflict, the Scrolls were reunited but the unpublished texts remained under the supervision of de Vaux's international team, now under the auspices of what

---

[11] The quotation comes from Zeitlin, "Propaganda, part III," 219.
[12] Fields, *Dead Sea Scrolls*, 191–239, writes apologetically about the secretive and slow work of the team assembled by De Vaux and Gerald Harding, the Director of the Jordan Department of Antiquities.

would become the Israel Antiquities Authority. Throughout the 1970s and 1980s, international pressure to make the Scrolls accessible to international scholarship had little success. (De Vaux was succeeded at his death by another Roman Catholic priest, Pierre Benoit; upon Benoit's retirement in 1984 John Strugnell, a secular academic and longtime member of the Scrolls team, took the helm.)

The suspicious secrecy of the Scrolls lingers in the background of the Gospel Thrillers. When Jack Gould, the academic hero of Easterman's *The Judas Testament*, is shown a bounty of ancient texts hidden deep in a Soviet library, he remarks to his friend Iosif: "'You think this could end up another Dead Sea Scrolls fiasco, with one little group of scholars appointing themselves guardians of the texts, keeping it all to themselves and letting information out as and when they see fit. That's what you're afraid of, isn't it?'" (p. 135) Two academics discussing new first-century finds in *The Negev Project* also acknowledge that "being clandestine ... was what had gotten some of the Dead Sea Scrolls editors in trouble" (p. 113). Rocha's *Pope's Assassin* takes this secrecy even further: the Scrolls discovered by Ben Isaac (and passed off as the find of Bedouin goatherds) remain under lock and key, seen by no one, subject to an ongoing and renewable secret agreement between Isaac, the Israeli government, and the Vatican. In Meade's *Second Messiah*, the Vatican and the Israeli government have a long-term agreement in place to conceal any discovery that might harm Catholics or Jews; this covert agreement leads to the tragic death of two archaeologists in the 1990s and panic in the Vatican and in Tel Aviv in the present-day when a new Pope promises to throw open the Vatican Secret Archives.

This aura of secrecy also fueled the shadowy promise of revelation, evident in modern reception of the Scrolls and amplified in their fictional framing in Gospel Thrillers. Almost from the beginning, both scholars and an eager public looked to the Scrolls as a new source for Christian origins. Was a bombshell about Christianity waiting to be discovered among the finds? Was it perhaps already ticking away in some secret scholarly lab, suppressed by the guardians of the Scrolls? That the Scrolls should tell the world *something* about Christian origins seemed self-evident. Wilson in his *New Yorker* article called the "monastery" excavated at Qumran "more than Bethlehem or Nazareth, the cradle of Christianity," even going to so far as to speculate that Jesus or John the Baptist might have "been a member

of the sect" at the Dead Sea since, after all, "Bethlehem itself is not
very far."[13]

In his 1955 essay and later book, Wilson relied heavily on the
speculations of French scholar André Dupont-Sommer, whose insistence on theological links between the sectarian Scrolls community and
the Jesus movement were pushed even more emphatically by John
Allegro, a British member of the Dead Sea Scrolls team working under
de Vaux. In the mid-1950s, Allegro began speaking publicly about his
sense of the strong links between the Dead Sea Scrolls and the Jesus
movement. In his slender 1956 popular introduction, *The Dead Sea
Scrolls: A Reappraisal*, Allegro speculated that John the Baptist may
have been "adopted by the Qumran sect as a boy." His final chapter,
on "Jesus and Scrolls," is only a little more circumspect. Allegro's
insistence on finding the roots of Jesus's movement in Qumran were
highly publicized, signaling the eagerness of the public for such revelations. Other members of the Dead Sea Scrolls team opposed this
Christian reading of the Scrolls, even going so far as to write a letter
to the *Times* of London, distancing themselves from "Mr.
Allegro's" interpretation.[14]

In the preface to his 1963 update to *Dead Sea Scrolls*, Allegro was
scathing about the "appalling situation" of Scrolls scholarship. He
decried the slow pace of publication and the inattention of scholars
of Christian origins to the Scrolls. He castigated "rather naïve attempts
on the part of Christian apologists to counter what they feared were
attempts to undermine the faith of believers." Without naming de
Vaux or the international team, Allegro hinted at deceit and
suppression:

What is perhaps even more disturbing ... is the cloak of secrecy that has
hung over the acquisition and disposal of these vital and often most controversial documents since 1956. *Scrolls have been secretly unearthed by the
Bedouin, fleetingly glimpsed by specialists, and then allowed to "disappear"
off the face of the earth.* Even when others from the same cache have early on

---

[13] Wilson, "Scrolls," 113, 116.

[14] John Allegro, *The Dead Sea Scrolls: A Reappraisal*, rev. ed. (London: Penguin,
1963), at 158. See Collins, *Dead Sea Scrolls*, 104–08. Later Allegro promoted
controversial theories about the role of psychedelic drugs in the origins of
Christianity, which effectively ended his academic career: *The Sacred Mushroom
and the Cross: A Study of the Nature and Origins of Christianity Within the
Fertility Cults of the Ancient Near East* (London: Hodder and Stoughton, 1970).

been rescued by the prompt action of the Jordanian Department of Antiquities, they have lain hidden away in the vaults of a foreign-controlled museum for several years, and only the vaguest information on their contents has been allowed to reach the outside world (emphasis added).[15]

Given his positive statements about Jordan here and later in this unhappy preface, the "foreign control" Allegro refers to may be the French government which had oversight of de Vaux's École Biblique; it may also be a subtle swipe at the Roman Catholic church. The oblique references to secret, lost, and suppressed documents are as tantalizing as they are vague. When Allegro soon after insists that he (unlike others) has "no axe to grind, religious or academic" we may surmise both of these as motives for the sinister suppression at work.

Insinuations of suppression and even conspiracy continued through the 1970s and 1980s. In Chapter 2, I discussed Donovan Joyce's conspiratorial claims in his 1972 *The Jesus Scroll*: a shocking discovery at Masada, an unscrupulous archaeologist looking to cash in, and a presumed cover-up by the Vatican tie together many of the threads floating around in scholarly and popular Dead Sea Scrolls discourse. In 1991, conspiracy raconteurs Michael Baigent and Richard Leigh made their own contribution to the Dead Sea Scrolls conspiracy discourse with the provocatively titled *The Dead Sea Scrolls Deception*. Despite the title, however, the volume is relatively tame compared to their previous offerings, coauthored with Henry Lincoln: *The Holy Blood and the Holy Grail*, which posited a secret royal bloodline descended from Jesus and Mary Magdalene, and *The Messianic Legacy*, which explored the historical Jesus and continued tracing the various secret societies linked to his purported descendants.[16]

Dead Sea Scrolls Deception builds on the first part of *Messianic Legacy* in an attempt to figure out what can be known and what has been suppressed about the historical Jesus. They mainly rely on the theories of Allegro and the more recent work of Robert Eisenman, a professor in California who developed particular theories about the relationship of Jesus, James (Jesus's brother), and Paul to the

---

[15] Allegro, *Dead Sea Scrolls*, 11–13.
[16] Donovan Joyce, *The Jesus Scroll* (Sydney: Angus and Robertson, 1972); Michael Baigent, Richard Leigh, and Henry Lincoln, *The Holy Blood and the Holy Grail* (London: Jonathan Cape, 1982) and *The Messianic Legacy* (London: Jonathan Cape, 1986); Michael Baigent and Richard Leigh, *The Dead Sea Scrolls Deception* (London: Jonathan Cape, 1991).

community at Qumran. Eisenman was one of the many scholars clamoring for open access to the Scrolls and acted as a ready source not only for scholarship into Jesus and Qumran but also for the convoluted politics surrounding Scrolls scholarship. A clear target for Baigent's and Leigh's conspiratorial thinking emerges already in their preface, as they describe how their investigations took them all the way "to the corridors of the Vatican and, even more ominously, into the offices of the Inquisition."[17]

Baigent and Leigh exculpate the Israeli authorities for not exercising authority over the "Scrollery" overseen by de Vaux but work hard to trace ties between de Vaux (whom they describe as an anti-Semite with youthful ties to right-wing French nationalists) and the Vatican's Pontifical Biblical Institute and the Congregation for the Doctrine of the Faith (what had formerly been known as the Inquisition). Their assumption, making explicit what was tacit for Allegro, is that the Roman Catholic commitments dominating the "Scrollery" could not possibly allow the official guardians of the Scrolls to publish and interpret the Qumran materials with academic rigor or honesty. They hint at "suppression of materials" and warn that "everything we ever learn about the Qumran texts will be subject to the censorship machinery of the Congregation for the Doctrine of the Faith – will be, in effect, filtered and edited for us by the Inquisition."[18]

While decrying the lack of access to the Scrolls and the possibility of suppression, Baigent and Leigh nevertheless spin out detailed theories based almost entirely on Eisenman's work: the relationship of John the Baptist and Jesus to Qumran; the Dead Sea settlements as a center for early Christian activity; and a critical conflict between James, preserving Jesus's Qumran-like message, and Paul, a "heretic" (and possible agent of the Roman Empire) who managed to wrench Jesus's message away from its origins and founded a religion that had little to do with Jesus. That Baigent and Leigh (and Eisenman) could produce this elaborate reimagination of Christian origins using published materials from Qumran, along with creative interpretation of New Testament texts, calls into question the efficacy of the Vatican-led "deception" they spend the first half of the book outlining. If Baigent and Leigh can

---

[17] Robert Eisenman, *Maccabees, Zadokites, Christians and Qumran: A New Hypothesis of Qumran Origins* (Leiden: Brill, 1984); *James the Just in the Habakkuk Pesher* (Leiden: Brill, 1986).
[18] Baigent and Leigh, *Dead Sea Scrolls*, 129, 125.

reveal the shocking truth about Jesus and Christian origins that the
Inquisition doesn't want you to know, how much of a conspiracy can
it be?

The idea that secrets about Jesus are being suppressed continues,
even though since the early 1990s all of the Scrolls photographed and
catalogued by the international team have been made public (and,
since then, the Israel Antiquities Authority has relaxed its tight reins
on access). The public collapse of the Scrolls director, John Strugnell,
led to a loss of confidence in the project. In 1991, two publications
effectively broke the embargo: Hershel Shanks, the editor of *Biblical
Archaeology Review*, published a facsimile of the Scrolls that had been
produced by graduate student Martin Abegg and his advisor, Ben Zion
Wacholder, using a concordance of the Scrolls. That same year the
Director of the Library at the Huntington Library in San Marino,
California, decided to make public the photographic plates of the
Scrolls that had, through a circuitous route, come into the
Huntington's collections. Litigation over publication continued, but
the Scrolls were now, after almost forty years, public. The whiff of
secrecy and conspiracy, however, has never fully dissipated.[19]

These scholarly conspiracy theories condense a more diffuse and
persistent desire for secrets and revelations from the Dead Sea: the
hope that the suppressed truth will emerge or that a newly discovered
scroll will provide the smoking gun to put all the pieces into place and
reveal a new truth about Jesus. It is possible some startling new
document will emerge: the state of Israel has recently embarked on a
sweeping survey of the caves around the Dead Sea in search of new
antiquities. It is equally likely that a forgery will emerge, passed off as
proof of the various theories put forward since the 1950s.

Gospel Thrillers do not need to wait for painstaking archaeological
investigation nor are they constrained by the uncertainty of a new
scroll suddenly appearing after so long. They can explore, amplify,
and push in new directions the tensions, hopes, and desires that have
surrounded the Dead Sea Scrolls in the West since Wilson's *New
Yorker* piece introduced the Scrolls and all their wild possibilities.
The promise and the stakes are both ramped up in these novels. The
novels agree that the secrets emerging from the desert will be explosive:

[19] On the publication of the Scrolls and their aftermath, see Collins, *Dead Sea
Scrolls*, 218–36.

a "bombshell" in *The Lost Testament* (p. 7); "shattering" and "over-whelming" in *The Judas Gospel* (p. 84); "'it will cause a lot of trouble when it's published,'" asserts the scholar-hero of *The Judas Testament*, to which his friend replies, "'That is an understatement'" (p. 143). In *The 13th Apostle* the protagonists realize they have "uncovered the most important document in the history of mankind" (p. 260). In Gold's *The Lost Testament*, the mere hint that a "Testament of Christ" might exist *somewhere* in the world leads to a media frenzy:

The world's popular press gave the story a sensational coverage, with blown-up pictures of the twelve scholars accompanying headlines that would have done credit to a Hollywood movie ... Television stations went wild, running footage from the press conference repeatedly along with thirty second grabs from their archives of anyone who had speculated on Jesus in the past. (p. 22)

If the stakes are higher so are the conspiratorial machinations put in motion to suppress these dangerous new truths. Gospel Thrillers imagine enormous international resources deployed to block our prot-agonists from finding or disseminating the truth. Many of them amp-lify the fears of religious interference posited by Baigent and Leigh. In *The Judas Gospel*, the Pope, after receiving a crude blackmail attempt from Geoffrey Mallory, dispatches a highly skilled assassin known as The Dominican to recover the gospel and eliminate any evidence of its existence (including Mallory, his wife, and their unfortunate friends). *The Masada Scroll* posits an even more elaborate fantasy of Catholic conspiracy in the Via Dei, a reactionary group working to hide the truth about Jesus since the time of the apostles. Other fundamentalist religious groups stalk our protagonists: Islamist and white supremacist groups in *The 13th Apostle* and a racist and antisemitic televangelist allied with the ultra-right Israeli Orthodox in *The Lost Testament*. Perhaps the most elaborate global conspiracy is found in *The Judas Testament*: the Crux Orientalis, or League of the Eastern Cross, a racist and antisemitic European Christian conspiracy seeking to estab-lish a new Holy Roman Empire. These novels are punctuated with conspiratorial violence meant to underscore the stakes of the newly found (or newly sought) gospel: from quiet assassinations in hotel rooms and private apartments to cars driven off the road or blown up with whole city blocks, the quest for the truth about Jesus emerges from the desert and wreaks violence far and wide. These are secrets that people will kill and die for. These are also secrets that could only emerge from one place: the home of the Dead Sea Scrolls, the dangerous and generative biblical sands of the land of Israel.[20]

Biblical Israel

In 1946, Bartley C. Crum, a liberal-minded California attorney, was tapped to serve as a US delegate on the Anglo-American Committee of Inquiry, an ultimately unsuccessful attempt to solve the political problem of Palestine after World War II. The Committee spent a few weeks touring Palestine before drafting their report; in 1947 Crum published a memoir of this tour of the Middle East. Crum was dazzled by the positive effects Jewish colonization was having on Palestine and, more amazingly, the transformative effects of colonization on the Jewish settlers. He wrote:

Many of the Jewish children I saw were blond and blue-eyed, a mass mutation that, I was told, is yet to be adequately explained. It is the most remarkable because the majority of the Jews of Palestine are of east European Jewish stock, traditionally dark-haired and dark-eyed. One might assert that a new Jewish folk is being created in Palestine: the vast majority almost a head taller than their parents, a sturdy people more a throwback to the farmers and fisherman of Jesus' day than the products of the sons and daughters of the cities of eastern and central Europe.[21]

In this reverie on fortuitous mutation, Crum condenses a century of US Orientalist fantasies about the Middle East, fantasies that came to view Jewish settlement and, eventually, nationalism as the antidote to perennial Arab backwardness. The literal whitening of the Middle East envisioned a whiter future recuperating a whiter past, a time before the

---

[20] Hotel rooms and apartments: Peters, *Dead Sea Cipher*, 9–14, 26–28; Van Greenaway, *Judas Gospel*, 234–38. Car bombs and accidents: Easterman, *Judas Testament*, 166–67; Van Greenaway, *Judas Gospel*, 217–18. I also discuss the particular hazards to academics in Chapter 5.

[21] Bartley C. Crum, *Behind the Silken Curtain: A Personal Account of Anglo-American Diplomacy in Palestine and the Middle East* (New York: Simon & Schuster, 1947), 192 cited by Amy Kaplan, *Our American Israel: The Story of an Entangled Alliance* (Cambridge, MA: Harvard University Press, 2018), 32. See generally Douglas Little, *American Orientalism: The United States and the Middle East Since 1945* (Chapel Hill, NC: University of North Carolina Press, 2009), 9–42.

"farmers and fisherman of Jesus' day" were displaced by – or descended into? – the nonwhite bodies of indolent Arabs.

Crum's vision of sturdy white bodies both in the time of Jesus and in
the future Jewish state also condenses much of the anxiety of white US
Protestants concerning the Bible's Middle Eastern origins. In *Innocents
Abroad*, Mark Twain popularized the cognitive dissonance of white
Protestants touring a biblical "holy land" populated with shifty and
categorically nonwhite "beggars and relic-peddlers." Crum's
bracketing off of those nonwhite bodies with the "farmers and fisherman of Jesus' day" and the mutated settlers' children of the 1940s
could secure a palatably familiar, and whiter, point of origin for the
western Christian Bible. But the uncertainty of those white
bodies – would they revert to their dark hair and eyes if transplanted
back into the "cities of eastern Europe"? – could also hint at the
uncertainty of that familiarly white Bible.[22]

Crum's fantasy of white, western bodies reclaiming a white,
Christian point of biblical origin becomes something more ambiguous
in Gospel Thrillers centered on a new discovery from Israel. Part of
that ambiguity comes in the split religious affiliations of many of these
novels' protagonists, to which I return below. But more fundamentally
these novels question the fantasy of a white Israel producing a white
Bible, in the deep past as well as in the present. Israel is viewed, as it has
come to be in so much popular US media, as western*ized* which is not
the same as *western*. We see this most clearly in the way Israel's
"westernness" is transmuted in these novels from a racial or ethnic
fantasy into a technological one: Crum's blond-haired, blue-eyed
farmer-settlers become olive-skinned, dark-haired hyperskilled soldiers
and scholars.[23]

Israel in these novels is thoroughly militarized. On the one hand, the
insistence on the military prowess of Israel reinforces the overall view
of the land we saw in the find narratives: it is generative but dangerous.
It also reflects popular portrayals of Israel in US media, particularly

---

[22] Mark Twain, *Innocents Abroad or, The New Pilgrim's Progress; Being Some
Account of the Steamship Quaker City's Pleasure Excursion to Europe and the
Holy Land* (Hartford, CT: American Publishing Company, 1869), 352. See
Hilton Obenzinger, *American Palestine: Melville, Twain, and the Holy Land*
(Princeton, NJ: Princeton University Press, 1999), 159–273.

[23] My distinction between *western* and *westernized* draws on the critical insights of
Frantz Fanon, *Black Skin, White Masks* (New York: Grove Press, 1967).

after the territorial expansions of 1967 and the military success of 1973. The military skill of Israeli soldiers also draws a contrast with the western visitors who become embroiled in biblical conspiracy in these novels. We have already seen the presence of Israel's military in *The Judas Gospel*, calmly and competently rescuing Geoffrey Mallory after the terrorist ambush on his camp. These same soldiers appear at the beginning of the novel, too, escorting Mallory, Lonsdale, and the rest of their doomed expedition to their desert camp. They help set up the tents, stay for a companionable cup of coffee, and then drive off in jeeps, laughing at the foolhardiness of the explorers, "back to the safety of base some miles distant in Hebron" (p. 7). When they come upon the lone survivor, Mallory, they demonstrate a practiced sang-froid the Englishman pointedly lacks:

While they examined the remnants with dispassionate interest he felt the need to vomit and turned away as the lieutenant, the same one who'd escorted them to their starting point, approached wiping his soiled hand with a khaki handkerchief. It had to do with Lonsdale's blood. (p. 59)

When Mallory ham-handedly insults the lieutenant ("'You're very intelligent for an army officer'") the soldier replies affably, "'We do not all graduate from Mr Waugh's academy for callow subalterns. I am, in happier times, a post-graduate student at Haifa University'" (p. 62). The lieutenant at once demonstrates intimate knowledge of British culture ("Mr Waugh") while mocking it and distancing himself from it.[24]

The reference to postgraduate education is no mere throwaway, either. Throughout these novels Israelis combine military efficiency with advanced technical skill. Western media from early on used the technological advances of the new Israeli state (agricultural, archaeological, and military) to draw a contrast with the "backward" Arab populations. The novels frequently merge military and technological expertise in the character of the soldier-scholar, a former (or sometimes current or undercover) member of the Israeli military or secret police who is also a scholar assisting in uncovering the truth about the new find.[25]

---

[24] "Military escorts" are also present in Peters, *Dead Sea Cipher*, 234.

[25] Alan George, "'Making the Desert Bloom': A Myth Examined," *Journal of Palestine Studies* 8 (1979): 88–100.

A key figure in *The Negev Project* is "an old eccentric archaeologist named Simon Rabin, an Israeli soldier-scholar who had been part of the team that had dug up ancient Jerusalem" (p. 11). Rabin is obviously modeled on Yigael Yadin, the Palestine-born son of Eleazar Sukenik who was a soldier, politician, and archaeologist famous, among other things, for excavating Masada and popularizing the site as an emblem of Israeli nationalist heroism. *The Negev Project* even links Rabin to Yadin, although without naming the "onetime commander of the Haganah":[26]

Rabin was by every measure the soldier-scholar so romanticized in his country. His work on the archaeological excavations of Jerusalem sealed his reputation, and put him in a second echelon alongside the general-poets, a type characterized by the man who was excavation leader – a onetime commander of the Haganah, the Jewish underground defense force. Israeli generals modeled themselves on Old Testament military heroes. Digging up the past was self-affirming patriotism. (p. 30)

Here the Gospel Thriller engages with the romanticized view of a "Biblical archaeology" in Israel that yoked the muscular militarism of Zionism to the authenticating aura of a biblical past, wrenched from the ground by strength and skill.

In many ways, the soldier-scholar in these novels disrupts western (especially Euro-American) claims to biblical patrimony. Rabin's own recollection of his patriotic archaeological past in *The Negev Project* is nostalgic but rueful, and his life's work (the titular "project") is a peace-seeking endeavor in partnership with a renowned Muslim imam. Archaeology, through the collection and dissemination of potentially first-century Christian remains, now complicates the Zionist agenda of his past. Even more fundamentally, however, this "patriotic" Israeli biblical archaeology is not in the service of a western recovery of a (white, ultimately Christian and Protestant) Bible. It is instead a west-er*nized* use of the (literal) tools of earlier Euro-American biblical

---

[26] On Yadin see Neil Asher Silberman, *A Prophet from Amongst You: The Life of Yigael Yadin: Soldier, Scholar, and Mythmaker of Modern Israel* (Reading: Addison-Wesley, 1993). On Yadin's role in the "mythmaking" of Masada, see Jodi Magness, *Masada: From Jewish Revolt to Modern Myth* (Princeton, NJ: Princeton University Press, 2019), 187–200 alongside Yigael Yadin, *Masada: Herod's Fortress and the Zealots' Last Stand*, trans. Moshe Pearlman (New York: Random House, 1966). Yadin also merits a mention (as "Professor Yadin") in Kiefer, *The Pontius Pilate Papers*, 36.

archaeologists to reconstruct their biblical history *in* the Middle East (the land of "Old Testament military heroes") rather than to extract it *from* the Middle East.[27]

The nation-state defended and excavated by these soldier-scholars was not the white outpost Crum and others imagined in the 1940s. Yadin and other members of the founding generation of Israel staked their claim not only on history but on their embeddedness in the land as natives. Yadin biographer Neil Silberman describes his subject at one of the excavations that established his reputation: "Yadin was seen as the personification of the sabra soldier-scholar." Later, in assessing Yadin's scholarly legacy, Silberman adds: "Yigael Yadin did not invent Israeli archaeology – his gruff and ambitious father has a much better claim to that honor. Yadin was, rather, its personification: a sabra soldier and scholar in search of his past."[28]

Labeling native-born Israelis *sabra*, after the prickly cactus pear with a soft interior, supposedly dates to the 1930s wave of Jewish settlers and, in the early days of Israel, served to characterize the tough exterior and hardiness of the founding generation. Comparing first-generation settlers to a native desert fruit recalls Crum's assertion that Jewish children born in Palestine were somehow transformed and mutated into something different. But whereas Crum and others fantasized about white colonization, the invocation of the sabra relocates Israelis from their European ancestry into Middle Eastern "natives." (Yadin's Russian-born father Sukenik, while "gruff and ambitious," was no sabra). Yadin, the quintessential "sabra soldier and scholar" did not just excavate Israel but "personified" the process of historical recovery from soil that is generative but dangerous.[29]

Although the myth of the sabra was determinedly masculine, the Gospel Thrillers prefer their sabras to be women. Here we see another

[27] Anna Shapira, "The Bible and Israeli Identity," *AJS Review* 28 (2004): 11–42.
[28] Silberman, *A Prophet Amongst You*, 243, 377.
[29] Oz Almog, *The Sabra: The Creation of the New Jew*, trans. Haim Watzman (Berkeley, CA: University of California Press, 2000) and Yael Ben-zvi, "Blind Spots in Portraiture: On Oz Almog's *Ha-tsabar—Dyokan, Sabra: The Creation of the New Jew*," *Jewish Social Studies* 7 (2000): 167–74. Raz Yosef, *Beyond Flesh: Queer Masculinities and Nationalism in Israeli Cinema* (New Brunswick, NJ: Rutgers University Press, 2004), describes how the sabra male ideal was meant to align Ashkenazi (i.e., European) Jewish settlers more closely with colonial whiteness (in contrast with Mizrahi, i.e., Middle Eastern, Jewish settlers).

way in which these novels struggle to reconcile the desire for new (white, Protestant) biblical truths with the foreign otherness of modern Israel, western*ized* but not western. These women soldier-scholars are not the central protagonists of the novels, but rather adjuncts and love interests to the non-Israeli male main characters. In *The Masada Scroll*, the US professor Preston Lewkis is immediately impressed by the Israeli soldier, Lieutenant Sarah Arad, sent to meet him and his companion, Roman Catholic priest Michael Flannery, at an archaeological dig on Masada: "The woman – in her late twenties, thirty at the most, Preston guessed – was disconcertingly attractive, with high cheekbones, olive complexion, chocolate brown eyes, and raven hair pulled up beneath a military beret." Father Flannery seems equally compelled "by the incongruity of such beauty packaged in khaki battle-dress utilities and heavy black boots, accented by an Uzi over the right shoulder, barrel pointed down" (p. 11). The next day, while entering a secret lab where the Gospel of Dismas awaits study, they encounter the lieutenant again and learn that she "has a degree in forensic archaeology, and she's something of an expert on the Masada ruins" (p. 17). More evocations of Yadin, but here in the shapely guise of an intellectual partner and love interest for the protagonist. While Preston and Father Flannery make sense of the recovered gospel, Sarah provides intellectual and military support, "'soldier, archaeologist, and secret agent, all in one'" (p. 263).[30]

In *The Second Messiah*, the Israeli love interest for the US protagonist is a police investigator (although, since she is nearly forty, readers can assume she completed mandatory military service in her youth). Lela Raul knew Jack Cane as a teenager: he accompanied his parents on their dig near Qumran and she lived with her father, a police officer (and former soldier), at a nearby kibbutz. As a teenager, Jack developed a crush on Lela: "Lela was smart and kind, with chocolate brown eyes, a sensuous mouth, and long black hair, and she'd made a big impression on a gangly, awkward nineteen-year-old" (p. 23). When they meet again twenty years later, after a murder at another dig near Qumran where Jack is working, Lela is the police investigator assigned to investigate: now "in her late thirties" but still "with

---

[30] Some Gospel Thrillers do feature Israeli heroes (such as Gabriel Allon in Daniel Silva's 2020 *The Order*) but, notably, not those centered on finds from Israel. Ben Isaacs, one of the protagonists of *The Pope's Assassin*, is an Israeli living permanently abroad in England.

chocolate brown eyes, her dark hair tied back in a ponytail" (p. 55).
Roped into cooperating with Israeli secret intelligence, Lela ends up
working with Jack across Israel and Europe to find the truth about
Dead Sea Scrolls past and present.

At the beginning of *The Lost Testament*, protagonist Michael Farber
returns from Australia to Israel, where he had studied as a young man,
on the hunt for a rumored Dead Sea Scroll penned by Jesus himself.
There he meets up with his long-lost love, Judith Abramovich, whom
he has not seen in twenty years. A successful archaeologist like
Michael, Judith shows up to their reunion "wearing the uniform of
an Israeli army colonel. Crisp, efficient" (p. 50). Judith – whose name,
of course, means *Jewess* – literally embodies the swaggering, swarthy
potency of Israel: when they dated in graduate school, "men would
wonder what an Israeli beauty saw in this emaciated Anglo." Judith
describes her Israeli husband, whom she is about to divorce, as "'a
typical Sabra. Cold, hard, precise'" and then tenderly assures Michael
"'he has none of the qualities I love in you'" (p. 172). While wandering
alone through the ruins of Masada, praying for comfort, one image
comes to Michael: "An image from a simpler time. The sharply
defined, dark-skinned, Semitic beauty, Judith" (p. 124).[31]

These are not subtle images (Gospel Thrillers, and thrillers generally,
are not a subtle genre). The least subtle feminine embodiment of the
sabra soldier-scholar is found in *The 13th Apostle*, in the person of
Sabbie Karaim (whose given name, revealed toward the end of the
novel, is actually Sabra). Sabbie is an Israeli translator and freelancer
working with the novel's protagonist, US cyber whiz Gil Pearson. Like
Sarah, Lela, and Judith, Sabbie is ethnically sexualized ("tall, with dark
straight hair to her shoulders, and high, full breasts that strained
against her ivory silk blouse" [p. 14]); she is also, as it turns out, a
former Israeli spy and trained soldier who ensures that Pearson can
crack the code and decipher the Gospel of Micah. While she is Gil's
love interest, she also sacrifices her life to save Gil's.

---

[31] My concern here is primarily with US cultural perceptions of Israel's not-quite-
whiteness. The question of whiteness in Israel is vastly more complicated: see
Orna Sasson-Levy, "A Different Kind of Whiteness: Marking and Unmarking of
Social Boundaries in the Construction of Hegemonic Ethnicity," *Sociological
Forum* 28 (2013): 27–50 and Johannes Becke, "Dismantling the Villa in the
Jungle: Matzpen, Zochrot, and the Whitening of Israel," *Interventions:
International Journal of Postcolonial Studies* 21 (2019): 874–91.

On one level we can understand this parade of swarthy, smart, and deadly Israeli women as required by the elements of the genre: they provide exotic color and love interests for the (non-Israeli) male prot-agonists. But beyond that they allow these novels to domesticate their fictional biblical discoveries, gospels which, like these women, are colored by the fruitful and dangerous sands of Israel from which they emerge. These women embody for readers the desirable otherness of the new biblical find – and, by extension, that of the canonical Bible that also once emerged from these hot sands. They differ from the off-putting, foreign otherness that provided fodder for Twain's humorous anecdotes or that Crum believed was making way for tall, bright Jewish settlers' children. The sabra soldier-scholar love interest is western*ized* but also semit*ized*, adapted to the Middle Eastern climes but also suitable for the Euro-American hero.

Natalie Yphantis in *The Mystery of Mar Saba*, which I discussed in Chapter 1, played a similar role as the love interest of the stalwart US hero, Tony Medhurst: the daughter of a Jewish mother (of unknown national origin) and a Greek father, Natalie symbolized the ancient Levantine origins of the Bible now converted into a suitable Protestant whiteness. These sabra women, however, are not bleached into a semblance of Euro-American femininity: they are exotic, yet accessible; they are dangerous, yet loyal; they are highly skilled, but always in the service of uncovering the hidden truth at the heart of the Gospel Thriller for the white, male protagonists. So, too, the gospel finds they symbolize retain more than a little tinge of Middle Eastern otherness, and danger (although ultimately in the service of white Protestant Christianity). Theologically this tinge of otherness is located in the person of Jesus revealed by the secret gospel.

Jew*ish* Jesus

In April 1956, *The New Republic* published a panel of biblical studies scholars assessing the significance of the Dead Sea Scrolls for a popular audience. Among their number, W. F. Albright, respected patriarch of biblical archaeology, put the kibosh on any hope of new finds about Jesus from the Dead Sea: "It is often supposed that the scrolls throw *direct light* on the life of Christ, either confirming or disproving situ-ations and events of the Gospels. This is entirely false; it is in the highest degree improbable that anything of the sort will ever be discovered" (emphasis added). While "direct light" will not shine forth, Albright does agree that the Dead Sea Scrolls community influenced the rituals and practices of the earliest Christians. The larger significance for understanding the (Christian) Bible is clear for Albright:

> In my opinion the new discoveries prove that New Testament Christianity was even more intimately related to parent Judaism than we were justified in thinking before 1948. From the Christian point of view, the bond between Old and New Testament becomes historically indissoluble. Our common heritage is greater than a great many Christians and Jews had believed.[32]

For Albright, as for most of the contributors to this magazine forum, the significance of the Dead Sea Scrolls for Christianity is indirect but indisputable, pointing out the deep and positive roots of Christianity in "parent Judaism."

Albright's larger point here is not only historical but theological, reflecting a key turn in Christian theology following World War II and the horrors of the Holocaust. Particularly as the scope and scale of the Shoah became known in the 1950s and 1960s, Christian theologians in the United States and Europe took stock of the deep well of antisemitic theology that had undergirded Nazi anti-Jewish ideology. What role had antisemitic theologies of supersessionism (the belief that Christians replaced Jews as the chosen people) played in the deaths of millions of Jews and how could Christianity reimagine a nonadversarial relationship to Judaism? On the pastoral side came new calls for "Jewish-Christian dialogue," as in the conciliatory Roman Catholic papal proclamation "Nostra aetate." Biblical studies scholars, for their part, began to reassess the Jewish context for Jesus and his movement in the first century.[33]

---

[32] W. F. Albright, "Not Likely to Change Beliefs," 19–20 in "The Dead Sea Scrolls: How Do They Affect Traditional Beliefs?" *The New Republic* 134.15 (April 9, 1956): 12–25.

[33] "Nostra aetate" is available on the Vatican website, www.vatican.va/archive/hist_councils/ii_vatican_council/documents/vat-ii_decl_19651028_nostra-aetate_en.html; see also Edward Kessler, "'I Am Joseph, Your Brother': A Jewish Perspective on Christian-Jewish Relations since Nostra Aetate 4," *Theological Studies* 74 (2013): 48–72. More generally, see Barbara U. Meyer, *Jesus the Jew in Christian Memory: Theological and Philosophical Explorations* (Cambridge: Cambridge University Press, 2020).

The relationship between the biblical text, the historical person of Jesus, and the Christian messiah has never been straightforward. For much of Christian history, there was no meaningful historicization of the figure of Jesus apart from his role as the Son of God incarnate. The advent of Higher Criticism in the eighteenth and nineteenth centuries led to a variety of attempts to extract a historical figure from his literary representations with varying results. In the early twentieth century, nonetheless, Albert Schweitzer pronounced that a century of efforts to recover a historical Jesus from the New Testament evidence were fundamentally theological exercises: "There is no historical task which so reveals a man's true self as the writing of a Life of Jesus." Irish Catholic modernist George Tyrell, around the same time, put it more bluntly: "The Christ that Harnack [a German theological contemporary] sees, looking back through nineteen centuries of Catholic darkness, is only the reflection of a Liberal Protestant face, seen at the bottom of a deep well." For much of the nineteenth and twentieth centuries, the Jesus of history stood in stark opposition to Jews and Judaism, denouncing Pharisees, sacrifices, and temple to proclaim a new faith to the gentiles.[34]

After World War II, reconstructions of Jesus took a decidedly Jewish turn as part of an effort to undo the historical harm of a Jesus divorced from his Jewish context. If German biblical scholars of Nazi Germany had tried to produce an "Aryan Jesus" suitable for an antisemitic Third Reich, New Testament studies from the 1960s onward insisted on locating Jesus in his Jewish context. But which Jewish context was that? This same period has seen historians dramatically expand the scope and variety of Judaism in the first century due only in part to the discoveries along the Dead Sea. This variety of Jewish contexts has licensed a variety of Jewish Jesuses: a progressive Jesus sympathetic to social liberation; a revolutionary Jesus opposed to Roman rule; a philosophical Jesus, wandering like a Cynic preacher; and, his most popular recent iteration, an apocalyptic prophet of the end of the world. Each of these variously Jewish Jesuses creates challenges and

---

[34] Albert Schweitzer, *The Quest of the Historical Jesus: A Critical Study of Its Progress from Reimarus to Wrede*, 2nd ed., trans. W. Montgomery (London: Adam and Charles Black, 1911), 4; George Tyrell, *Christianity at the Crossroads* (London: Longmans, Green, & Co., 1909), 44. For a lucid overview of historical Jesus studies, see Jens Schröter, "The Quest for the Historical Jesus: Current Debates and Prospects," *Early Christianity* 11 (2020): 283–96.

opportunities for Christian theologians attentive to biblical history, creatively reworking existing materials (above all, the four canonical gospels) to arrive at their specific Jewish Jesus.[35]

Influenced by these trends in biblical studies, Gospel Thrillers are free to ignore W. F. Albright's stern warning against expecting anything new to shed "direct light" on Jesus's life. Novels centered on new discoveries from Israel tackle head on these two interrelated questions: How Jewish was Jesus? How was Jesus Jewish? Because these finds are authentically from the hands of Jesus or his first followers they can cut through the endless iterations of Jesus that historians reconstruct out of later texts and contexts. These novels explore contradictory Christian theological desires for and anxieties about a Jewish past. In some novels, the Jewish Jesus is bold and revolutionary, a fierce Middle Eastern warrior fighting against Roman oppression. In other novels, however, the Jewish Jesus is more ecumenical, a preacher of universal values and comity whose message travels easily from his own time into ours.

The coyest novel on the subject of Jesus's Jewishness is also the oldest of the novels set in Israel: Peters's *Dead Sea Cipher*. Layard, the disgraced archaeologist who discovered the cache of manuscripts on the shores of the Dead Sea, left behind a list of their contents in the cryptic style of the Dead Sea Scrolls (the titular "cipher"):

2QMICb
1QOBa
1MHOSa
2MAMb
1QMATb
1QCHRa
1QAMa
1QVIRa
4QEXz

---

[35] Susannah Heschel, *The Aryan Jesus: Christian Theologians and the Bible in Nazi Germany* (Princeton, NJ: Princeton University Press, 2008); Paula Fredriksen and Adele Reinhartz (eds.), *Jesus, Judaism, and Christian Anti-Judaism: Reading the New Testament after the Holocaust*, (Louisville, KY: Westminster/John Knox Press, 2002). James G. Crossley, "A 'Very Jewish' Jesus: Perpetuating the Myth of Superiority," *Journal for the Study of the Historical Jesus* 11 (2013): 109–29, at 113 notes the significance of attitudes toward Israel after 1967 in bolstering work on the Jewish Jesus.

1MNEHa
1QEXb
1QMICa
1QLJESb (p. 116)

While Dinah, the protagonist of the novel, at first mistakes this list for
a code, her eventual partner in uncovering the truth, a scruffy but
attractive US archaeologist named Jeff Smith, explains that all Dead
Sea Scrolls are labeled in this way: a number indicating a cave; a "Q"
or "M" indicating the location of that cave (Wadi Qumran or Wadi
Muraba'at), an abbreviation of the contents (often a biblical book),
and a letter indicating it is one of several fragments (pp. 175, 202–03).
For Layard to have labeled all his finds he must have read enough to
ascertain their contents.

Eventually Dinah and Jeff realize what the various abbreviations
mean: in addition to canonical books of the Hebrew Bible (like Exodus
and Nehemiah), Layard has stumbled upon Aramaic versions of the
canonical gospels ("1QMATb") and, even more astounding, hitherto
unknown accounts of Mary ("1QVIRa") and Jesus ("1QLJESb"). At a
climactic moment in the novel, however, when Jeff and Dinah find
Layard's cache of texts and are beginning to read them, they are
apprehended by the primary antagonist, a sinister mercenary named
Cartwright who wants to sell the finds to the highest bidder.
Cartwright, however, is dispatched by a motley crew of spies, repre-
senting various national and religious interests. United in their mission,
these spies allow one of their number – the US Jesuit Father Benedetto,
hazily foreshadowing Baigent and Leigh's conspiracy theories about
Catholic suppression of the Scrolls – to bury the explosive documents
under an avalanche of stones (pp. 271–86). The Aramaic versions of
the canonical gospels survive, but the Lives of Jesus and Mary remain a
mystery to Dinah, Jeff, and the readers.

Peters's coyness reflects the debates still ranging in the 1960s about
Qumran, the Dead Sea Scrolls, and Christian origins. By placing these
documents in the caves at Qumran and Mubara'at, *The Dead Sea
Cipher* also places Jesus in some relationship to the Jewish sectarians
who left behind the Dead Sea Scrolls. There are even hints that the
"Life of Jesus" discovered by Layard was penned by Jesus himself. The
climactic scene of discovery and destruction is preceded by a lengthy
explanation of the "Jewish sect" in whose library the lives of Jesus and

Mary (along with "originals" of the four gospels) were kept (pp. 239–41). The novel's readers are therefore primed to associate Jesus with a Jewish, sectarian group, rendering him potentially more alien to a modern, US readership.

At the same time the novel contextualizes Jesus's potentially alienating Jewishness with the revelation of other surprising Christian documents found alongside the lives of Jesus and Mary: that is, early, Aramaic versions of the canonical gospels Matthew, Mark, Luke, and John. When Dinah consoles Jeff that the conspirators "left the others" for him to study and publish, he responds sullenly, "'You can be damned sure there's nothing interesting in them, or those devils would have destroyed them as well'" (p. 289). On the one hand, the fact that these early versions of the canonical texts hew so closely enough to the received versions that the protagonists (and readers) would not find them "interesting" may also suggest that whatever Jewish surprises awaited us in the "Life of Jesus" would be similarly disappointing (or perhaps, from another perspective, reassuring). Beyond that, however, there is the comforting fact that these "original" versions of the canonical gospels are to be found in the library of a "Jewish sect" in Israel: whatever discomfort a US readership might experience with a Bible derived from the darkened sands of the Middle East is tempered by the certainty that it was always already the (white, Protestant) Bible familiar to them.

Other novels after *The Dead Sea Cipher* pivot between the anxiety of an alien Jesus, perhaps too deeply colored by the Middle Eastern climate, and a comforting and familiar Jesus, always stretching his hand toward a broader, universal (that is, western) Christian truth. According to Judas's first-person account in *The Judas Gospel*, Jesus colluded with a clearheaded and steel-hearted Judas to violently overthrow the Roman military in Jerusalem; when their plot failed (due, Judas suggests, to a treacherous Simon Peter), Judas watched helplessly as Jesus was condemned to death (pp. 90–100). Jesus's message of political liberation, readers also learn, directly opposed the coercive power of both state and religion. At Jesus's trial Judas laments: "So long as priests and state are one there can be no escape from tyranny. Priests and state, mind and body – by these nails men hang from the cross" (p. 97) Furthermore, unlike the potential alignment of secret and canonical gospels Peters hints at in *The Dead Sea Cipher*, *The Judas Gospel* is clear that the "Judas Testimony" stands in stark contrast to the falsified accounts spread by the disciples, "written in ink ground from the dried blood of their 'Messiah'" (p. 100).

The mealy treachery of the disciples in Jesus's day continues on in the institutional Christianity of the present day in *The Judas Gospel*. The Vatican assassin, "The Dominican," acts on the orders of the Pope as he dons several disguises and flies around Europe to dispatch anyone with knowledge of the "Judas testimony" and to recover the scroll. The startling denouement of the novel further divides Jesus, the resolute champion of truth and liberty, from the devious machinations of "the Church" and instead aligns him with the modern state of Israel. It turns out the soldiers who rescued Mallory suspected Mallory of deceit. They discovered the scroll and extracted it from his belongings during his unconscious hospitalization. Recognizing its value, they copied it and had it transcribed and translated. (The efficient soldier-scholars at work again.)

Only after news spread of Mallory's death and the theft of the scroll do the Israeli authorities release their transcription along with translations into multiple languages. They also release an official announcement explaining their reluctance to go public earlier:

> To have permitted publication *at that time* in a land deeply conscious of latent divisions born of history, between Christianity and Jewry, must inevitably and perhaps understandably have drawn upon Israel a renewal of old hatreds and suspicions – even the maledictions of Christians everywhere. (p. 293, emphasis in original)

Israel positions itself here beyond and apart from the petty bigotries and "old hatreds" of modern Christianity, echoing Jesus's earlier resistance to intolerant religious institutions as reported by Judas in his "testimony." Here the truth about Jesus belongs squarely to the non-Christian Middle East.

The potential for Jesus's Jewishness to divide him from Christianity (and, in some sense, the West) is strongest in Easterman's *The Judas Testament*. Here, "Judas" is not a noun but an adjective: this secret gospel (another first-person account from the hands of Jesus) will betray the modern Christian church just as Judas betrayed Christ. The discovery reveals that Jesus, the "son of a rabbi," abandoned a comfortable life to become not just a member but a leader of the separatist sect at Qumran. The Soviet professor who has uncovered the firebrand document in state-run archives explains: "'He is what we would today call a Jewish fundamentalist. The Law of Moses, he says, is to be obeyed above all things. Those who infringe it and those who desecrate God's Holy Temple, they must be driven from Israel or put to the sword.'" The letter from Jesus's own hand "'is a call to arms'" (p. 142). Easterman's Jesus is thus fully incompatible with the Christianity that followed him.

A hasty meeting of Roman Catholic cardinals and associates in the backroom of a Roman restaurant makes this dilemma clear partway through the novel. One of their number asserts that this letter from Jesus, if proven authentic, "'will serve only to give succor to those Judaizers who seek to make sacred history a battleground for their sordid dispute ... those scholars ... who maintain that Our Saviour was nothing more than a Jewish teacher, a Galilean rabbi, a political extremist, an Essene'" (p. 426). The same hard-nosed cardinal warns: "'Believe me, the Jews will make a laughing-stock of us'" (p. 427). Even more worried about the gospel than a hushed meeting of cardinals is the flamboyant conspiracy of the Crux Orientalis comprising ex-Nazis and European royalists (pp. 283–90). The cartoonishly violent and antisemitic conspirators want Jesus's letter to blackmail the skittish Vatican and establish a new Holy Roman Empire to fill the vacuum of post-Cold War politics.

Easterman's thoroughly Jewish Jesus wreaks geopolitical havoc from London to Moscow, revealing to its readers the enormous stakes involved in Judaizing – and therefore, it seems, de-Christianizing – Jesus Christ. When, as I noted above, the protagonist smuggles the document back into Israel to hide it near the Dead Sea for future "official" discovery, we are meant to understand the deep and alienating truth about this Jesus: he was always and will always be literally rooted in the Jewish, Middle Eastern soil from which he (and the Bible) grew. All hope for the familiar, white, Christian Jesus of popular imagination dissipates.

Other novels try to ameliorate the alienating Jewishness of Jesus, often by making that Jewishness a precursor to a more expansive, universal understanding of religious truth. In *The 13th Apostle*, the copper scroll being decoded by Gil Pearson, with the able assistance of Sabra "Sabbie" Karaim, bears the testimony of an otherwise unknown disciple of Jesus named Micah. (It turns out that Micah is both the "beloved disciple" of the Gospel of John and the mysterious naked "young man" fleeing from Jesus's arrest in the Gospel of Mark [p. 260].) Micah reveals a Jewish Jesus by now familiar to us: "Yeshua" was a "trouble-maker" and "rabble-rouser," preaching revolution against Roman rule and Jewish corruption (pp. 230, 281). As in earlier novels, the apostles are blamed for betraying Jesus's revolutionary message and founding a Christianity stripped of his Jewish fervor (pp. 279–81). Yet *The 13th Apostle* pushes the significance of this new gospel even further, as it also contains a mystical message about world salvation and the "thirty-six *tzaddikim*" (or righteous ones) whose existence sustains and promises peace throughout the world. This ultimate message from Yeshua transcends history, geopolitics, or religious division. Jesus's message is at once deeply embedded in ancient revolution and medieval Jewish mysticism *and* transcendent and universal: it embodies the tensions and anxieties of a Jewish Jesus and new gospel from Israel.

We see a similar attempt to move from Jewish specificity to ecumenical universality in Gold's *The Lost Testament*. Here the rumored gospel turns out to be a first-person memoir by "Jeshua," after he has grown up "among the Desert People of the Book," that is, the Qumran sectarians (p. 1). Readers do not read the testimony but learn about it indirectly from a series of flashbacks: after years of following the rigid "rule" of the Community, awaiting an apocalyptic war against the sinful world outside, Jeshua has decided to leave and preach God's message of love to that sinful outside world (pp. 83–96). Before embarking on his preaching mission, Jeshua leaves his testimony behind among the sectarians; it is later secreted away and winds up hidden in Ethiopia (where the "treasures of King Solomon" are kept). Jeshua's message of "love, and peace and understanding" (p. 89) received directly from his "Father" (p. 95) stands in explicit contrast to the apocalyptic militancy of the Qumran sectarians and points the way to a new, universal message of love and peace. Jesus's universal message, traveling outward from the Dead Sea, counters the stark and violent religious divisions throughout the novel.

The Masada Scroll also uses flashbacks and global interreligious strife to underscore the universal message of Jesus embedded in its "Gospel of Dismas." Violent turmoil suffered by Jews and Christians in the first century overlaps with Islamic terrorist attacks and violent Vatican conspiracies in the twentieth century. The mystical secret discovered at Masada is the "trevia Dei," a monotheistic universalism that aligns Judaism, Christianity, and Islam through a miraculous symbol combining the Star of David, the cross, and the crescent. (When Father Flannery complains "'that's nonsense ... None of those symbols existed two thousand years ago,'" he is told, "'All things are possible to him who created the universe and time'" [p. 336].) Already from the time of the apostles, it turns out, clandestine forces have conspired to sow division and violence, while the peaceful, universal message of Jesus has been passed down covertly from keeper to keeper, awaiting the discovery of Dismas's testimony in our present day.

Gospel Thrillers struggle to make sense of Jesus's Jewishness, either so deeply embedded in the theopolitics of his first-century context as to be alien to contemporary religious consciousness or breaking out of that context to inspire a new (still Jew*ish*) universal view of God and humanity. The ambiguous Jewishness of Jesus in the Gospel Thrillers aligns the theological and geopolitical ambiguity attached to a westernized (but not quite western) Israel, likewise split in US cultural consciousness. This tension, as I noted above, already permeates biblical studies and Christian theologies that attempt to take seriously the historical Jewishness of Jesus. These novels are not sites to resolve that tension but rather to confront it, grapple with it, and then contain it safely in the fictional story of an "improbable" discovery.

Good Guys and Bad Guys: "Half a Jew" versus Nazi Spies

Conspiracy narratives pit individual protagonists, often teamed up with other like-minded individuals, against shadowy networks of enemies seeking power and control no matter the costs. In Gospel Thrillers this conflict of characters reflects the personal investments that US reading publics associate with the production of a good or correct Bible: protagonists seek biblical truth while antagonists work to pervert the Bible through forgery or through suppression of secret gospels, long hidden or newly discovered. These personal motives are deeply intertwined with the geopolitical and theopolitical themes I trace above: the ambivalent status of Israel (western*ized*, but not western) and the ambiguous status of Jesus (Jew*ish*, but how and how much?).

It is notable that very few of the protagonists in these Dead Sea Scrolls novels are themselves Jewish or Israeli, with a few exceptions. Ben Isaacs, in *The Pope's Assassin*, was an Israeli archaeologist in his youth but lives the life of a wealthy retired banker in London. In any case, Isaacs is not the main protagonist of the novel seeking the truth, but a victim of the violence of conspirators who have kidnapped his son. In *The Secret Scroll*, the hero Josh Cohan is a US archaeologist whose Jewish identity is both overdetermined yet oddly attenuated. His name, *Cohan*, signals Jewish roots: the surname of Jewish families claiming descent from the ancient Israelite priestly line (*kohanim*); yet we learn early on that he is not religious ("a cultural Jew if not a practicing one" [p. 2]) and that he was, in fact, adopted as a baby by the Cohans (p. 36), so he is (probably?) not of the Jewish priestly line. By the end of the novel, readers are even led to believe that Josh Cohan ("J. C."), with his indeterminate Jewish identity, may be a new messianic figure.

Other Dead Sea Scrolls Gospel Thrillers use their protagonists' identities to probe the familiar strangeness of a Middle Eastern Bible. We have already seen the displacement of Israeli Jewish (sabra) identity onto the women love interests of the non-Israeli, non-Jewish male protagonists. In addition, several of the protagonists themselves are of ambivalent Jewish heritage. One of the few women protagonists of a Gospel Thriller is Dinah van der Lyn, who is described in the opening pages of *The Dead Sea Cipher* as "a respectable young woman, traveling alone, the daughter of a minister, touring the Lands of the Bible under parental auspices, and with parental funds" (p. 2). Her minister father is in fact "an authority on biblical archaeology" (p. 9; on p. 19 Dinah also recalls "being fed biblical archaeology with her strained food"), not just an amateur but (as Jeff Smith later marvels) "the guy who writes articles for *The Biblical Archaeologist*" (p. 100).

More of Dinah's background emerges under interrogation by a suspicious Lebanese police officer investigating a murder in her hotel. Bristling at the accusation that she might be mixed up with spies, Dinah remarks: "'How can you possibly think I could be mixed up in your politics here? I'm an American.'"

"Yes. And are you not also, mademoiselle, half a Jew?"

"Half a –" Dinah stared. The Inspector's flat expressionless eyes met hers and did not turn away. "You have been busy, haven't you?" she said.

"Routine inquiries. Is it not true that your mother's name was Goldberg? Is that not a Jewish name?"

"Yes. To both questions." (p. 72)

Dinah is defensive but proud: "'My mother was Jewish, yes,'" she replies. "'I'm proud of it and of her. She was a rabbi's daughter, as well as a fine scholar and a compassionate, beautiful human being.

The other is just – just a fact, like being Presbyterian or of Irish descent. It doesn't *mean* anything, not in the way you're thinking!'" (p. 73, emphasis in original).

Dinah's fluster at the accusation of Jewishness is matched by the pride in her pedigree: not merely the daughter of a Jewish woman, but the granddaughter of a rabbi. Readers know, along with Dinah, that her Jewish identity really is irrelevant to the narrative, although she brings it up herself to Jeff, perhaps as a way of testing his tolerance or claiming her own kind of "native" expertise: "'My father is a minister, a biblical specialist. And my mother,' Dinah added deliberately, 'was a rabbi's daughter'" (p. 100). As I noted above, Jeff is suitably impressed by her father's expertise; he ignores Dinah's "Jewish half," and it is never mentioned again in the novel. Dinah, it seems, is just Jewish *enough* to embark on a quest for the truth about Jesus the Jew and the Bible (which, as we saw above, remains unseen and unthreatening).

Warren Kiefer's 1976 novel *The Pontius Pilate Papers* is the first novel to inscribe the tensions of a partially Jewish protagonist along the fault lines of Israeli and diaspora Jewish identity. The result is a marked tension surrounding issues of Jewish ethnicity, religious faith, Israeli nationality, and the quest for biblical truth. The novel's protagonist (and narrator) refers breezily to his hybrid ethno-religious identity: "That's me – Jay Brian Marcus, surgeon *manqué*, dilettante digger, wandering Irish-American Jew" (p. 8). Marcus has used some of his inherited wealth to endow the Marcus Archaeological Museum in Jerusalem and it is the remarkable discovery of Victor Lanholtz, "renowned paleographer and the most distinguished member of the museum staff" (p. 11), that brings Marcus back to Israel from his "dilettante digger" life across Europe and the Mediterranean. Lanholtz has uncovered sheafs of papyrus codices at an archaeological dig in Caesarea, including correspondence from the household of Pontius Pilate. As I noted above, *The Pontius Pilate Papers* is the only Dead Sea Scrolls novel to center on what is revealed, in the end, to be a forgery, perpetrated by Lanholtz.

While Marcus's Jewish identity is minimized throughout the novel ("'But you're so Irish!'" his love interest exclaims at one point [p. 151]), Lanholtz's is shaped by his experiences escaping Nazi persecution and working for the US army as an intelligence officer during World War II. Although religiously he is an atheist he is nonetheless "'a Super-Jew when it came to emotions,'" a colleague remarks:

"'otherwise he never would have come here [i.e., to Israel] after the war.'" Lanholtz's Zionist dedication to Jewish survival is matched by his deep sensitivity to antisemitism: "'He regarded practically every non-Jew in the world as a kinetic anti-Semite'" (p. 64). Lanholtz's sense of historical Jewish grievance led him to forge ancient letters exculpating Jews for killing Jesus and laying all the blame at Pilate's feet. His murder, and the disappearance of the titular "papers," leads Marcus on his quest for the truth.

The contrast between Marcus and Lanholtz, and the forgery plot of *Pontius Pilate Papers*, adds a new wrinkle to the Dead Sea Scrolls Gospel Thrillers. Lanholtz the "Super-Jew" is unable to set aside his personal motivations; Marcus the "wandering" (that is, Diaspora) "Irish-American Jew" is more clear-sighted. Marcus's relationship to Israel is that of the philanthropic Diaspora Jew, and even then it is his Jewish grandfather's name on the museum, not his own, and it is administered by his Jewish paternal uncle. Marcus's emotional and ethnic distance from Jewishness and Israel renders him better equipped to assess the dangerous secrets emerging from Israel's past; by contrast, Lanholtz's fervor acts as a warning against the rare, but always potentially present, excesses of Jewish scholars in the Jewish State motivated by strong Jewish feeling to obscure the biblical truth.

Other Gospel Thrillers similarly present readers with ex-Jewish and half-Jewish protagonists as the appropriate seekers of secret gospel truths about the Jewish Jesus from Israel. Michael, the main character in Gold's *The Lost Testament*, is a convert from Judaism to Roman Catholicism. He first appears in the novel kneeling for a traditional, Latin Catholic mass and remembering the heartbreak of his "old Jewish father" and "his forgiving mother" following his conversion (pp. 7–9). Yet Michael's former Jewishness is grounded not only in his Jewish identity but in the land of Israel itself. He had gone to Israel for graduate study in biblical archaeology and his "decision to convert to Christianity was made on the Via Dolorosa, walking up the steep, narrow cobbled path where Jesus had carried His cross" (p. 49).

Michael's ex-Jewishness makes him the ideal protagonist to uncover the truth about Jesus, the Jew from Israel. While Michael is on his search for Jesus's Testament, beginning to suspect it might be in Africa, Romain de La Tour, the head of the Dead Sea Scrolls project, flies to the Vatican to meet with Cardinal Franz Kitzinger. Kitzinger congratulates De La Tour on keeping so many volatile scrolls under wraps for so long, and then expresses concern that this dangerous new "Testament" will be found. "'Does Farber pose such a threat?'" he asks. "'Yes, unquestionably,'" is the reply, "'and not just because he's a maverick. It's also because he's both Jew and Christian. Because he sees things from both sides. He's a devout Catholic now . . . but one can still see the Jew in him'" (348–39).

Michael's mirror image in *The Lost Testament* is David Berg, a radicalized and violent "compulsive political Zionist" who, like Michael, was converted by his time in Israel. Whereas the gentle archaeologist was transformed in Israel by an affinity with Christ, Berg, previously "professing no heartfelt beliefs," was inspired by a visit to the Western ("Wailing") Wall, the remains of the Jewish Temple, to give up his career as a physician in the United States to become an ultra-orthodox rabbi and rabid Zionist. He briefly returned to the United States to lead a militant Zionist organization prone to protest and violence before returning to Israel and winning election to the Israeli Knesset, "rallying the extreme right and Zionistic causes under his banner" (pp. 127–29). Unlike Michael, David can only see one side, and goes to violent lengths to stop Michael from finding the Testament. As he tells a crowd of raucous followers (before leading an assault on the tomb of the Holy Sepulcher): "'We've suffered for two thousand years because of the Christians. Is this Testament going to condemn us to another two thousand? A Testament by an apostate Jew. I'll tell you what we should do with this Testament. We should find it and burn it. What right does it have to be in our land?'" (p. 126) Michael embodies peace and interreligious reconciliation; David wants to incite a holy war on the Temple Mount. We already know where the sympathies of Jeshua lie.

We have seen this tension between a fanatical, isolationist Jewish identity and an expansive, universal one embodied theologically in these novels in the figure of Jesus. *The Lost Testament* reinscribes this tension not only in the opposition of protagonist and antagonist but in their geographic loyalties, as well. Michael and Judith initially seek the Testament near Masada, that Zionist symbol of militant resistance to outside empire. But they find it at last among the Agau tribe of Jews of Ethiopia (called throughout the novel *Falashas* [pp. 278–29, 311–21] a term in common use when the novel was written but now widely recognized as derogatory). Ethiopian Jews have been a flashpoint for tensions about race, religion, and the limits of Jewish diaspora identity since the 1980s. In the novel, Michael and Judith find Binyoussef, the last of the "Guardians," who explains that "'for thousands of years, since the time of King Josiah, there have been Guardians who have protected the greatest secret of the Agau'" (p. 490): the treasures of the Temple of Solomon. That the Testament of Jesus is found among these Ethiopian *Jews* and not the ancient community of Ethiopian *Christians* further emphasizes the role of the Jewish Jesus and the ex-Jew Michael in this novel: to expand outward the ecumenical significance of the Jewish Bible to encompass multiple faiths, territories, and races.[36]

Finally, in *The Judas Testament*, we meet another part/ex-Jewish protagonist. Jack Gould is an Irish scholar with a Jewish father and a Catholic mother. Flashbacks reveal that Jack had been married to an English woman named Caitlin who died tragically. Only toward the end of the novel is it revealed that Jack's wife was in fact the daughter of the novel's main antagonist: Stefan Rosewicz, a fabulously wealthy manuscript collector in the UK who is in reality Andrija Omrcanin, a former Nazi concentration camp guard (pp. 283–88). Rosewicz/Omrcanin and his fellow ex- and neo-Nazis have instituted the Crux Orientalis, a new and virulent antisemitic coalition bent on European domination.

Nazis make repeated appearances in many Gospel Thrillers, in their original form or reimagined into new incarnations. Among the cluster of conspirators out to stop Gil Pearson in *The 13th Apostle* are a white supremacist fundamentalist group known as "White Americans to Save Christianity" or "WATSC," pronounced to rhyme with "Nazi" (the comparison is made directly at least once in the novel) (p. 56). The sinister leader of an antisemitic heretical sect in *The Secret Scroll* was born in a concentration camp (although to his horror he finds he was born to a Jewish couple and adopted by Christians) (p. 300). In *The Lost Testament* Michael's Jewish father was interned in a concentration camp (p. 12) and one of the antagonists out to find (and possibly destroy) the Testament of Jesus is Jimmy Wilson, a drug-addled, abusive, racist leader of a US Pentecostalist megachurch who has modeled his speaking style on that of Adolf Hitler (p. 69).

---

[36] Ethiopian Jews are more typically known by the name *Beta Israel* (House of Israel in Ge'ez). See Steven Kaplan, "Can the Ethiopian Change His Skin? The Beta Israel (Ethiopian Jews) and Racial Discourse," *African Affairs* 98 (1999): 535–50 and Tudor Parfitt, *Black Jews in Africa and the Americas* (Cambridge, MA: Harvard University Press, 2013).

Nazis antagonists appear with surprising frequency in a genre of thriller that first appeared decades after World War II and continue to the present day. In these novels concerned with the Jewishness of the Bible – its origins in the Middle East, the theological manifestation in Jesus, and the personal identities of the novels' protagonists – Nazis play a special role as quintessential "bad guys." They embody the intersection of anti-US and antisemitic sentiment: the wartime opponents of US freedom and the monsters of Jewish history. Their opposition to the truth of a new manuscript by (or about) the Jewish Jesus aligns the Jewishness of the Bible with forthright (Christian, US) identity.

Such an alignment can never be perfect. Christians have struggled for centuries with the Jewish roots of Christianity and more recently that struggle has centered on the historical person of Jesus and the material origins of the biblical texts, both impelled in part by discoveries near the Dead Sea and the nearly simultaneous creation of the state of Israel. Many US Christians with deep devotion to biblical truth have difficulty navigating away from a supersessionist theology that sees Jews as former partners in a covenant with God, Israel as the site of the coming (Christian) apocalypse, and the Bible as the blueprint for both ideas.[37]

Gospel Thrillers, however, are more expansive in their thinking about these issues. These novels are not interested in simply aligning traditional biblical (white, Protestant) Christianity with US culture through a domestication of the Middle East and Israel. They create a space to imagine, for a moment, the questions that have been swirling around since the first headline proclaimed the finds at Qumran: What if a new biblical text emerged from Israel? What if Jesus's Jewish message is not what we thought? What if nefarious forces have been conspiring to keep the truth hidden? These novels potentially render the Bible more alien to traditional (white Protestant) biblical Christianity and so potentially liberate US culture and politics from its influence. They allow tension around a western scripture – and messiah – with a Middle Eastern pedigree to haunt biblical Christianity. Like all good ghost stories, however, part of the pleasure comes in containment: Gospel Thrillers are free to be expansive in their explorations precisely because they give readers closure and finitude, and the cover of fictionality. Whatever disturbance their questions bring dissolves with the closing of the back cover.

---

[37] Amy-Jill Levine, "Supersessionism: Admit and Address rather than Debate or Deny," *Religions* 13.155 (2022): 1–12.

4 | *Texts and Sects*

Two Discoveries: The Bank Box and the Basement

I begin with stories of two lost gospels recovered from unlikely places. The first nonfictional gospel was (according to the widely accepted public story) placed in a safety deposit box in a bank in Hicksville, New York, in 1985, by an Egyptian who had come to the United States in hopes of selling it. It remained there for nearly twenty years, forgotten or neglected, until a Swiss antiquities dealer who had heard rumors about it sought it out. Securing its purchase from the Egyptian, Frieda Tchacos Nussberger "rescued" the manuscript – by then in seriously decayed condition – and eventually had it restored with care by experts in Switzerland. In 2006, the most spectacular portion of what was now called "Codex Tchacos" was unveiled to the world: a long-lost Gospel of Judas.[1]

A fictional version of this Gospel of Judas turned up not far from that Hicksville bank in the 2010 novel *The Judas Conspiracy*, by Leslie Winfield Williams. As a young man, Paul Guilford summered at his grandfather's New Haven mansion and, to keep himself occupied, he began cataloguing the trunks and boxes of heirlooms and books stored in the basement. Years later, the Guilford family – Paul, now a New Testament professor; his uncle Malcolm, a lawyer who now owns the house; and his other uncle Andrew, Dean of Yale Divinity School – realize that among these musty old books were a piece of Greek papyrus and a Latin codex that preserved a full and complete version of the Gospel of Judas. On the eve of a conference dedicated to this new gospel, soon to be donated to Yale University, Malcolm's house is robbed, his wife is murdered, and the manuscripts are stolen.

Both Judas discoveries raise a host of unanswered questions about provenance (the official transmission history of an artifact): how did

---

[1] The story is recounted by Herbert Krosney, *The Lost Gospel: The Quest for the Gospel of Judas Iscariot* (Washington, DC: National Geographic, 2006).

the Guilford family originally acquire these precious manuscripts that lay concealed for centuries ("'They'd come over on the Mayflower with our ancestors from England,' said Andrew. 'Not the Mayflower,' corrected Malcolm" [p. 47])? How did Nussberger manage to track down the owner and the correct bank, and why did it take her almost four years to make any effort at restoring the damaged codex? (I discuss the strange tale of Codex Tchacos in Chapter 6.) That these manuscripts have a murky provenance does not make them unique in the shadowy world of biblical antiquities, to be sure. But this murk highlights a key feature of "heretical" gospels in the public imagination: they are marked by displacement.

Throughout this book I have interwoven and juxtaposed real-world concerns about the vulnerability of the Christian Bible to new discoveries with the florid and exaggerated narratives found in Gospel Thrillers. I continue that juxtaposition and interweaving here but want to make clear once more that my goal throughout is neither to pinpoint the origins of Gospel Thrillers nor to point out the influence of these novels on popular culture. As we shall see acutely in this chapter, the speculations of academics, the fantasies of Gospel Thrillers, and the suspicions of the biblically curious readers of both emerge from a common well of fears and desires, the *what ifs* that perennially emanate from a Christian Bible open, and vulnerable, to transformation.

So when we catch sight of this mobile heresy inscribed in Gospel Thrillers we should see it as a reflection, amplification, and contemplation of this broader awareness of Christian heresy's rootless meandering. Unlike the Dead Sea Scrolls gospels of Chapter 3, slumbering in the volatile sands of Israel, these lost gospels wander from to site to site (and drift from one language into another) until they come to rest in the most unlikely of places. Their origins are mysterious, their histories circuitous. In J. G. Sandom's 1992 *Gospel Truths*, a primitive version of the Gospel of Thomas lies buried in a Carolingian crypt in the cathedral of Chartres. In *The Prophetess*, by Barbara Wood (1996), the seventh "Scroll of Sabrina," a mystical revelation of universalism, is squirreled away in a convent in rural Vermont. In Jonathan Rabb's *The Book of Q* (2001), Jesus's liberating admonitions about individual spirituality and gender equality are concealed beneath a medieval fountain in the Bosnian town of Visegrad. In a winky reference to the famous Nag Hammadi finds of the 1940s, Paul Christopher's 2006 *The Lucifer Gospel* places Jesus's lost account of a faked crucifixion in the "Little Egypt" region of Illinois. In a direct reference to those Nag Hammadi finds, Greg Loomis's *The Coptic Secret* (2009) imagines a lost volume of those codices surfacing in the present in the possession of a wealthy Englishman; on the eve of his unveiling the volume at the British Museum, the volume is stolen and eventually recovered from a secret Catholic order in Rome. In Gospel Thrillers *heresy*, that fearsome deviation from orthodox truth, is compelling but rootless, spreading across the history of Christianity like spores in the wind.

The Buried Jar

The most famous discovery of unorthodox early Christian texts epitomizes this compelling rootlessness: the discovery of gnostic books near Nag Hammadi, Egypt, in 1945. I gave some of the familiar details of this story in Chapter 1; there I emphasized its similarities to the nearly contemporaneous discovery of the Dead Sea Scrolls. The first Dead Sea Scrolls were supposedly discovered by young men throwing a rock in a cave to recover a lost goat. The jar containing the Coptic codices, the "heretical" library of Nag Hammadi, was supposedly unearthed by "Arab peasants" digging for fertilizer. Both are tales of routine rustic activity uncovering surprising precious biblical antiquities. Their differences, however, are as important as their similarities.

Here's how Elaine Pagels recounts the story of Nag Hammadi in her popular nonfiction book, *The Gnostic Gospels*:

Thirty years [after the 1945 discovery] the discoverer himself, Muḥammad 'Alī al-Sammān, told what happened. Shortly before he and his brother avenged their father's murder in a blood feud, they had saddled their camels and gone out to the Jabal to dig for *sakakh*, a soft soil they used to fertilize their crops. Digging around a massive boulder, they hit a red earthenware jar, almost a meter high. Muḥammad 'Alī hesitated to break the jar, considering that a *jinn*, or spirit, might live inside. But realizing that it might also contain gold, he raised his mattock, smashed the jar, and discovered inside thirteen papyrus books, bound in leather.[2]

Pagels adds other details: Muḥammad's mother ('Umm-Aḥmad) burned "much of the papyrus" for fuel; after avenging their father,

---

[2] Elaine Pagels, *The Gnostic Gospels* (New York: Random House, 1979), xiii.

Muḥammad handed over the books for safekeeping to a priest from whom, eventually, most were confiscated by the Egyptian government; one codex was smuggled out of Egypt to Europe where it became a birthday present for Swiss psychoanalyst Carl Jung. An international cast of characters populates the story: "Bahīj ʿAlī, a one-eyed outlaw from al-Qaṣr," "Albert Eid, a Belgian antiquities dealer," "French Egyptologist Jean Doresse." Eventually all of the codices were reunited for study by a committee of (mostly) western scholars working under the auspices of UNESCO and the Egyptian Department of Antiquities.[3]

Pagels's account is heavy on local Egyptian detail: the careful diacritics on the Arabic names, the italicized native terms for fertilizer and spirits, the "blood feud" that impels much of the action. Much of this local color recalls similar details spun out by Edmund Wilson in his foundational account of the Dead Sea Scrolls in the 1950s. The crucial difference, however, lies in the nature of the discovery. Whereas the stone-throwing goatherders "discovered" parchments that had been composed and concealed in situ, the leather-bound codices sealed and concealed in a tall jar were transplants multiple times over. These texts had been translated from Greek into Coptic, copied from originals into newly bound books in the fourth century, buried some distance from wherever they had been produced and read. These were not primeval texts disgorged from their native soil; these were migrant texts from other obscure times and places.

Much of the Nag Hammadi find story was pieced together over time and remains even today subject to revision and scrutiny. James Robinson, the chair of the UNESCO committee overseeing the transcription and translation of the codices, was the first to popularize the story of Muḥammad ʿAlī and the buried jar in the 1970s and 1980s (Pagels based her account on Robinson's). In the 2000s, as the concluding chapter of his UNESCO responsibilities, Robinson compiled an exhaustive two-volume account of the discovery, collection, and study of the texts from the 1940s to the 1970s. Around the same time, North American scholars of the New Testament and early Christianity began to question the Robinson-Muḥammad ʿAlī story: Mark Goodacre in a 2013 piece in the *Journal for the Study of the New Testament* and Justine Ariel Blount and Nicola Denzey Lewis in a

---

[3] Pagels, *Gnostic Gospels*, xiv, xxv.

2014 article in the *Journal of Biblical Literature*. Their skepticism was prompted by the inconsistent nature of the story over time and its reliance on age-old colonialist stereotypes and caricatures.[4]

In 2016, a series of articles in the *Bulletin for the Study of Religion* reassessed the state of affairs. Experts in archaeology, papyrology, apocrypha, and biblical studies concluded that the true story of the Nag Hammadi find was unlikely ever to be established. Instead (as the editor of this special issue notes) we are left to contemplate "the mirrors and windows that we – as scholars – internalize in our treatment of our sources." Papyrologist Brent Nongbri, after assessing the bewildering and contradictory array of archaeological data and assumptions used in retelling the story, counsels that "it might be best to adopt a more, shall we say, agnostic view of the circumstances of the deposition and discovery of the Nag Hammadi codices."[5]

As Nongbri's pairing of "deposition and discovery" suggests, the confusion over the find replicates debates over where these books came from and how they came to be sealed in a jar (if they were) which was deposited under a rock (if it was). This confusion stems from the particular nature of these books. They were written in a late dialect of Egyptian known as Coptic, but almost certainly translated from earlier Greek originals (older Greek fragments of some Nag Hammadi texts, like the Gospel of Thomas, were found elsewhere in Egypt). The scrap papyrus used in the binding of the codices shows they were bound together sometime after the mid- to late-300s – but when? and by whom? for what reason? Why were they sealed in a jar? Why were they buried?

---

[4] James M. Robinson, *The Nag Hammadi Story*, 2 vols., Nag Hammadi and Manichaean Studies 86 (Leiden: Brill, 2014). Mark Goodacre, "How Reliable Is the Story of Nag Hammadi?" *Journal for the Study of the New Testament* 35 (2013): 303–22; Nicola Denzey Lewis and Justin Ariel Blount, "Rethinking the Origins of the Nag Hammadi Codices," *Journal of Biblical Literature* 133 (2014): 399–419. Denzey Lewis later published an additional essay: "(Still) Rethinking the Origins of the Nag Hammadi Codices," *Marginalia Review of Books* (July 6, 2018), online at https://themarginaliareview.com/still-rethinking-the-origins-of-the-nag-hammadi-codices.

[5] *Bulletin for the Study of Religion* 45 (2016), with an introduction by Philip L. Tite ("Windows and Mirrors: Texts, Religions, and Stories of Origin," 2–3), and essays by Dylan Burns, Brent Nongbri ("Finding Early Christian Books at Nag Hammadi and Beyond," 11–19), Eva Mroczek, Tony Burke, and Paul-Hubert Poirier.

Things do not become clearer as we push back further toward the origins of these texts. When and why were they translated from Greek into Coptic? When and why were they originally composed in Greek? Under what circumstances, by whom, for what audiences or communities? From the moment the texts entered into scholarly conversation in the twentieth century, they have generated long chains of unanswerable questions about origins, transmission, and provenance. Of course, scholars have made careers answering all these questions, producing a rich bibliography on Gnosticism that grows longer every year. My point is not to deconstruct the field of Gnostic studies (although scholars of so-called Gnosticism do that routinely), but rather to ponder how this find narrative, and the ancillary narratives about production and transmission that precede it, are fundamentally a story of texts always on the move.[6]

Religion scholar Maia Kotrosits has shifted attention away from the veracity of the find narrative to explore how the story continues to generate "*a particular set* of feelings – in this case, allure, romance, fascination, and excitement" (emphasis in original). The "allure" and "fascination" come from the transgressive nature of the Nag Hammadi find, locked in place through a highly Orientalizing narrative. Kotrosits points out how these noncanonical texts interact pleasurably with the constraints of the biblical canon and the normalizing boundaries of theological orthodoxy: "How can one fully know the comfort, the paternalistic safety of one's institution without an excursion into thrill (anxiety) inducing foreign territory?" The foreignness of the Dead Sea Scrolls is in some ways easier to accommodate: clear in their provenance, reassuringly more canonical (although not entirely so), and imaginatively adjacent to Christ's milieu (although in a distinctly Middle Eastern way that requires some intellectual agility). The "foreign territory" of the Nag Hammadi texts and the heretical otherness they represent is more distant and less secure. Texts buried in a jar have been transported from elsewhere, a hazy "foreign territory" for which the Egyptian sands are a mere waystation. These are texts with a

---

[6] Two accessible scholarly volumes that deconstruct the term "gnosticism": Michael A. Williams, *Rethinking "Gnosticism": An Argument for Dismantling a Dubious Category* (Princeton, NJ: Princeton University Press, 1996) and Karen L. King, *What Is Gnosticism?* (Cambridge, MA: Harvard University Press, 2003). But see also David Brakke, *The Gnostics* (Cambridge, MA: Harvard University Press, 2010).

mysterious past that matches the dangerous allure of their contents: heresy.[7]

Heresy and Apocrypha: Sects and Texts

The Greek word from which heresy derives originally meant *choice* but in the first Christian centuries came to signal *deviance*: a willful and even demonic turn away from the Christian truth. Heresy was similar enough to orthodoxy to fool the uneducated but was nonetheless a certain path into damnation: premodern Christians were taught to be on high alert for heresy. Their traditional theological narrative posited a single true faith, continuous from the time of Christ, which from time to time threw off heretical malformations that needed to be identified, isolated, and eliminated. From the second century onward, "ortho-dox" Christians penned vituperative and slanderous treatises against "heretics," accusing them not only of deviant theology but immoral activity. The religious communion of heretics was shaped as much by ethical aberration as by theological error. Whether or not this unceas-ing parade of covert heretical communities actually existed remains open to debate; what is certain is that the "orthodox" could not stop thinking and writing about heretics.[8]

This deep suspicion of heresy, this link between deviant belief and immoral action, was from early on highly textualized. According to their orthodox detractors, depraved heretics targeted naïve Christians in order to seduce them over to their theological aberrations (the language was often highly sexualized and gendered). Their instruments in this endeavor were texts that *seemed* biblical but were, in fact, forgeries: *apocrypha*, they were called (from a Greek term for "secret things"). Texts that purported to be by apostles, or recount their lives and teachings, were produced by these nefarious heretics in order to fool the orthodox into believing the wrong things and, ultimately, into joining their new heretical coreligionists in perversion and sin. One of the most famous anti-heretical writers in antiquity, a bishop named Epiphanius, recalled a time in his youth when gnostic heretics tried to

---

[7] Maia Kotrosits, "Romance and Danger at Nag Hammadi," *The Bible and Critical Theory* 8 (2012): 39–52, at 42 and 44.

[8] Todd Berzon, *Classifying Christians: Ethnography, Heresy, and the Limits of Knowledge in Late Antiquity* (Oakland, CA: University of California Press, 2016); G. R. Evans, *A Short History of Heresy* (Oxford: Blackwell, 2003).

lure him into their sexual misadventures by showing him a library of apocryphal texts (he escaped their clutches and reported them for discipline to the local bishop).[9]

The place of so-called apocrypha among orthodox Christians has never been straightforward: while these texts were not included in the canonical New Testament they also circulated widely and provided familiar narratives about Jesus, the apostles, and Christian origins: the childhood of the Virgin Mary, the martyrdom of Paul, the foundation of the church in Rome were all first recounted in ancient "apocryphal" texts. At the same time apocryphal texts could also be blamed for turning the faithful away from orthodoxy into heresy. These texts that *seemed* biblical but were in fact heretical demonstrate early and persistent anxieties about the textual vulnerability of the Bible: susceptible to revision, alteration, and mimicry. Just as orthodox Christians exhibited a constant fascination for and fear of heresy, so too they were drawn to but fearful of apocrypha.[10]

The forceful bifurcation of *orthodoxy* and *heresy* took a sharp turn in the early modern period, as the proliferation of denominationalism in Europe promoted a willingness to agree to disagree about certain ideas and practices and allowed for differing versions of the Bible to be read among different Christian communities (although not without occasional conflict, as I discuss in Chapter 2). The antiquarian and philological predilections of some early Enlightenment freethinkers also led to a positive reevaluation of "apocrypha" as testimony to the lost origins of Christianity. Historian of religions Annette Yoshiko Reed elucidates how the writings of Irish Deist John Toland (d. 1722) reversed previous equations of *apocrypha* and *falsehood*. In works like *Amyntor* and *Nazarenus*, Toland posited that, far from being heretical inventions, apocryphal (or "apostolic") texts should be seen as suppressed early witnesses to authentic Christianity. Toland asserted that orthodox writers covered up this authentic teaching; they

---

[9] I have written elsewhere about Epiphanius (d. 403) and this incident: *Epiphanius of Cyprus: A Cultural Biography of Late Antiquity*, Christianity in Late Antiquity 2 (Oakland, CA: University of California Press, 2016), 97–99.

[10] For an overview see Brandon Hawk, *Apocrypha for Beginners: A Guide to Understanding and Exploring Scriptures Beyond the Bible* (Emeryville, CA: Rockbridge Press, 2021). For an invaluable, regularly updated catalogue of "apocrypha" see the website of the North American Society for the Study of Christian Apocryphal Literature, http://nasscal.com.

maligned these texts as forgeries and their readers as heretics. The sanitized and adulterated witness of "the New Testament" was (to quote Reed) "defended . . . by power-hungry clerics who must resort to censorship to monopolize their own power over the Christian past."[11]

Reevaluation of apocrypha as occasionally useful sources and not just scurrilous forgeries has continued. Scholars from the nineteenth century to the present have, on different occasions, viewed these texts as evidence both for an alternative narrative of Christian origins and for heretical beliefs. In another essay, Reed traces this early modern appraisal of apocryphal New Testament texts as a "countercanon" in the centuries following Toland: William Hone in the 1820s and M. R. James in the 1920s published English translations of these texts entitled *Apocryphal New Testament*, a title that suggests the Christian Bible could be either updated or totally supplanted by "suppressed" texts. (James's volume has been updated in recent decades by J. K. Elliott.) On the one hand such collections made otherwise esoteric texts like the *Acts of John* or *Epistle of Barnabas* more accessible to a wider readership; on the other hand, they conveyed to readers, either explicitly or implicitly, that they were viewing "secret" texts as (in Reed's summation) "potential sources for exposing the suppressed truth, which undermine ecclesiastical claims about the canon and, hence, the church's authority to censor diversity of opinion."[12]

At the same time that these "secret" or "lost" texts were undergoing reevaluation among scholars and some general readers, so too was the very notion of *heresy*. In the 1930s, German New Testament scholar Walter Bauer wrote a wide-ranging volume entitled *Rechtglaübkeit und Ketzerei im ältesten Christentum* (Orthodoxy and Heresy in Earliest Christianity) in which he turned the traditional narrative of

---

[11] Annette Yoshiko Reed, *Jewish-Christianity and the History of Judaism*, Texts and Studies in Ancient Judaism 171 (Tübingen: Mohr Siebeck, 2018), 264–69, at 267. John Toland, *Nazarenus, or: Jewish, Gentile, and Mahometan Christianity* (London: J. Brown without Temple-Bar, 1718); *Amyntor, or: A Defence of Milton's Life* (London: Booksellers of London & Westminster, 1699). On the surge of interest in apocrypha in Toland's time, see Tony Burke and Gregory Peter Fewster, "*Opera Evangelica*: A Lost Collection of Christian Apocrypha," *New Testament Studies* 67 (2021): 356–87.

[12] William Hone, *The Apocryphal New Testament* (London: Ludgate Hill, 1820); M. R. James, *The Apocryphal New Testament* (Oxford: Clarendon Press, 1924), updated by J. K. Elliott in 1993. Annette Yoshiko Reed, "The Afterlives of New Testament Apocrypha," *Journal of Biblical Literature* 133 (2015): 401–25, at 415.

Christian orthodoxy on its head: Bauer argued that Christian movements later labeled *heresy* were actually the original forms of
Christianity in various parts of the ancient world. Part of Bauer's
argument derived from the early and wide circulation of purportedly
heretical apocrypha.[13]

The political strife of 1930s Germany prevented Bauer's book from
having much impact outside of German theological circles. When it
was republished in German in 1964, however, it began to make
headway in US scholarly circles (due primarily to German-educated
scholars teaching in US universities). In the late 1960s, a cadre of US
scholars collaborated on an English translation that, when published,
helped make Bauer's revisionary history enormously influential. It was
no coincidence that this new German edition, and subsequent English
translation, appeared just as the first public versions of gnostic texts
from Nag Hammadi were also becoming known: a time when conspiratorial thinking about the Bible and Christian origins was beginning to grapple with the possibility of Jesus himself as unorthodox. It is
also no coincidence that at this time of political and religious upheaval
in the United States the possibility of unorthodox Christian origins
should move so swiftly and dramatically from the corridors of academia onto the bookshelves of the reading public.[14]

"A Powerful Alternative": Alluring Heresy

Elaine Pagels first encountered the Nag Hammadi texts as a graduate
student at Harvard University in the late 1960s. At the time, scholars at
only two universities in the United States had access to the entire

---

[13] Walter Bauer, *Rechtglaübkeit und Ketzerei im ältesten Christentum* (Tübingen:
J. C. B. Mohr, 1934); English translation: *Orthodoxy and Heresy in Earliest
Christianity*, trans. Robert A. Kraft, Gerhard Kroedel, and a team from the
Philadelphia Seminar on Christian Origins (Philadelphia, PA: Fortress
Press, 1971).

[14] On this political, religious, scholarly timeline see Matthew Dillon, "The
Heretical Revival: The Nag Hammadi Library in American Religion and
Culture," PhD dissertation (Houston, TX: Rice University, 2017). As Dillon
points out (pp. 17–29), Los Angeles journalist John Dart became an early
popularizer of the Nag Hammadi texts, publishing dozens of articles and a
book, *The Laughing Savior: The Discovery and Significance of the Nag
Hammadi Library* (New York: Harper & Row, 1976; republished and
expanded as *The Jesus of Heresy and History: The Discovery and Meaning of
the Nag Hammadi Gnostic Library* [New York: Harper & Row, 1988]).

library: Harvard University and Claremont Graduate School, in southern California (where James Robinson taught). Some more exciting texts, like the Gospel of Thomas (on which more below), were already published in the late 1950s, but it took a bit longer for the more esoteric texts to make their way into the scholarly and public consciousness. As Pagels recounts in several of her popular works, these texts spoke with startling immediacy to students of religion (professional or otherwise) on the search for spiritual truth outside of traditional religious institutions. In her conclusion to *The Gnostic Gospels*, Pagels explicitly linked those ancient texts with modern spiritual desires:[15]

When Muḥammed [*sic*] 'Alī smashed that jar and was disappointed not to find gold, he could not have imagined the implications of his accidental find ... They remained hidden until the twentieth century, when our own cultural experience has given us a new perspective on the issues they raise. Today we read them with different eyes, not merely as "madness and blasphemy" but as Christians in the first century experienced them – a powerful alternative to what we know as orthodox Christian tradition.[16]

Pagels's "smashed jar" releasing its potent texts into our modern religious atmosphere conjures up the image of the very *jinn* Muḥammad 'Alī supposedly feared: a spirit that might be benevolent or malicious, that might grant wishes or bring down curses. Heresy as a curse ("madness and blasphemy") or a blessing ("a powerful alternative") gracefully captures its doubled role in popular consciousness, a doubled role that will fuel a particular subset of Gospel Thrillers.

Pagels plots these two modes, curse and blessing, historically: in the past, the views contained in these "hidden" texts were seen as "madness and blasphemy" (she is citing here a second-century Christian writer against heresy, Irenaeus of Lyons, who serves as a foil for much of *The Gnostic Gospels*). "Today we read them with different eyes," she explains, positioning her reader as part of a "we" – western, Christian, liberal – freed from the blinkered views of "what we know as orthodox Christian tradition." Pagels relies on the dominant scholarly view of orthodoxy and heresy that held sway in the Euro-

---

[15] Pagels has recounted these personal and professional moments of discovery in many books, most recently in her memoir: *Why Religion? A Personal Story* (New York: HarperCollins, 2018), 21–23.
[16] Pagels, *Gnostic Gospels*, 152.

American academy for much of the twentieth century and which has
percolated, to various degrees, into the cultural consciousness of US
reading publics.

Nag Hammadi's "powerful alternative" to the rigidity of institutional Christianity landed on a ready audience, especially in 1970s and
1980s United States. (I wager *The Gnostic Gospels* was one of the only
books on esoteric early Christian texts to receive a glowing review in
Rolling Stone magazine.) In Chapter 2, I touched on the religious ennui
pervasive among a middle-class, predominantly white US public during
the Cold War (recall the 1966 issue of *Time* magazine asking: "IS GOD
DEAD?"). Not just ennui but active resistance to the patriarchal norms
of religious life was finding new expression in politically infused
debates roiling US churches: questions about women's ordination; calls
for civil rights and racial justice; aspirations for individual spiritual
achievement over against the staid and static institutional churches;
and, above all, inspired, even poetic interpretations of sacred texts over
against fundamentalist adherence to letter over spirit.[17]

From early in the twentieth century, and the early days of the Nag
Hammadi discoveries, gnostic Christianity had been praised by some
as a spiritual refutation of the stale institutionalism of traditional orthodoxy. Now, in the heady 1960s and 1970s, that spiritual discovery
found an easy entry point into progressive US political culture as a kind
of liberation from the trap of patriarchy. Didn't the appearance of divine
female figures in the texts break the mold of the dire and stern Father
God of traditional Christianity? Didn't the presence of female apostles in
these texts, especially Mary Magdalene, speak to the antiquity of gender
equality, a freedom for women quashed by later religious leaders? The
"countercanon" (to use Reed's term) now emerging from the halo of the
gnostic gospels resonated with the countercultural politics still echoing
from the 1960s and 1970s: a theopolitics that valued liberating heresy
and apocrypha over stultifying orthodoxy and canon.[18]

In contrast to the modern resonance between the countercanonical
and the countercultural, Pagels is clear in her work that the gnostics
had a limited appeal in antiquity. The social conservativism and tight
institutionalism of the orthodox spoke more directly to ancient

[17] Greil Marcus, "Pagels Says: Don't Knock the Gnostics," *Rolling Stone* 312
(March 6, 1980): 36.
[18] Dillon, "Heretical Revival," 6–9 on the tenor of the times; 160–211 on
Mary Magdalene.

Christians and likely ensured the eventual success of institutional Christianity: "The concerns of gnostic Christians survived only as a suppressed current, like a river driven underground," Pagel writes. That underground river would emerge throughout Christian history, carrying on its cloudy waters some of the more provocative European figures who "found themselves at the edges of orthodoxy." These figures (like Blake, Rembrandt, and Nietzsche) "found themselves in revolt against orthodox institutions," Pagels writes, continuing: "An increasing number of people today share their experience":

All the old questions – the original questions, sharply debated at the beginning of Christianity – are being reopened: How is one to understand the resurrection? What about women's participation in priestly and episcopal office? Who was Christ, and how does he relate to the believer? What are the similarities between Christianity and other world religions?[19]

The time had come for the jar to be smashed, the "old questions" to be reopened, the gnostic streams to burst once more into public view. If ancient Christians were too hidebound to heed calls for spiritual expansion, women's leadership, enlightened embodiment, and interreligious fellowship, their modern descendants might not be.

The continued success of *Gnostic Gospels* and other works that followed in its wake reveals a US reading public eager for the "powerful alternative" to orthodoxy the Nag Hammadi texts suggested: a readership hungry for heresy. Since the 1970s, lost gospels have rarely left the shelves of bookstores, promising to readers "secret," "forgotten," and suppressed truths that just might go back to the time of Jesus. The same qualities that once made heresy fearsome now make it attractive: its deviation from a rigid norm, its freedom from institutional constraint, its revelation of new possibilities. Gospel Thrillers that imagine gospels linked to historical heresies play with these twin responses of fear and desire and, in this, they work in tandem with modern scholarship on ancient Christian heresy.

Not Doubting Thomas

In imagining the possibility of "nonorthodox" gospels in the first century, Gospel Thrillers are also following the lead of scholars of

---

[19] Pagels, *Gnostic Gospels*, 150.

New Testament apocrypha. While surviving texts are usually dated to
the second, third, or fourth centuries, readers of noncanonical sources
often seek to push these unorthodox views back into the time of Jesus
himself. This desire for original heresy is evident in the popular press
whenever a new "heretical" text comes to light, as I discuss with regard
to several such texts in Chapter 6. This desire frequently finds its way
into scholarly assessment of texts, as well.[20]

The Gospel of Thomas is one of the Nag Hammadi texts that has
been working its way back into the first century since it first entered the
scholarly and public conversation in the 1950s. A set of 114 sayings in
the Coptic version (some sayings in Greek were also found in the trash
piles of Oxyrrhyncus, Egypt, in the late nineteenth century), this
"sayings gospel" early on captivated readers as an evocative doppel-
ganger of the canonical gospels. It contains some sayings found in
Matthew, Mark, and Luke, some variations of those canonical sayings,
and then some sayings entirely alien to the canonical worldview. Barely
a decade after the full gospel's discovery some scholars proposed that
Thomas – or some version of it – originated in a time and place closer
to Jesus than the canonical texts; the argument has recurred in many
forms every decade since.[21]

In an Oxford lecture in 1957 (later published as an article), Dutch
scholar of Gnosticism Gilles Quispel posited that the Gospel of
Thomas provided precious evidence for a lost (but lurking) "Gospel
of the Hebrews" of "Palestinian origin" and thus "may have preserved
something of the words of Jesus in a form more primitive than that
found in the canonical Gospels." In the 1960s, Helmut Koester (Elaine
Pagels's doctoral advisor) published an influential essay that similarly
argued for an early origin point for the materials in Thomas on the
sayings genre, "the most original 'Gattung' [i.e., genre] of the Jesus
tradition." In the early 1980s, Stevan Davies argued that Thomas was
not gnostic but part of a "Jewish wisdom tradition" that "might have
conceivably characterized Jesus' own teaching" and was probably
originally produced "between 45 and 70 AD." The 1990s saw a slew
of publications that placed Thomas alongside the canonical gospels as
a "fifth gospel" and potential source for the historical Jesus (see my

[20] The catalogue of popular scholarship on gnostic texts is vast, including several
reader-friendly anthologies of the Nag Hammadi Scriptures since the 1970s.
[21] J. Gregory Given, "'Finding' the *Gospel of Thomas* in Edessa," *Journal of Early
Christian Studies* 25 (2017): 501–30 for analysis of early scholarship.

discussion in Chapter 6). More recently, April DeConick has assessed previous theories of Thomas's composition and proposed a "rolling corpus": a "kernel" gospel from close to Jesus's time that was shaped by different hands, at different times, in different places, passing through Palestine, Syria, and ending up, at last, in Egypt, in Coptic, buried in a jar.[22]

All of these readings of Thomas distinguish between the "origins" of the text (its "kernel"), close to (if not from) Jesus himself, and the Coptic text found at Nag Hammadi, a later redaction. In this method, of course, they follow standard source criticism and redaction criticism as they are practiced in modern biblical studies: the careful unspooling of an existing text to isolate and study its prior (if lost) sources and an analysis of their subsequent rearrangement and editing. But in the case of the Gospel of Thomas, this chronological and theological layering also reinforces the rootless wandering of heresy as it meanders through time and space from some nebulous point close to (if not from) Jesus himself, through different languages, cultures, and traditions until remerging from a smashed jar into our present moment.

The Gospel of Thomas has enjoyed a long life among scholars and in the popular press: Pagels, for instance, published *Beyond Belief: The Secret Gospel of Thomas* in 2004 and made it to the *New York Times* Best Seller list. Thomas's popularity among scholars and general audiences is due to its accessible strangeness: comprising primarily sayings, many of which echo familiar sayings from the canonical gospels, it's also just strange enough to surprise a reader. Other Nag Hammadi texts delve so deeply into the mythopoetic realms of "gnostic" creation and redemption that they are rarely accessible to general readers. Thomas *feels* familiar while also registering at times as mystical and even esoteric. Its familiar strangeness also hints at long-ago acts of

---

[22] All of these authors published numerous articles and books on the Gospel of Thomas, but I quote here from a few of their representative articles: Gilles Quispel, "The Gospel of Thomas and the New Testament," *Vigiliae Christianae* 11 (1957): 189–207; Helmut Koester, "ΓΝΩΜΑΙ ΔΙΑΦΟΡΟΙ: The Origin and Nature of Diversification in the History of Early Christianity," *Harvard Theological Review* 58 (1965): 160–203 (I cite Koester due to his influence in this trajectory of study; recently, Elaine Pagels has revealed that he sexually assaulted her when he was her graduate advisor at Harvard); Stevan Davies, "Thomas: The Fourth Synoptic Gospel," *Biblical Archaeologist* 46 (1983): 6–14; April D. DeConick, "The Original *Gospel of Thomas*," *Vigiliae Christianae* 56 (2002): 167–99.

omission and suppression. Pagels already said it in *The Gnostic Gospels*: this "powerful alternative" survived as a "suppressed current." Later in *Beyond Belief* she recalls discovering Thomas and other "secret writings" in graduate school that "revealed diversity within the Christian movement that later, 'official' version of Christian history had suppressed." Upon reading them, Pagels was "surprised to find in them unexpected spiritual power." The frisson of the "secret Gospel of Thomas" comes from recognizing that historical suppression and becoming an insider to that suppressed truth.[23]

Gospel Thrillers likewise plunge readers into a world in which secret truths of ancient heretical teachings, going back to Jesus himself, have been suppressed for centuries and brought to light to modern eyes. They can go further, of course, than modern scholars, who must work with hypothetical lost sources and theoretical editorial accretions. Gospel Thrillers imagine the recovery of a lost gospel, from Jesus's own time, that reveals an "original" Christianity at odds with institutional orthodoxy: Jesus's teachings as heresy. These novels dwell at length on the perpetrators of that "suppression," often some secret order tucked away in the back rooms of a venerable institution (like the Roman Catholic Church). They also grapple with the tension between an exciting text bursting with secret, liberating truths and nefarious sects, animated by, and perhaps even perverted by, those secret truths. Heresy in the novels is a double-edged sword: "madness and blasphemy" on the one hand, a "powerful alternative" on the other. At the center of that tension lies the conflicted relationship between texts, truths, and religious institutions.

You Cannot Escape the *Concilium*: Dangerous Orthodoxy

One Gospel Thriller follows the long lead of scholars positing a first-century Gospel of Thomas that might reveal Jesus's shocking lack of orthodoxy. In *Gospel Truths*, an ancient Hebrew copy of "The Book of Thomas the Contender" (one of the Coptic texts uncovered at Nag Hammadi) has turned up in a cathedral in France. It ends up in the hands of the head of the Vatican bank, Archbishop Kazimierz Grabowski, who has been involved in various money-laundering

---

[23] Elaine Pagels, *Beyond Belief: The Secret Gospel of Thomas* (New York: Random House, 2004), 32.

schemes with nefarious co-conspirators in and out of the Roman Catholic hierarchy. Grabowski has the text examined by an expert, a monsignor who pronounces that this ancient relic is very likely a version of "Q," the lost source for the canonical gospels. But that is just the beginning of his exposition: for this version of "Thomas the Contender" found at Amiens is linked to even older version of the "Gospel of Thomas" supposedly hidden in the cathedral at Chartres that would record Christ's actual words.

Grabowski asks concerning this "Gospel of Thomas": "'How valuable would it be, if someone were to find it?'" His colleague answers: "'You don't understand. It doesn't have any intrinsic value, or relatively little. But it would be of inestimable value to suppress it ... Because it would mean the end ... The end of the church as we know it.'" The monsignor continues in panic:

"And then think what would happen if those sayings happened to be Gnostic ... if the ideas which Christ espoused were not at all the same as those the Church has come to stand for. Can you see the headlines now: Christ Found To Be a Heretic! It would mean anarchy." (pp. 147–48)

Grabowski is swept up in the race to find this original Gospel of Thomas and becomes, in the process, the perfect representation of the religiously affiliated conspirators who suppress heretical gospel truths: driven by equal parts institutional loyalty, monetary greed, and desire for personal power. Belief rarely enters into religious conspirators' considerations; archbishops, cardinals, clerics, and monsignors are not moved by the sincere conviction that the canonical gospels, as interpreted by religious authorities, are theologically correct. Instead, power, wealth, and control drive the institutional desire to suppress the truth.

In Gospel Thrillers, the suppression of the heretical origins of Christianity is often the work of secret religious orders, fantasy projections of longstanding conspiratorial fantasies about the Roman Catholic church in US popular culture. Anti-Catholicism stretches back deep into the colonial prehistory of the United States, reanimated by white racist panic about immigration in the nineteenth century and linked to global conspiracy in the early twentieth century and the period of the Cold War. At various moments that pervasive anti-Catholic sentiment has entered into the biblical realm, as in nineteenth-century debates over which version of the Christian Bible to use in public schools or twentieth-century suspicions about the Catholic custodianship of the Dead Sea Scrolls (see my discussion of these moments in Chapter 2 and Chapter 3). The novels take the conspiratorial kernel of US anti-Catholicism and blow it up into fantastical proportions.[24]

In at least one novel, *The Judas Gospel*, the Pope himself is directly responsible for the violent attempts at suppressing a newfound testament by Judas, sending out an assassin known as "The Dominican." More typically the conspiratorial force is not the Roman Catholic church per se, but rather some small subset within it: a secret order, a sub rosa alliance flourishing for centuries in back corridors of the Vatican. Narratively, this containment of Catholic conspiracy allows the novels to paint a multifaceted and even ambivalent picture of institutional religion. On the one hand, the entire Roman Catholic Church is not held responsible for suppression and conspiracy; indeed, several novels feature Catholic protagonists working to reveal long-hidden truths (*Book of Q*, *The Masada Scroll*, *The Order*). On the other hand, the orthodox institution par excellence is an amenable site for pockets of suppression and conspiracy to flourish.

In *Gospel Truths*, Grabowski is working with Informazione Quatro (or IQ), a mostly secular conspiratorial network formed outside the Vatican after a banking scandal the year before (based on the real collapse of the Banco Ambrosiano in 1982). Other novels have a penchant for the secret society within the Vatican but set apart from its official hierarchy. Only one novel, Luis Rocha's *The Pope's Assassin* (2011), uses a real-life Catholic group, imagining a sinister German priest leading the Jesuits on a violent rampage. More often, the novels invent a colorful and evocatively named secret group: the Guardians (*Keepers of the Secret*), the Via Dei (*The Masada Scroll*), the Knights of Malta (*The Coptic Secret*, echoing a similarly named Catholic lay movement), the *concilium* (*The Lost Tomb*), and the Order of St. Helena (*The Order*) all spring into violent action to recover, contain, or suppress a dangerous secret gospel that threatens the power and prestige of the Roman Catholic church by calling into question the

---

[24] See Mark Massa, *Anti-Catholicism in America: The Last Acceptable Prejudice* (New York: Crossroad, 2003) and "Anti-Catholicism in the United States," in *The Cambridge Companion to American Catholicism*, ed. Margaret M. McGuinness and Thomas F. Rzeznik (Cambridge: Cambridge University Press, 2021), 197–215.

truth of traditional orthodoxy. Many of these groups in fact date back to the very origins of Christianity, millennia-old conspiracies that have kept the truth out of the Christian Bible since its formation. Others have emerged more recently out of power-hungry modern international conspiracies that see in the Vatican's global reach an opportunity for more wealth and power. All of them leverage their immense resources to hatch immoral schemes to cover up the truth and hold on to power.

In some novels, like *Gospel Truths*, institutional religious forces partner with unsavory, secular co-conspirators: in James Becker's *The First Apostle* (2008), a cardinal in charge of the Congregation for the Doctrine of the Faith ("the direct descendant of the Roman Inquisition" [p. 35]) gets a mysterious phone call from an Italian *mafioso* whose criminal syndicate has been charged for more than a century with tracking ancient documents that could bring down the Church. In other novels, a secret religious group apart from, but with curious ties, to Roman Catholicism stands between the protagonists and the truth: the Greek Orthodox Order of Xenope in *The Gemini Contenders* (1976); the Crux Orientalis in *The Judas Testament* (1994); the Knights of Saint Clement in *The Testament* (2006); Operation Leonardo in *Secret of the Templars* (2015).

Like Grabowski in *Gospel Truths*, none of these secret societies is motivated by sincere theological belief: they all already know (or at least suspect) the truth that they are covering up. Conspiracies in thrillers are motivated by selfish desires for power and control and when Gospel Thrillers draw on the worst stereotypes about institutional religion – especially US cultural stereotypes about Roman Catholicism – they see it as the natural site of a violent conspiracy to hide the truth. Orthodoxy, embodied in these power-hungry religious groups, becomes the foil for the "powerful alternative" that will be unleashed when the secret gospel comes to light and truth defeats secrecy. It is perhaps unsurprising, then, that so often the heretical truth of earliest Christianity revealed in these texts strikes at the very foundations of institutional religious truths.

Lost Texts

Gospel Thrillers imagine that their new gospels will counter institutional sterility and reveal a lost teaching of Jesus that will free his followers from the shackles of patriarchal orthodoxy. An early "heretical" Gospel Thriller, *Keepers of the Secret* by Barnaby Conrad and Nico Mastorakis from 1983, accomplishes this revelation in perhaps the bluntest fashion. It features dashing widower and investigative journalist Jason van Cleve who, during a restful Mediterranean cruise, is confronted with evidence of a lost gospel written by the apostle John, unearthed in the walls of a house in Ephesus in the 1930s. The old man who had discovered "the Ephesus scrolls" in his youth is murdered before he can reveal to Jason the complete text or its present-day location. Accompanied by Taylor Phillips, an ex-diplomat and amateur archaeologist (and love interest), van Cleve sets off to find the truth; they dodge the murderous machinations of the Guardians of the Faith, a centuries-old conspiracy within the Roman Catholic church who take as their mission protecting the glory and prestige of Christianity.

The shocking secret at the heart of the Ephesus scrolls is that the true messiah, the miraculous child of Mary, was a girl named Mary Lael; Jesus was her foster-brother, picked up by the side of the road in Egypt and adopted by Mary and Joseph. It was Lael who received divine teachings and performed the miracles found in the gospels (while making them seem like the work of Jesus); it was to Lael that Jesus cried out on the cross, asking why she had abandoned him; and it was Lael who went into the tomb and removed Jesus's body, leading to the story of the resurrection. Apart from the denial of the resurrection (which features in many Gospel Thrillers), there is very little by the way of radical teaching in *Keepers of the Secret*. Lael does recite some "wisdom sayings" that draw from gnostic texts; after resurrecting a goat, Lael pronounces: "'If you bring forth what is within you, what you bring forth will save you. If you do not bring forth what is within you, what you do not bring forth will destroy you'" (p. 17). This saying from the Gospel of Thomas (*logion* 70) is often interpreted along highly individual, spiritual terms, an antidote to institutional religious authoritarianism. But apart from one or two references to humility and the "brotherhood of man," Lael's teachings are not as significant as the fact that the messiah was a woman.

While initially making light of this new discovery ("'What are you planning – a book called *She, Jesus?*'" [p. 49]), Taylor later ponders the effect a woman messiah would have: "'With the Messiah, the words He left us with cannot be taken separately – they cannot be divorced from the man, from His life, from His sacrifices, from His crucifixion and His resurrection. Yes, it would matter'" (p. 89). The various characters who encounter or hear about the Ephesus scrolls tend to agree that the revelation about Lael would be catastrophic. As one cardinal puts it (while commissioning a hitman to stop Jason and Taylor): "'Not only the Catholic Church but every branch of the Christian religion. Two thousand years, down the drain'" (p. 103). Even the Pope, when he finally learns about the scrolls, concedes that he's not sure he wouldn't destroy them if given the chance and says: "'Perhaps these scrolls would not be as damaging as a third world war, but they would certainly weaken the faith, hoax or not'" (p. 132). Readers are told, time and again, that the scrolls' secrets are a shocking "bomb" waiting to go off (pp. 2, 25 90). The "bomb" does not, in the end go off: Jason manages to save his lover and her child and defeat the villainous Guardians, but all evidence of the scrolls literally goes up in smoke.

Keepers of the Secret appeared as the Nag Hammadi finds were just beginning to make inroads in the popular imagination, and references to the "gnostic chronicles" and even direct citations from texts like the Gospel of Philip pepper the pages (pp. 87, 107, 110). While critical scholarly work on Gnosticism and gender would appear in the coming years, in this Gospel Thriller the mere fact of a woman messiah seems sufficiently radical to threaten patriarchal orthodoxy. There is no discussion of women's ordination, and the decision to make Lael Jesus's sister rather than, say, his wife removes discussion of priestly celibacy and sexuality from the story, as well. Just the hint of gender politics attaching to the origins of Christianity is enough to threaten to set the world on fire.[25]

Gospel Truths takes readers on a circuitous journey through multiple lost gospels that have been concealed for centuries in European cathedrals. An Italian banker named Pontevecchio, mixed up in recent Vatican banking scandals, has been found dead, hanged beneath Blackfriars Bridge in London; before his death, he was on the hunt for lost gospels that would give him leverage against his Informazione Quatro co-conspirators. (Pontevecchio is based on Italian banker

---

[25] On the more radical gender politics being produced within academia around the same time, see Karen L. King (ed.), *Images of the Feminine in Gnosticism*, Studies in Antiquity and Christianity (Philadelphia, PA: Fortress Press, 1988).

Roberto Calvi, who was found dead in similar circumstances in 1982.)
Pontevecchio had in fact acquired a copy of the Book of Thomas the
Contender; in this novel, as I noted above, the Book of Thomas is an
early version of "Q," an edited list of sayings of Jesus circulating after
his death. But the prize at the heart of this Gospel Thriller is an earlier
version of the Gospel of Thomas containing Jesus's unedited words.[26]

According to this primitive Gospel of Thomas, Jesus's original teachings consist of "'gnosis, a kind of mystical secret knowledge [that] also
meant you didn't need the Church, the organization,'" as one character
explains, adding: "'Obviously, the centralized Church in Rome felt
threatened'" (pp. 128–29). One of the protagonists, a US mathematician investigating numerological codes in Gothic cathedrals, remarks
that "their philosophy sounds almost Eastern" (p. 129). This "philosophy" is also directly compared to modern liberation theology. For
another protagonist, an undercover London cop, the links are clear:

He began to understand the power of this latest heresy [i.e., liberation
theology]. It was the same power for which the Gnostic Book of Thomas
the Contender had been banned so long ago. And, somehow, it was the
power which had slipped a nylon rope around Pontevecchio's neck. (p. 123)

Later the cop explains to the mathematician why so many have killed
and died for this gospel: "'The fact that the sayings could be Christ's
own words, and Gnostic words at that. Heresy, Joseph'" (p. 270).

Jesus's words are not only "heresy," inimical to the power and
prestige of "the Church," they are not even really Christian: "sounds
almost Eastern," one character notes. This easternness is elaborated by
a mysterious French Countess Irene de Rochambaud: "'The link of the
tradition spanned from the Magian Brotherhood in Babylon, through
the Gnostics and the Manicheans, past the Paulicians and Catharists to
the Templars and Freemasons of today'" (p. 202). The Countess is
herself, as it turns out, "matriarch" of the "Grand Loge Féminin," a
present-day group of "Speculative Masons" also on the hunt for
Jesus's heretical teachings. Just as some Dead Sea Scrolls in Gospel

---

[26] The death of Calvi (known as "God's Banker") has fueled Vatican conspiracy
theories for decades: see John Allen, Jr., "Power, Secrecy Feed Conspiracy
Theories in Vatican City," *National Catholic Reporter* 34.35 (July 31, 1998):
15–18, which lists the banking scandal and Calvi's death first in its list of seven
famous Vatican conspiracy theories (as of 1998).

Thrillers made Jesus so Jewish that any links to Christianity were tenuous or broken, so these heretical Gospel Thrillers often threaten to push Jesus's teachings beyond the Christian pale into the more intriguing realm of "eastern philosophy."

As in *Keepers of the Secret*, everyone on the hunt for this Gospel of Thomas is certain that it will bring down institutional Christianity: "'the end of the Church as we know it'" (p. 147), "who could have faith in a Church that was founded on a lie?" (p. 156), "a document so old – and so heretical, apparently – that its publication alone would cause irreparable damage to the Church" (pp. 185–86), capable of "'toppling the Church'" (pp. 275, 276). Unlike *Keepers of the Secret*, however, the lost gospel is recovered and set to be unleashed on the world, sent to a publisher by Countess Irene. Readers don't see the effects of this gospel on the world, though: whether the "eastern" truth of Jesus's liberatory teachings really does help dismantle institutional patriarchy remains unknown. (More on this lack of theopolitical denouement below.)

David Gibbins's 2008 *The Lost Tomb* (originally published in the UK as *The Last Gospel*) likewise links Jesus's teachings to Christian heresy and the potential dismantling of the institutional Church. Early in the novel, a group of underwater archaeologists prepare to enter unexcavated rooms in the Villa of the Papyri in Herculaneum, buried in the first century by the eruption of Mount Vesuvius. Even before excavation has begun, the shadow of "the Church" lingers over the possibility of new discoveries, as one of their number remarks: "'Like other sacred sites, like the caves of the Dead Sea Scrolls in Israel, people yearn to find out what lies inside, yet they also fear it. And believe me, there is one very powerful body in Italy that would rather not have any more written records from the first century AD'" (p. 44). Once inside the Villa the protagonist, Jack Howard, makes a shocking discovery: a scrap of papyrus in which reference is made to Jesus's written words, preserved by the Roman Emperor Claudius.

The team begins a hunt that takes them around the world: from Herculaneum to London, where they find the hidden tomb of the Celtic rebel Boudicca and their next clue; to a monastery in California that was the early twentieth-century refuge for a brilliant and idiosyncratic British codebreaker; to a secret crypt hidden beneath the Church of the Holy Sepulcher in Jerusalem: our reminder that heresy is relentlessly mobile. Along the way Jack and his companions get clues about the content of Jesus's sayings as well the surviving traces of Jesus's original "heresy." Brought by Claudius himself to ancient Britain, this pre-Roman Christianity survived into antiquity as the heresy of Pelagius, defined as "'people having control and responsibility for their own actions, their own destiny'" (p. 267). An inheritor of Jesus's "personal religion" version of Christianity, Pelagius came into conflict with the "domination"-centered Christianity of Augustine. The authentic, heretical religion of Jesus, focused on personal freedom, also made room for women as equals to men (pp. 312–13).

The *concilium*, the secret Vatican conspiracy out to stop Howard and his team, has existed from the very beginnings of Christianity to suppress this heretical teaching of Jesus: created by Claudius's freedman Narcissus along with the apostle Paul, throughout history the *concilium ecclesiasticum Sanctus Paulus* (*sic*) has acted to thwart the Pelagianism of Jesus. A mysterious stranger tells them:

"Over the centuries the *concilium* fought off the most pernicious of heresies, the ones the Inquisition of the Holy See was unable to defeat. In Britain they fought the Pelagians ... They fought the Protestants after the Reformation ... After the New World was discovered the *concilium* ordered the destruction of the Maya and the Aztec and the Inca, fearing a prophecy of the ancient Sibyl that foretold a coming darkness from the west." (p. 338)

The hyperinstitutional *concilium*, caring only for the survival of the Church, ends up being precisely what Jesus preached against:

The Kingdom of Heaven is on earth,
Men shall not stand in the way of the word of God.
And the Kingdom of Heaven shall be the House of the Lord.
There shall be no priests.
And there shall be no temples ...

(p. 481)

Jesus even mistrusts the idea of Scriptures: "The written word stands in the way of the Kingdom of Heaven" (p. 478). One member of the *concilium* calls this teaching: "'The heresy of those who would deny the sanctity of the ordained'" (p. 165).

At the end of *The Lost Tomb*, readers are once more promised that this explosive lost gospel will be released to the world and that it will have the ability to defeat the violence and domination of institutional religion: "'Freedom for people to choose their own spiritual path, without fear, guilt, persecution, the *concilium*'"(p. 450). Yet, as in other novels that will reveal the heretical origins of Christianity, readers never see the fruits of this liberating revelation.

Found Sects

Gospel Thrillers not only fantasize about a heretical Jesus preaching liberation; they also catastrophize about the theological anarchy of ancient heresies surviving into our own day. In *The Book of Q* a text is found under Rome that is somehow related to Manicheism, an ancient dualist heresy (in which a God of Light is eternally squaring off against a God of Darkness). When the archaeologist who made the discovery dies mysteriously, US Jesuit and scholar Ian Pearse sets about unraveling the mystery. It turns out Manicheism did not go extinct "fifteen hundred years ago," as Pearse and everyone else believe. It merely went underground, growing and even flourishing throughout the world: its adherents supposedly number close to ten million members. It's led by a sinister Austrian Cardinal, Erich von Neurath, who is plotting to take over the Roman Catholic church. Pearse and von Neurath race to discover a lost text, the *Hagia Hodoporia* (Holy Journey), for which the Roman discovery is a kind of treasure map. Von Neurath thinks it will secure his Manichean triumph; Pearse hopes that Christ's own words recorded in this lost text will bring a new clarity to his lagging Catholic faith.

The novel distinguishes between the Manichean sect which has survived from antiquity and the truly Gnostic Christianity of Christ supposedly preserved in the *Hagia Hodoporia*. Pearse consults with an Italian expert, Cecilia Angeli, who explains that the basics of Gnosticism are spiritual enlightenment and rejection of institutional authority. "'The Gnostics ... claim that self-knowledge – the highest form of attainment – is actually knowledge of God. So, self and Divine become identical at a certain point of self-awareness.'" Pearse replies: "'That's [*sic*] sounds like a very Eastern view of spiritual growth'" (p. 73). As in *Gospel Truths*, Jesus's "heresy" distances him from western Christianity. Angeli continues that since "'Self and Divine are identical ... there's no need for a resurrection or a papal authority, with its subsequent structure'" (p. 73). Pearse replies: "'It sounds like you're saying we don't need a church'" (p. 74).

When Angeli turns to the Manicheans, however, she distinguishes their material obsessions from the spiritual enlightenment of true Gnostics:

"Unlike your basic Christians, or even Gnostics, the Manicheans believed that light and darkness were substances scattered within the material world. For instance, they actually thought that melons and cucumbers held a great deal of light, meats and wines the dark elements. Eat a melon, promote good. Eat a chicken, foment evil."

"And that was what Mani developed out of Gnosticism? Evil foods?" (p. 103)

Pearse's joke highlights what readers learn is a primary failure of the modern Manicheans: their hatred of the "material world" that has led them to "'a kind of hyperasceticism'" (p. 104), a rejection of sex and worldly comforts. This rejection of the material world even licenses some of the more horrific actions of the Manichean conspirators in the novel: not only engineering a takeover of the Catholic church – von Neurath manages to be named Pope Lucius the Fourth – but launching a global religious war by bombing thousands of Christian churches worldwide (including the Vatican) and blaming non-Christian terrorists.

Pearse does find the *Hagia Hodoporia*, which turns out to be the lost sayings source Q, recording Jesus's actual words: "a source contemporary with Christ, and thus unlike any of the four gospels" (p. 331). It resonates with the spiritual enlightenment Angeli ascribed to the Gnostics and, as Pearse himself had intuited, this "gnostic" wisdom of Jesus expands beyond traditional Christianity, "drawn from the pages of Cynicism, Indian mysticism, and Essene wisdom" (p. 336). Its message of universal love and spiritual autonomy recalls some of the more popular gnostic sayings of a text like Thomas: "Blessed are those who have grown confident and have found faith for themselves" (p. 33). It is also a radically egalitarian message. As Pearse reads this lost gospel he marvels:

Except for the passages on the Resurrection [which it denies], Q put forward an image of Jesus and faith that the modern church would have been only too happy to embrace. Q's commitment to individual rights and responsibility, and its view of women and their role in the church – anathema to a fifth- or sixteenth-century mind – were perfectly designed to resolve any number of contentious debates now ripping Catholicism apart. (p. 336)

Moreover, the text the Manicheans have been hunting for disproves their entire belief system, lacking their "hyperasceticism" and hidden "gnosis" and instead giving plain wisdom that "might actually be the device to save the church from itself" (pp. 336–37).

Pearse returns to Rome with his amazing find, Pope Lucius's reign of terror ends in assassination, and the last Manichean conspirators are rooted out of the Vatican. Pearse, along with Professor Angeli and a sympathetic Cardinal Peretti (who will be the next Pope), decide to demoralize the global Manichean sect and rejuvenate orthodoxy by releasing Q. Before they do so, however, they excise from the text forty verses disproving the resurrection of Christ and insert "restored" passages that will confirm the Eucharist and other sacraments of the church (pp. 362–64). Cardinal Peretti expresses shock: "'We're talking about the Holy Word of Christ. You can't overlook that.'" Pearse replies: "'The Gospel writers did … Maybe that's what the church needs now in order to survive in the next millennium. Another dose of selective editing'" (p. 362). The restorative truth, the "powerful alternative," proves in the end too heretical for public consumption.

The Book of Q provides the most optimistic view of what would happen should a lost, heretical gospel face off against a secret, heretical form of Christianity, and even it pulls its punches at the very end. Other Gospel Thrillers are less sanguine about the ability of heretical texts to defeat the machinations of heretical sects. In Leslie Winfield Williams's *The Judas Conspiracy*, as I mentioned at the beginning of this chapter, an early medieval translation of the full Gospel of Judas has been found in the New Haven mansion of the late father of the Dean of Yale Divinity School, but the Dean's sister-in-law is murdered and the text is stolen. The culprits are a millennia-old gnostic sect, the Sethian Brotherhood, working through their assassin, called Gabriel. Gabriel kills more people, first in New Haven and then at the nearby meeting of the American Academy of Religion in New York City, in order to protect the Brotherhood's secrecy and get vengeance on their theological detractors. (At the end of the novel, Gabriel is revealed to be the angelic nom de guerre given to a troubled young man named Jeeter Smythe at his Sethian initiation.)

The novel's protagonists are Isabella, a brilliant woman detective who had once studied for the ministry, and Paul, the handsome academic nephew of the Yale Divinity dean and translator of the full Gospel. Throughout the book they are hot on the Sethian Brotherhood's trail. By the end of the novel, they have thwarted the Brotherhood's plot to blow up the National Cathedral in Washington, DC, on Thanksgiving Day and have unmasked Paul's own uncle, the Dean's lawyer brother, as the American Patriarch of the Sethian

Brotherhood. The Gospel is never recovered (in fact, it is destroyed in a fire at the Scottish manor house of the Sethian Grand Patriarch, who himself dies soon after) and readers have no idea if the Brotherhood will continue.

Unlike the disalignment of sect and text in *The Book of Q*, what little readers learn about the Gospel of Judas and the Sethian Brotherhood in *The Judas Conspiracy* suggests they are in theological sync. The gospel promises Judas eventual triumph and preaches that embodiment is an obstacle to salvation (licensing some of the group's atrocities). The text contains what Paul colorfully calls "the Black Beatitudes," several of which are left on ominous postcards near the Brotherhood's murder victims. "Blessed are the merciless, for they shall see the truth. Blessed are those who value knowledge more than life, for they will be given secret wisdom" (pp. 67, 95). These warped versions of Jesus's sayings from the Sermon on the Mount suggest a fundamentally different moral universe. The full Gospel of Judas also records that Judas had twin sons: David founded the Sethian Brotherhood, to preserve his father's memory and the anti-material teachings of the gnostic Jesus, while Jesse "became a Christian" (p. 52). Thus, the bona fides of the Sethian Brotherhood is at least as ancient and authentic as that of orthodox Christianity.

The sect is just as twisted as the text. In their investigations, Isabella and Paul discover traces of the Brotherhood's murderous past, including involvement with Nazis, Al Qaida, and the Kennedy assassination. Their Grand Patriarch is a ludicrously effeminate and depraved wealthy Englishman, who leads the Brotherhood ineptly and accidentally burns down his manor house along with the Gospel of Judas while dancing around in his ceremonial robes. The movement thrives on appeals to broken masculinity. Gabriel, the Sethian assassin, is a former drug addict who found salvation in the elitist message of the Brotherhood. Paul's Sethian uncle Malcolm is also shown in the novel turning to the Sethian Brotherhood in a crisis of masculinity (his wife had an affair with his brother). Both Malcolm and Gabriel find in the gnostic text and sect an illusory power and satisfaction denied to them in their "straight" lives.

The most disturbing alignment of heretical text and heretical sect comes in Adam Blake's *The Dead Sea Deception* (2011). As in *The Judas Conspiracy*, the lost gospel in this case is a more complete version of the Gospel of Judas. It has been discovered by an ancient historian in the UK who crowdsourced the extraction of a coded text concealed in a medieval manuscript known as "the Rotgut Codex." Barlow, the British historian, derived some unspecified code from a fragment of the Dead Sea Scrolls (thus the title of the novel, which otherwise has nothing to do with the Dead Sea Scrolls) and uncovered not only a complete version of Jesus's gnostic instructions to Judas but a kind of "community rule" for Judas's descendants and followers. Barlow and most of the participants in his crowdsourced endeavor are soon murdered by bizarre assassins.[27]

We soon learn that there does, in fact, exist a group of followers of Judas's gnostic Christianity that has survived for centuries, literally underground, relocating whenever they fear discovery. Living lives of total isolation, speaking Aramaic and worshipping according to the secret gospel's instructions, the "Judas people" send two types of secret agents out into the word: *Elohim* (Messengers), trained assassins fueled by drugs and wielding ancient weapons to eliminate threats to the sect; and *Kelim* (Vessels), women chosen by lot to go out and marry healthy men, bear three children, and then return with their invigorated offspring to live among the Judas people. (Many *Kelim*, feeling polluted by their time in the world, choose to die upon their return.) One such spurned husband, Leo Tillman, has spent nearly fifteen years training to be a mercenary to track down the man he thinks kidnapped his wife and children.

Heather Kennedy, the London police officer charged with investigating Barlow's murder, slowly puts all these pieces together. She learns from another scholar who has also decoded the lost gospel that its "'hidden message is heresy on the most breathtaking scale imaginable'" (p. 371). The gnostic mistrust of the imperfect created world creates a communal sense of opposition and resistance, a fundamentally suspicious and isolated moral perspective radically different from our own (pp. 380–83). This radically different morality is on display throughout the novel: lives brutally taken, a plane brought down, and a barely thwarted plot to poison the water supply to Mexico City and kill twenty million people.

The Judas people are not only morally distinct from those outside their sect; they have become physically distinct (thus the need to diversify their gene pool): pale from living underground, speaking a dead

---

[27] Blake is the pseudonym of a popular cartoonist Mike Carey.

and alien language, emerging into the light only to guard their secrets
and fortify their community. The drugs used by the *Elohim* to increase
their murderous efficiency even cause them to cry tears of blood. More
than once Kennedy thinks of them as more than just a heresy: "an
entire race that had retreated from the world and scuffed sand over
their own footprints so that nobody would know they'd existed"
(p. 401). When she attempts to explain all of this to Tillman, she says:
"'They've lived like a big secret society for at least the last two
millennia ... But actually, that's a lousy simile for what they are.
Because they're also a race. A secret race'" (p. 505). This idea that
gnostics are a distinct subset of humanity appears in ancient gnostic
texts, in which "those in the know" understand themselves to be a
different "generation" of humans, destined for salvation while this
tainted world falls away. *The Dead Sea Deception* takes this notion
seriously, positing a text and sect that divide humanity utterly.[28]

The plot to poison Mexico City is averted and one of the sinister
leaders of the Judas people is killed in a final conflict with Tillman and
Kennedy. But the Judas people themselves relocate and, presumably,
continue their covert existence fueled by paranoia and violence until
their time comes. (The next year, Blake published an apocalyptic sequel
to *The Dead Sea Deception* entitled *The Demon Code* in which the
Judas people continue their violent ways.) The gospel is recovered and,
one assumes, published (Emil Gassan, its second translator and exposi-
tor, survives to appear in the sequel) but the "powerful alternative"
encoded in its text and embodied by the Judas people is not the
liberation hoped for by some scholars or hinted at in other Gospel
Thrillers, such as *Keepers of the Secret* or *The Book of Q*. For *The
Dead Sea Deception*, heresy is "madness and blasphemy," a
frightening glimpse into what happens when the "powerful" heretical
alternative is allowed to grow and thrive underground.[29]

These frightening gnostic sects lurking in this set of heretical Gospel
Thrillers stand in a complex imaginative relationship to the institutions
of orthodox Christianity against which (in other Gospel Thrillers) the
liberating heretical texts stand opposed. On the one hand, these sects

[28] On gnostic separatism, see Guy G. Stroumsa, *Another Seed: Studies in Gnostic
Mythology*, Nag Hammadi Studies 24 (Leiden: Brill, 1984) and Dylan Burns,
Apocalypse of the Alien God: Platonism and the Exile of Sethian Gnosticism,
Divinations (Philadelphia PA: University of Pennsylvania, 2014).
[29] Adam Blake, *The Demon Code* (London: Little, Brown and Co., 2012).

provide a foil for the "good orthodox," from whose ranks emerge several well-meaning protagonists and their helpful colleagues. We've already met Ian Pearse, the handsome and resourceful Jesuit in *The Book of Q*, working side by side with future pope Cardinal Peretti to root out the Manichean infiltrators of the Church. When the novel begins, Pearse is a priest who fled into the world of arcane scholarship from the "confusion" of the priesthood: "too much responsibility ceded by a willing congregation; too easy a reliance on detached hierarchy. Church dogma had a way of clouding everything" (p. 34). It's precisely in his quest for the truth, in his opposition to the violence of the heretical Manicheans, that Pearse finds his way back to the comforting stability of the Roman Catholic church (chastened by the newly found Q).

At the same time, those Manicheans reflect and amplify some of the worst stereotypes about the Vatican and other wealthy global religious institutions. The worldwide network of Manicheans cloaks its sinister aspirations for world power under the veneer of charitable good deeds. In a quiet confrontation with one of the last Manicheans to be unmasked (a gaunt Roman monk who, under guise of friendship, had first brought Pearse into the search for the gospel), the parallels are made clear.

"You really think we're some group of fanatics don't you?"

"Why should I think that? ... The church bombings, the Vatican, the bank, the hysteria over Islamic fundamentalism. Am I missing anything? Oh, and of course, the one true and holy church for the initiated." (p. 358)

Pearse means to underscore the depravities of heresy although his examples, on an uncharitable reading (and apart from the church bombings), might apply to Roman Catholicism as well. His former friend quickly points this parallel out:

"Unlike the Catholic church, Father? ... What if I told you we've got child-welfare initiatives, drug-abuse programs, planned-parenting centers, all set up by the hundreds, both here in Europe and in the States? Would you think differently? In the abstract I suppose it does sound like fanaticism. But not when it has a practical face to it ... Fifteen hundred years ago, we wanted to destroy you because of the corruption of certain theological truths. Now we simply want to put you out of your misery, turn the church into something that has real power and that can make the world whole again." (p. 359)

Heresy and orthodoxy, once mortal enemies, have dovetailed over the centuries until – at least, from the heretics' perspective – they are interchangeable in terms of their methods and goals: real power.

The Sethian Brotherhood in *The Judas Conspiracy* also evokes some of the most damaging stereotypes about institutional religion: a secretive and unimaginably wealthy cadre of all-male initiates, whose leader engages in pederastic fantasies ("He had found a new website that brought together his love of the Holy Land and his interest in young boys" [p. 56]), using "hidden influence and money to steer the course of history" (pp. 135–36). Even though the Sethians see themselves as deeply opposed to orthodoxy, "'working to bring down the false Christ and destroy Christendom forever'" (p. 88), the distinction is not so clear to Isabella the detective. She says to seminary professor (and love interest) Paul: "'The Sethians are willing to kill and die for their belief in the Pleroma and the triumph of Judas. I need you to tell me why the Christian God is better than Pleroma'" (p. 245). Paul's answer ("'God loves *me*. God loves *you*. Pleroma . . . is impersonal'") is unsatisfying to Isabella, but eventually she makes piece with Paul's "faith" (p. 301)

It is true that in the novels that feature underground heretical sects, the heretics are portrayed (or portray themselves) as not-quite-human: Malcolm, in *The Judas Conspiracy*, proudly proclaims that the Sethian Brotherhood are "'the incorruptible generation, and we have important work to do on earth'" (p. 289); Heather in *The Dead Sea Deception*, as we've seen, refers to the Judas people as "a secret race." Yet just as in science fiction the portrayal of aliens is a way to reconsider the foibles, failures, and possibilities of humankind so too, the moral deviations of heresy in Gospel Thrillers – sometimes cloaked in charitable works, often driven by power and greed – reflect back to readers the chilling possibilities of unrestrained orthodoxy.

Status Quo

What would it mean for the world to discover that heresy had preceded orthodoxy, and that the Christian institutions we know today were the products of centuries of suppression of revelatory texts? When modern readers are drawn to the idea of an original heresy displaced by a less authentic orthodoxy, what exactly are they drawn to? In 2003, New Testament scholar Bart Ehrman (who has written many subsequent popular books on Christian origins) published *Lost Christianities: The Battles for Scripture and the Faiths We Never Knew*. (The same year he also published a companion reader with the less provocative title *Lost Scriptures: Books that Did Not Make It into the New Testament*). The cover of *Lost Christianities* features the last page of the Gospel of Thomas from the Nag Hammadi find. The title implies a readership ("we never knew") from whom the truth about Christian origins has been hidden.[30]

Much of *Lost Christianities* explains how diverse early Christianity was, focused on texts from the "second and third centuries" later deemed apocryphal and, in most cases, heretical. But the book poses larger questions, as well. "Throughout the course of our study," Ehrman writes, "I will be asking the question: What if it had been otherwise? What if some other form of Christianity had become dominant, instead of the one that did?" In his conclusion, Ehrman ponders the "intolerance" of the "proto-orthodox" (his name for the early Christian group that "won" the "battle for Scripture") as perhaps the most unfortunate legacy of orthodox Christianity. But, much like Pagels in the 1970s, he then concludes that "we" in the present are more open to a message of tolerance that might be gleaned from those "lost" texts: "There is ... a sense that alternative understandings of Christianity from the past can be cherished yet today, that they can provide insights even now for those of us who are concerned about the world and our place in it." *Lost Christianities*, like *Gnostic Gospels* almost a quarter century earlier, becomes an invitation to more open-minded seekers ("those of us") to imagine *what if heresy became orthodoxy*.[31]

Gospel Thrillers can take up that invitation with gusto, imagining texts from Jesus's time, including Jesus's own words, that reveal orthodoxy as the result of centuries of deception and suppression. The question is no longer *what would have happened* but rather *what will happen now?* Truth has been revealed; orthodoxy has been unmasked; heresy has been redeemed. Yet these novels consistently stop short of reimagining a Christianity rewritten in the image of heresy, or replaced

---

[30] Bart D. Ehrman, *Lost Christianities: The Battle for Scripture and the Faiths We Never Knew* (New York: Oxford University Press, 2003); *Lost Scriptures: Books that Did Not Make It into the New Testament* (New York: Oxford University Press, 2003).

[31] Ehrman, *Lost Christianities*, 4–5, 256–57.

altogether by universalist spirituality (the explicit message of Wood's *The Prophetess* and the implicit message of the multiple Gospel Thrillers that marvel at how "eastern" Jesus's true teachings sound). Despite giving readers a glimpse of the "powerful alternative" that has been covered up for centuries, Gospel Thrillers never actually allow that alternative to upset the Christian status quo.

In the novels that yoke together a secret heretical sect with a heretical text filled with "madness and blasphemy," status quo is preserved when the text is revealed and the sect unmasked. In *The Judas Conspiracy* and *The Dead Sea Deception* readers are led to believe that the contents of the shocking secret gospel will be made known to the public: in *The Judas Conspiracy* the original text is lost but it has already been translated and studied by Paul, the protagonist. In *The Dead Sea Deception*, although the original decoders of the Rotgut Codex have been murdered, another British scholar has succeeded in deciphering its "breathtaking" heresy and has even prepared a copy for the London police officer to read (p. 388). Revealing the horrifying truth of a lost gospel that licenses deceit and murder reinforces the positive status of the Christian Bible. The pairing of depraved and "alien" sect with "mad" and "blasphemous" text allows the reader to set both aside and leave orthodoxy and canon in place.

As we've seen these fictional heresies do not so much function as sites of liberation as twisted, fantastic refractions of the worst stereotypes about repression and exploitation in "traditional," orthodox Christianity. They also open up a space to reconsider the appeal of that orthodoxy if only it could be freed of its patriarchal rigidity. We see this in *The Book of Q*; the gnostic liberation of the *Hagia Hodoporia* is released to the world, full of social liberation, but with its most radical verses – rejection of church and resurrection – purged before publication. The result is the defeat of heresy (the Manicheans) and the restoration of a reformed Roman Catholic orthodoxy, complete with a nice new Pope taking charge of the Vatican. A softening of orthodoxy might be on the horizon ("Q was helping people to regain focus" [p. 373]), but it is still a preservation of status quo.

Even when the heretical gospel is revealed, free from orthodox "correction" or association with violent heretics, status quo remains in place. At the end of *Keepers of the Secret*, the protagonist, Jason van Cleve, has recovered the photographs of the Ephesus scrolls and the English translation. He finds and confronts Cardinal Tobin, the cruel and sadistic leader of the Guardians who have suppressed the truth about Lael since the time of Christ. After a scuffle, Tobin is killed and Jason, instead of revealing the truth as he had originally intended, burns all evidence of the scrolls without looking back: status quo is maintained.

Some novels invent gospels that do live up to the promises of liberation that have animated so much interest in heresy and apocrypha in the twentieth and twenty-first centuries; nevertheless, readers do not see what effect, if any, the revelation of these heretical gospels will have. Both *Gospel Truths* and *The Lost Tomb* reveal to readers teachings of Jesus that unequivocally dismantle the patriarchal domination of the religion constructed in his name, instead promoting gender equality, personal spiritual liberation, and rejection of clerical authority. *The Lost Tomb* ends with the protagonists reading Jesus's words for the first time: Will this hardy band of independent archaeologists reveal the shocking new gospel to the world? Readers might assume so, but are not privy to what happens next. *The Lost Tomb* is the third of ten novels featuring Jack Howard recovering shocking artifacts and facing off against conspiratorial forces; the logic of such a series demands that no single discovery (which includes Atlantis, the spoils of the Jerusalem Temple, and remains from the Trojan War) can ever effectively disrupt the status quo or the series would come to an end. That an author would include a heretical gospel among his amazing but ineffective discoveries shows that keeping the status quo is just as important as imagining, even briefly, its disruption.[32]

Similarly in *Gospel Truths*, the gnostic Gospel of Thomas, with its theology of liberation, is sent by the head of the Grand Loge Féminin to a US publisher who presumably is going to reveal its explosive truths to the world. Once again, though, readers are deprived of a resolution. When J. G. Sandom published a sequel in 2009, *The God Machine*, the strange lack of resolution persists as mention is made of the Gospel of Thomas hidden "in France" but no one seems to have seen it or knows what it contained. Narratively, leaving readers with a lack of denoue-ment leaves the orthodox status quo in place, as well.[33]

---

[32] The final scene of *Raiders of the Lost Ark* lampooned this logic of the serial relic-hunter by showing the titular Ark locked away in a cavernous government warehouse.

[33] J. G. Sandom, *The God Machine* (New York: Bantam Book, 2009).

Why this reticence to imagine Christianity beyond the status quo, to imagine liberating heresy displacing restrictive orthodoxy? Gospel Thrillers exist in a world of imagination and fantasy unavailable to real-world explorations of orthodoxy, heresy, and apocrypha. But at this crucial moment, the novels pull their metaphorical punches. One scene in *The Testament* frames this reticence as a fear of the unknown. At the end of this novel, the protagonist Braverman "Bravo" Shaw is debating whether or not to disclose The Testament of Jesus to the world. This "Testament" is, in fact, a fuller version of the Secret Gospel of Mark, a real and highly controversial "discovery" that I discuss in Chapter 6. In *The Testament*, this lost gospel reveals that Jesus was not a miracle worker at all but possessed a miraculous life-giving elixir. A kindly mentor warns Bravo: "'What it contains – the words of Jesus – has the power to upend all Christianity. Is this what you want?'" (p. 557) Bravo does not answer "yes" or "no"; all he can say is, "'But it's the truth.'" (Since Bravo's adventures also continue in sequels, the ultimate answer will be "no.")

This reticence to answer *yes* or *no* belongs also to the authors and readers of these heresy-curious Gospel Thrillers: the desire for a liberating truth is always tempered by a fear of what unleashing that truth will accomplish. Will the world be better off without the institutional guardrails of orthodoxy Christianity? Or will something even more fearsome take its place? Gospel Thrillers not only give readers space to imagine the possibilities of a liberating, heretical Jesus; they also give readers space to acknowledge the fear attached to promises of religious liberation. Promises of liberation are also threats to the status quo; what awaits us on the other side of change might be as benign as a Jesus preaching "individual rights and responsibility" or as radical as a plot to blow up the church (literally or even just metaphorically).

While the conspirators in thrillers are usually driven by antisocial and selfish motives, the ending of a massive conspiracy is not always represented as an unalloyed good: after all, the hidden levers of power and knowledge controlled by conspirators have kept the world as we know it functioning. What will that world look like with those conspiratorial controls removed? Will benevolent chaos be better than malevolent control? Likewise, the contemplation of the potential for heresy and apocrypha to displace canon and orthodoxy are reined in by Gospel Thrillers: not only by their finitude (a fictional story between two covers) but by their narrative reticence.

Kotrosits identified these dual tugs of pleasurable transgression and familiar restraint in her essay on the affective appeal of heretical gospels. At the outset of that essay, Kotrosits also evokes the jar in which the Nag Hammadi texts were (supposedly) discovered: "The jar at Nag Hammadi, keeper of long-hidden secrets, the earthen vessel that can 'offer tantalizing alternatives.'" As I noted earlier, the jar represents both the suppression of heretical secrets, waiting to be smashed open, but also the peculiar mobility of heresy: never at rest, always on the move. I want to focus, however, on the phrase that Kotrosits has in quotation marks: "offer tantalizing alternatives." This phrase comes from a defunct National Geographic webpage attached to the publication of the Gospel of Judas; Kotrosits used the full sentence from that website as an epigraph to her article: "The texts offer tantalizing alternative versions of Jesus' life and teachings."[34]

We forget, sometimes, the root of that verb *tantalize*: Tantalus in ancient Greek myth was punished by the gods to eternity in torment, always thirsty and hungry, food and drink always receding from his reach. The possibility of original heresy, a "powerful alternative" that could "upend all Christianity," is also kept always out of reach in Gospel Thrillers: it tantalizes but pulls away before it can be fully grasped. Gospel Thrillers narratively capture the tension that continues to surround the allure of heresy, the "tantalizing alternative," the "faiths we never knew": always visible enough to stoke desire, but never so close that it can exert its potentially destructive force. Heresy is the horizon that beckons the biblically curious reader.

---

[34] The webpage has since been removed but is still available through the internet Wayback Machine: https://web.archive.org/web/20170430114637/https://www .nationalgeographic.com/lostgospel/timeline_18.html.

5 | *Knowledge Brokers*

Two Forgers

The first forger is fictional and was revealed in the fast-paced final third of Irving Wallace's 1972 novel *The Word*. The second forger is nonfictional and was first unmasked in an electrifying article in *The Atlantic* by freelance journalist Ariel Sabar.[1]

The fictional forger is an elderly French ex-convict, traced by the novel's protagonist, Steve Randall, to a sunny café in Rome. Randall had already learned secondhand about Robert Lebrun and his dastardly plan to forge and expose a gospel written by Jesus's brother James. Now, in Randall's hotel room, over drinks from the lobby bar ("a whiskey, strong") Lebrun tells Randall his tragic life story and how he arrived at his daring attempt to topple the Roman Catholic Church and make his fortune. A talented forger condemned to the horrors of the French penal colony known as "Devil's Island," Lebrun was promised freedom but then betrayed by the Catholic priest there. He swore revenge: "'*Fumier et ordure* – garbage and manure on the Church! *Merde* on Christ! I will have my vengeance'" (p. 541). Upon his release he resolved to create and reveal a forgery that would destroy the church and earn him millions.

The nonfictional forger is a middle-aged German émigré living in Florida whose biography was pieced together in the article (and subsequent book) by Sabar. Walter Fritz was a bright boy with a troubled childhood who made his way to a prestigious German Egyptology program but dropped out to pursue more lucrative career paths. Sketchy involvement with an auto parts manufacturing company that went bankrupt was followed by a move to Florida, hazy attempts to deal in art and artifacts, and the creation of a small, online

---

[1] Ariel Sabar, "The Unbelievable Tale of Jesus' Wife," *The Atlantic* (July/ August 2016): 64–78 expanded into *Veritas: A Harvard Professor, a Con Man, and the Gospel of Jesus's Wife* (New York: Doubleday, 2020).

pornographic empire with his second wife. The owner of the Coptic fragment dubbed "The Gospel of Jesus's Wife," Fritz has never admitted to forging the suspicious fragment. Sabar nonetheless posits a handful of motives for forgery: greed, pride, and, ultimately, revenge against the Roman Catholic church for his childhood sexual assault by a priest. (I discuss Fritz, Sabar, and the "Gospel of Jesus's Wife" in more detail in Chapter 6.)

Lebrun and Fritz have a lot in common, besides the confession (Lebrun) and accusation (Fritz) of forging a bombshell gospel. They are both migrant Europeans, displaced by fortune and misfortune, who have along the way acquired the technical skills to forge a gospel; they are both schemers, through means legal, quasi-legal, and extra-legal; they are both portrayed as impelled by personal, ideological, and financial motives to perpetrate an outrageous fraud against global religious institutions. They also show us, in fact and fiction, the ways in which dangerous knowledge of new biblical discoveries is brokered by marginal and uncertain characters. Their foggy motives and hidden operations can reveal or obscure the truth about biblical origins.

When and how can we (the seekers of truth, in novels or in real life) know that newly discovered knowledge about the Bible is true and not corrupted by shady motivations? Or (to the contrary) how can we know that the Bible that we have is true, and that it has not been corrupted by shady motivations in the past, perhaps all the way back to the time of Jesus himself? The twisting, conspiratorial narratives of the Gospel Thrillers revolve around dangerous biblical knowledge and they explore that danger through the various characters who produce, reveal, hide, and distort the truth about Christian origins. That is, they place the personal at the center of their political and theological stories.

Conspiracy narratives are by definition about hidden knowledge. These stories presuppose that our knowledge of the way the world works has been obscured by secret forces; some select few have become aware of that secrecy and fight to disclose it; and some others have always known about that secrecy and fight to maintain it. In this chapter, I consider the various characters that Gospel Thrillers use to explore the dangerous circulation of secret biblical knowledge: the knowledge brokers. These characters highlight how important personal motivations and desires are in the quest for biblical truth, and the specific locations of these characters highlight for readers the key points at which political context, theological desires, and personal

motivations intersect. Time and again readers meet the ambitious
academic who always wants to know more; the "native" informant
who knows more than he says; the simple monk who may not be as
simple as he appears; and the satin-clad cleric for whom loyalty matters
more than the truth. Dangerous biblical knowledge circulates through
and around these characters in the Gospel Thrillers and, through them,
we get a sense of the fears and desires about biblical knowledge
animating their eager readers, fears and desires often obscured in the
professional world of biblical studies.

Forgeries, Cover-Ups, and the Wrong Hands

I started this chapter with two forgers but, in reality, only a few early
Gospel Thrillers revolve around a forgery: *The Q Document* (1964),
The Word (1972), and *The Pontius Pilate Papers* (1976) (as well as the
proto-Gospel Thriller I discuss in Chapter 1, *The Mystery of Mar
Saba*). The villainous forgers in *The Q Document* are Nazis (extorting
a Jewish scholar); in *The Word*, as we have seen above, it is a vengeful
ex-convict; and in *The Pontius Pilate Papers*, the eponymous papers
exculpating Jews for the death of Jesus have been forged by an Israeli
paleographer who survived the Holocaust. After *The Pontius Pilate
Papers*, however, the forged gospel at the heart of biblical conspiracy
fades away; more typical since then is the existence (or rumored
existence) of an authentic gospel whose contents would reveal the
Bible itself as the falsified product of conspiratorial forces. The cover-
up displaces the forgery.

Forgery and *cover-up* are, however, merely two sides of the same
coin. Both the forgery plot and the cover-up plot highlight the danger
the Bible faces from unscrupulous or untrustworthy knowledge
brokers. The earliest Gospel Thriller shows how closely intertwined
the forgery and cover-up plots are. In *The Q Document*, the protagonist, disillusioned expatriate academic George Cooper, is confronted
with first-century documents portraying Jesus as a madman and Paul
as a murderer, documents that might cause irreparable harm to believing Christians if they are made public. He confides in a friend and
colleague, a Roman Catholic priest who immediately urges Cooper to
take action by destroying the new "discoveries": "'Can you sit by and
watch Christianity destroyed?'" (p. 149). The longer Cooper investi-
gates the documents, the more he becomes convinced they are forged,

but he lacks proof. He decides that, if he can't find evidence of their forgery, he will destroy them: if the Chinese Communists offering to buy the documents are successful, he says, "'they'll kill Christianity once and for all. It's pretty easy to demote a religion if you can demote a god to the status of a mortal'" (p. 196). He is ready to cover up this explosive discovery. In the end, however, Cooper finds his evidence and doesn't need to cover up the documents' existence. In a moment the narrative flips: a possible conspiracy to cover up a shocking biblical secret becomes a thwarted conspiracy to perpetrate a fraud through forgery.

Cover-up and forgery also blur together in *The Book of Q*. After a breakneck race against a global network of heretical conspirators, Father Ian Pearse has recovered the original words of Jesus, the lost gospel Q, whose existence has been covered up for centuries. Pearse and his colleagues prepare to reveal Q's radical message to the world: "populist" preaching of a "brotherhood of believers," acknowledgement of women preachers, "individual rights and responsibilities," and, most shocking of all, a denial of Christ's resurrection. Before doing so, however, they alter the ancient text: by removing the denial of the resurrection, Pearse and his co-conspirators, scholar Cecilia Angeli and cleric Cardinal Peretti, are able to produce a new gospel that will defeat the heretics and restore the Roman Catholic church. When the heretics get their hand on the altered scroll, *they* move to destroy it, but are prevented by the protagonists. The back and forth between cover-up, falsification, cover-up, and revelation is dizzying precisely because the movements to hide or conceal keep us focused on what matters: the *dangerous knowledge*.

The conspiracies that animate Gospel Thrillers – forgeries, cover-ups, or otherwise – are at heart about knowledge in the wrong hands. Throughout this book I have tried to avoid the language of *heroes* and *villains*, particularly as the thriller genre, with its focus on individual agency versus blind conformity, so often challenges any easy moral calculus. It is not simply the case that secrecy is villainous and revelation is heroic in Gospel Thrillers; our protagonists and antagonists struggle to come to terms with the moral value of new biblical knowledge. Even as Cooper in *The Q Document* contemplates covering up the discovery of the defaming gospels, his gradual moral awakening over the course of the novel suggests he would be doing the right thing. In another early novel, Elizabeth Peters's 1970 *The Dead Sea Cipher*, a new cache of Dead Sea Scrolls, possibly including first-century lives of Jesus and his mother Mary, end up destroyed by a loosely united gang of international spies and operatives. One protagonist castigates them: "'Good for you, good for all the skulking, cautious cowards you represent. When you don't know for sure – destroy. When something might be dangerous – get rid of it. Truth is the one commodity governments can't tolerate'" (p. 287). One of the spies, a kindly American Jesuit, objects: "'Until the human race can accept a fact as a fact, instead of as an excuse for riots and pogroms, this sort of thing will have to be done. There are different kinds of truth, you know.'" Just as in *The Q Document*, the cover-up of dangerous knowledge is portrayed as a potential act of moral courage rather than sinister opportunism.

In most Gospel Thrillers the suspense hinges on this very question: *Will dangerous knowledge fall into the wrong hands?* That the dramatic tension lies in the possession of knowledge rather than the content of the knowledge itself is clear from the fact that around half of Gospel Thrillers to date concern "lost gospels" that are not discovered and revealed until the final pages (or, as in *The Dead Sea Cipher*, not even then). The novel's action is propelled by the mere rumor of a new gospel and the accompanying fear that this new gospel will be either suppressed or misused: that it will fall into the wrong hands.

In classic conspiracy narratives, the struggle over the truth follows the Cold War logic of freedom-seeking individuals squaring off against self-interested and power-hungry conspirators. In the right hands, knowledge sets us free; in the wrong hands, knowledge keeps us captive to the selfish desires of others. In many conspiracy thrillers this selfish desire may be no more articulated than a raw will-to-power: when the heroine of *The Stepford Wives* asks the mastermind of the anti-feminist conspiracy why they have gone to such horrific lengths to stifle their wives' freedom, he coolly answers: "Why? Because we can." Yet, as we've already seen in Chapter 4, the calculus can often be more complicated: the revelation of truth might be as dangerous as truth's suppression. In Gospel Thrillers, this tangle between individual freedom and power-hungry suppression often finds expression in two specific arenas: institutional religion and individual wealth.

In many of these Gospel Thrillers, the forces of truth and virtue square off against the sinister self-interests of institutional religions.

It's quite common to find protagonists in Gospel Thrillers in a frantic race for the truth against forces from the Vatican (whether in the form of direct papal delegates or small orders operating in secret) that seeks to suppress that truth. As I outlined in Chapter 4, "the Vatican" (with or without direct papal direction) often provides a convenient short-hand for the failures of organized religion – formalism, pietism, blind loyalty, deluded self-interest – drawing on decades of anti-Catholic stereotypes. It also provides a convenient shorthand for the ways in which love of power motivates the suppression of religious freedom and truth.

To return to one example: in David Gibbins's 2008 *The Lost Tomb*, archaeologists stumble upon a newly opened chamber in the buried city of Herculaneum. When they find a scroll that hints at "the words of Jesus" they draw the attention of the *concilium*, a secret Vatican enclave operating throughout history to fight off "the most pernicious of heresies, the ones the Inquisition of the Holy See were unable to defeat" (p. 388). These religious conspirators prize their own insti-tutional power over the truth. "'I suspect someone powerful in the Church is worried about some great revelation, some ancient docu-ment that might undermine their authority,'" protagonist Jack Howard speculates (p. 116). In a particularly apt twist, readers dis-cover at the end of this novel that the secret the *concilium* had worked for centuries to suppress was precisely Jesus's original message of individual liberation from the shackles of institutional religion:

> *The Kingdom of Heaven is on earth.*
> *Men shall not stand in the way of the word of God . . .*
> *There shall be no priests.*
> *And there shall be no temples . . .*
>
> (p. 481)

In other novels it is not the self-serving love of religious power that pits truth-seeking protagonists against nefarious antagonists, but the cor-rupting influence of personal wealth. In Barbara Wood's 1996 *The Prophetess*, the tough, feminist archaeologist Catherine Alexander races to find the lost "scroll of Sabrina" and reveal its theological mysteries before a ruthless and bloodthirsty billionaire can add it to his private collection and hide it away forever. Miles Havers is a "computer mogul whose net worth *Forbes* had pegged at $10.5 billion" (in a novel set in 1999). Havers is obsessed with his unparalleled collection of rare flowers, art, and artifacts. When word first reaches him that a first-century scroll about Jesus may be out there, his adrenaline kicks in: "This was the real high of being a collector – not in the acquisition, but in the anticipation. And the danger. There always had to be danger." He barks quick and ruthless commands to his hired gun: "'Find out if the basket is related to the papyrus fragment and if there are scrolls. If there are, *I want them*. Be discreet, but get them by whatever means necessary. And Zeke, don't leave any witnesses'" (pp. 26–27, emphasis in original). When later Alexander tries to use the collective support of the internet to escape Havers's clutches, the mogul's greed becomes animalistic: "Miles smiled and nodded to himself. *Very well, Dr. Alexander*, he thought. *You give me no choice*. Time for the tiger to move in for the kill" (p. 230).

Both greedy billionaires and power-mad cardinals prioritize their own selfish desires over the common good, an immoral perversion of the liberating power of knowledge that is always central to the conspiratorial plot of the thriller. But in the race for the truth between protagonists and antagonists in Gospel Thrillers stand intermediary characters, experts who assist the protagonists in finding, verifying, and understanding the lost gospel truth. These experts, too, are driven by diverse and complex motives, clogging up the circuits of knowledge. I start with the rarefied (and perilous) knowledge hoarded by academic experts and then turn to the artless (but equally perilous) knowledge offered by "local" experts on foreign locales. I then turn to two complementary sites of religious expertise: the premodern monastic grounds of Mount Athos and the closely guarded vaults of the Secret Vatican Archive.

"High Pitched Voice, High Strung Manner": Academic Experts

Gospel Thrillers are deeply ambivalent about the reliability of the academic biblical expert. In the very first Gospel Thriller, *The Q Document*, the specialized knowledge of academics is a double-edged sword. The arcane knowledge deployed by Cooper to unmask a Nazi forgery is identical to the arcane knowledge of the Jewish scholar coerced by Nazis into producing that forgery. The same expertise that allowed Cecilia Angeli, in *The Book of Q*, to help Father Ian Pearse find the lost gospel also allowed her to alter that gospel to remove information that might work against the liberalization of the church. In conspiratorial thrillers, a genre defined by the dangers of hidden knowledge, the obscure and rarefied information belonging to scholars makes them key brokers of biblical knowledge. That knowledge must be strange, yet ultimately accessible to our protagonists; likewise the keepers of that knowledge are often strange yet ultimately accessible.

In Paul Christopher's 2015 *Secret of the Templars*, the protagonist, ex-spy "Doc" Holliday, meets clandestinely with an old friend, Professor Spencer Maxwell Boatman: "in his mid-forties but he still had the air of a tall, slim figure from a Renaissance painting by Raphael." Boatman appears for only four pages in the novel but provides essential information on a lost Dead Sea Scroll stolen "by a professor" from the École Biblique in 1949. Boatman is loaded with memorable traits: "heterochromia" (one blue eye, one green eye), "an IQ of 224, an eidetic memory, doctorates in everything from chemistry and physics to archaeology and psychology as well as a background that included more wealth than several medium-sized countries" (pp. 43–44). This handsome and idiosyncratic supergenius (who has been friends with Holliday since they were both teenagers) has only to close his eyes to retrieve the necessary information from the recesses of his capacious memory. Boatman embodies one fantasy of academic knowledge at the service of the truth-seeking protagonist: the living encyclopedia. But even this fantasy academic has his unsafe side: "He was the kind of middle-aged man who young girls fell in love with as easily as taking in a deep breath. The kind of man people his own age knew to keep away from their daughters." The explosive knowledge acquired by academics is not for the weak or susceptible; fortunately, Holliday is no swooning teenage girl, but a mature man who can handle the truth.

Most of the academic characters in Gospel Thrillers are ancillary characters like Professor Boatman, sources of information (accurate or not) for the nonacademic protagonists of the stories who come from the worlds of law enforcement, public relations, or espionage (what Fredric Jameson in his study of conspiracy narratives called the "social detective"). The relegation of academic characters to the margins has a practical aspect in the novels, allowing authors to naturalize otherwise awkward exposition. When Steve Randall, the public relations expert on the search for the truth in *The Word*, has questions about biblical history, radiocarbon dating, or *Codex Sinaiticus* he (and readers) can

learn it through dialogue with an academic character. When Chris
Bronson – the hard-nosed London cop on the trail of biblical mysteries
in several novels written by James Becker – needs arcane information
about antiquities, his ex-wife and sidekick, a British Museum curator
named Angela Lewis, can call or email any number of erudite colleagues for handy explanations.

This narrative distance placed between the sources of arcane knowledge and the protagonists of Gospel Thrillers also allows the novels to
express ambivalence about these academic wielders of expertise. In *The
Word*, Randall arrives in the UK to meet the academics who have been
working on the newly discovered "Gospel of James." First he meets
with the head of the project, Dr. Bernard Jeffries: "barrel-chested, with
shaggy white hair, a small head with rheumy eyes, pinkish nose with
large pores, an untidy moustache, wrinkled face, striped bow tie,
dangling pincenez, and a blue suit in need of a pressing" (p. 130).
Jeffries, who is "the best in his field" (philology, papyrology, Holy
Scriptures, comparative religions) proceeds for almost a dozen pages to
explain the highs and lows of biblical archaeology for the past century
with unceasing verve. He prefaces his four pages on Tischendorf and
the *Codex Sinaiticus* by pronouncing "with evident relish": "'Here is
our thriller!'" (p. 134). It's unclear whether readers are supposed to be
enlightened, engrossed, or bored with these recitations (Randall seems
impressed), but what is clear is the image of the scholar as the untidy,
bookish, genial, and functionally inert source of knowledge.[2]

Soon afterward Randall meets Dr. Florian Knight, described to him
as "one of those precocious and eccentric English geniuses":

"Looks rather like Aubrey Beardsley. Have you ever seen a picture of
Beardsley? Kind of Buster Brown haircut, deep-set eyes, nose like the beak
of an eagle, pushed-out lower lip, big ears, long, thin hands. Well, that is Dr.
Knight. High-pitched voice, high-strung manner, nervous, but absolutely a
marvel on New Testament languages and scholarship." (pp. 115–16)

The nervous manner and mastery of knowledge seem to go together
naturally, as if full-time occupation with the abstruse workings of

---

[2] Richard R. Lingeman, in his review of *The Word* for the Sunday *New York Times*
Book Section, noted that Wallace "throws in large, partially digested chunks of
his research – what a codex is, the complexities of Aramaic, little-known theories
about the historical Jesus" ("Happy Irving Wallace Day!" *New York Times*
[March 15, 1972]: 45).

ancient "New Testament languages and scholarship" induced psychological abnormality. When Randall meets Knight he finds him much as
promised: "Florian Knight did resemble Aubrey Beardsley ... Only he
looked more so, more the esthete, more the eccentric. He was sipping
what Randall supposed was sherry from a wineglass" (p. 147). Knight
is also sickly (bedridden, with a hearing aid) and defensive about his
scholarly prowess. The two British academics, rheumy-eyed teddy bear
Jeffries and the sickly esthete Knight, are subtly feminized in contrast
to the manly heroics of the oversexed US flack Randall. Even the
attraction of *Secret of the Templar*'s "tall, slim" Professor Boatman
(also British, teaching mathematics in France) is more suitable to
enamored teenage girls than the mature love interests of Gospel
Thrillers protagonists.

Gospel Thrillers portray academics as *odd*, alienated from normal –
US, virile – manhood by their preoccupation with ancient languages
and texts. In some cases, this strangeness pushes the academic characters more squarely into the realm of antagonists who set out to suppress the revelation of new biblical truths through concealment or
chicanery. The unpleasant and sexually frustrated Semiticist Mallory
in *The Judas Gospel* (1973 [1972]) is willing to conceal the newly
found gospel in exchange for a payout from the Vatican. He is eventually eliminated by the more sinister Vatican forces he tried to extort.
The paleographer Victor Lanholtz, in *The Pontius Pilate Papers*
(1976), is a war hero, a Nazi-fighting Zionist whose keen sense of
antisemitic injustice led him to counterfeit evidence exculpating the
Jews for the death of Christ. While perhaps more morally upright (and
manly) than Mallory, Lanholtz nonetheless ends up murdered by the
fanatical Catholic patron who had sponsored his archaeological
explorations. That both Mallory and Lanholtz end up dead suggests
that while academics may at times want to tamper with biblical truth
through suppression or forgery, they will quickly find themselves out
of their depth.

Academics do on occasion appear as protagonists in Gospel
Thrillers, but usually only once they have been displaced from the
musty corridors of academia. Cooper in *The Q Document* is in self-
imposed exile from his academic post in the United States, as is Declan
Stewart, the tragedy-struck ex-archaeologist surfer living off the grid in
G. M. Lawrence's *Q: Awakening* (2012). Braverman "Bravo" Shaw
in *The Testament* (2006) is lured away from scholarly pursuits

(the study of medieval religions and cryptography) into private industry before taking up his true calling as one of the elite members of the
secretive "Order of the Gnostic Observantines." Jay Marcus, who
unlocks the mystery of *The Pontius Pilate Papers*, is an independently
wealthy freelance archaeologist. In similar fashion, Jack Howard, the
protagonist of *The Lost Tomb*, runs an independent "International
Maritime University" based on his ancestral British estate and his ship,
the *Seaquest II*, specializing in underwater recovery and excavation.
Finn Ryan, in Paul Christopher's 2006 *The Lucifer Gospel*, is not
herself an independently wealthy archaeologist but is a young and
resourceful illustrator working on her master's degree; she has been
hired to work on the dig of an independently wealthy archaeologist.
Archaeologist Nick Hampton in Larry Witham's *The Negev Project*
(1994) is soon to be unemployed due to his controversial publications
and opinions.

As this brief overview suggests, Gospel Thrillers prefer their academic protagonists to be archaeological rather than textual: tanned, fit,
and resourceful, unlike the wan and weedy Florian Knight rendered
pale and impotent by superfluous book-knowledge. Certainly, part of
this preference is a long tradition of the archaeological adventurer, the
Indiana Jones-type who combines technical expertise with inventive-
ness. Hampton in *The Negev Project* is a US archaeologist in Israel
with a "reputation for independence," whose first book on Bible
scholarship had "cut him loose from the establishment" and showed
he "had the wherewithal to take a risk" (pp. 11–12). Michael Farber,
in *The Lost Testament* (1992), has "a reputation as one of the world's
most original and audacious biblical scholars" (p. 16). Jack Cane, in
The Second Messiah (2011) comes from an archaeological family (his
parents died after making a shocking discovery at Qumran twenty
years earlier), but his own archaeological career seems to exist entirely
outside of any academic context. In *The Prophetess*, Catherine
Alexander is a maverick feminist archaeologist searching for evidence
of Moses's sister Miriam when she stumbles upon a first-century gospel
written by a woman. The archaeologist in the field embodies the
independent spirit of the truth-seeker, free from the constraints of
conventional and conservative institutions. This rigorous and quick-
witted independence has a gendered aspect; even when the archaeologist is a woman, like Alexander, she is doing more manly work than
her colleagues toiling in libraries and archives. The archaeological hero

also reinforces the ethnic logic of the Gospel Thrillers, intent on the extrication and verification of new gospel truths by western (i.e., white) hands from foreign lands.

Academic characters also become lightning rods for the conspiratorial violence surrounding new biblical discoveries. I've already discussed in Chapter 3 how the dangerous territory of Israel literally explodes around the valiant archaeologists seeking to unearth its secrets: Sir Max Lonsdale and his entire band of scholarly seekers fall prey to terrorist bombs, leaving Mallory alone to discover an incendiary gospel in *The Judas Gospel*. But the threats to the academic experts extend outside the dig site: a package bomb delivered to archaeologists on leave in London in *The Negev Project* (pp. 208–10); a car bomb blowing up the apartment block of a Soviet archivist in *The Judas Testament* (1994, p. 167); a museum specialist in ancient languages chased into traffic in *The First Apostle* (2008, p. 164). In *The Dead Sea Deception* (2011), a British paleographer about to decode the secret Gospel of Judas is pushed down the stairs by an assassin. The scholar in the Gospel Thrillers stands closest to the perilous truth that nefarious forces want to suppress and so frequently and spectacularly falls victim to conspiratorial violence.

In Leslie Winfield Williams's 2011 *The Judas Conspiracy*, death and mayhem tear an ever-widening path through the academy. The murder of the Yale Divinity School Dean's sister-in-law, who surprises the thief and assassin in the midst of stealing a newly found version of the Gospel of Judas, is just the beginning. The assassin, operating under the angelic pseudonym Gabriel, next murders Dr. Bonnie Barnes, a scholar from Oxford coming to Yale to deliver a talk on the Sethian sect. The violence fans outward from New Haven to the meeting of the American Academy of Religion and Society of Biblical Literature in New York City. The victims are not only those studying the new gospel but any scholar of Gnosticism getting close to discovering the secret existence of the Sethian Brotherhood or disparaging its gnostic worldview. When Dr. Henry Hawthorne begins a paper on "why the *Gospel of Judas* didn't measure up to the other gospels," he takes a quick gulp of water ("he looked nervous, a typical academic reading his lousy paper") and begins choking and sputtering before falling dead of poisoning before a shocked room of conference-goers (p. 154). The police and FBI descend on the conference when it's clear a serial killer is targeting scholars of religion.

Gabriel takes the morning off ("before his fourth murder, he planned to enjoy Belgian waffles" [p. 181]) and then goes to plant poisoned chocolate strawberries in the hotel room of Dr. Reginald Bloome. Bloome is scheduled to deliver a plenary address on "The Importance of Christian Orthodoxy in an Inclusive World" that evening. Unfortunately, this final assassination goes awry: Bloome returns to the hotel early, turns down the gift of strawberries ("'I'm allergic'"), and gives the sweets to a graduate student who happens to be passing through the hallway. "Charity Collins ... just finishing [her] degree at Duke Divinity School" accepts the gift and goes on her way (p. 183). In a gruesomely comic turn, Charity suffers from an eating disorder and escapes death through bulimia (p. 186).

Gabriel's murderous spree through an academic conference is by turns horrifying and humorous. Gabriel is lethal but also cartoonish in his near mustache-twirling villainy and ultimate incompetence. But the grim humor of the situation – a gnostic assassin on the loose at an international conference of religious studies scholars – derives from narrative exaggeration of a deadly serious point: new biblical knowledge is dangerous and to assist in brokering that knowledge invites peril. The academic characters in Gospel Thrillers have a unique relationship to that knowledge: the ability to authenticate, disseminate, or suppress that new and dangerous biblical truth. Some, lackluster in their manly fortitude, do little more than provide handy exposition; some more stalwart among those characters bravely face that danger; the more pusillanimous try to profit from it; and the more hapless fall prey to it, through spectacular explosions or gurgling helplessly at the podium of a scholarly talk.

"A Nice Little Man, Who Spoke Excellent English": Local Experts

A key trope of Gospel Thrillers (as with most thriller genres) is exotic travel in search of the truth; frequently chapter and section headings in these novels give days, times, and locations around the world, a typographic way of conjuring the suspenseful ticking of the clock and the whooshing spin of the globe. Capitalist travel consumption in Gospel Thrillers replaces the imperial adventuring of an earlier generation of Bible Hunters. In their travels, our protagonists frequently rely on the knowledge of local "experts," some of whom stand in close relationship to the lost gospel and its dangerous truths. These "native informants" play multiple roles in the novels. They reinforce by contrast the western-centric viewpoint of the novels, whose protagonists are usually from the United States or UK, usually male, and always white (where race is even specified). These characters also subtly remind readers that gospel truths are often hidden in "foreign" sites not easily accessible or even comprehensible to the western seeker.

In some novels, the purveyors of local knowledge are, like some academic knowledge brokers, colorful but otherwise inert sources of knowledge. This is the case with the various local workers and guides that the protagonist Dinah van der Lyn in *The Dead Sea Cipher* encounters on her group tour of the Near East. Their embeddedness as "local color" highlights the foreignness of the lands through which our white, Protestant protagonist is passing. Early in the novel, while staying in Beirut (where she will become witness to a murder), Dinah befriends Salwa, the chambermaid in her hotel: Salwa was "a student at the American University of Beirut, and the daughter of a poor but honest merchant in the city." Salwa is multilingual (her "French was much better than her English"; she also teaches Dinah "some Arabic") and they bond as friends of roughly the same age. At the same time, though, Dinah marvels at Salwa and "the educated young women of these countries, whose mothers and grandmothers for generations back had spent their lives in harems" (pp. 5–7). Of course, Dinah's US or German grandmothers might also be imagined as lacking basic civil rights, but it is only Salwa who evokes the image of sexual isolation in harems "for generations back."

Dinah similarly imagines the deep shadows of the past hovering around "Mr. Awad, the tour guide" during a trip to a crusader castle near the ruins of Byblos. Like Salwa, Mr. Awad is pleasant and harmless ("a nice little man, who spoke excellent English"). As his commentary on the castle drones on (unreported in the narrative), Dinah contemplates their divergent histories: "Studying Mr. Awad's calm brown face she wondered how he could describe so enthusiastically the subjugation of his homeland by a lot of bloody zealots, even though the subjugation was centuries past, and his listeners were descendants of those same zealots" (pp. 16–17). Whether contemplating sexual politics or holy wars, Dinah sees in her local "native" guides reminders of the non-western space through which she moves and in which biblical secrets are concealed.

When Dinah teams up with a US archaeologist, Jeff Smith, the presence of local experts become an opportunity show how effectively the western traveler can adapt to the foreign environment. Adaptation is, of course, necessary for the recovery of new gospel secrets emerging in foreign lands, but it also has its limitations. (The Arabic Dinah learns from Salwa is not enough to sustain conversation and she doesn't use it again in the novel.) While Jeff and Dinah are on the run from unknown bad guys, they encounter a young pickpocket whom Jeff recognizes: "'Mohammed el Zakhar. I might have known. Back to your old tricks, eh?' He went on in Arabic and the boy grinned" (p. 182). Mohammed wears the foreignness of the holy land on his body:

> The boy's face ... had the hard beauty of many young Arab faces. The planes of cheekbones and forehead had a rich brown patina, like polished wood ... One eye was dark and glowing with intelligence. The other was blind ... Either he was older than he looked, she decided, or children in this part of the world really did mature earlier than their Western counterparts. (p. 185)

Jeff and Mohammed trade barbs in Arabic and, for a moment, the native expert validates the acquired expertise of the western traveler. When Mohammed leads Jeff and Dinah to a series of unknown tunnels under Jerusalem, however, the suave and knowledgeable westerner Smith marvels at how much he has *not* been able to learn: "'Sometimes I feel like such a fool. The wisdom and scientific know-how of the West! We grub and dig and write dull learned reports, and these local people know more about the antiquities of the area than we could learn in a million years'" (p. 186). Only some level of local knowledge can ever be acquired by western travelers; they will always require the cooperation of the "natives" to lead the way to the hidden secrets.

In Meade's *The Second Messiah*, local expertise is central not only to the "discoveries" made by US archaeologists at Qumran but also to the various conspiratorial networks that suppress or subvert those "discoveries." Several "Bedu" characters (Meade's preferred term for the Bedouin) play central roles in uncovering new scrolls but also in illuminating the shadowy networks of smugglers (Arab and western) engaging in illicit antiquities trading. In a wry comment on the complicated relationship between local diggers, local smugglers, and US archaeologists, readers learn that the shocking discovery made by

Jack Cane in *Second Messiah* had actually been made "months earlier" by Josuf, "the chief Bedouin digger" (p. 52). Under instructions from wealthy art dealer Hassan (who came from a Bedu village and made his fortune smuggling antiquities), Josuf *reburied* the scroll so it would be found by Cane. In this way, Hassan wagered, he could circumvent the Israeli–Vatican conspirators who were keeping such explosive finds under wraps while still giving the scroll the necessary imprimatur of western "discovery."

While Meade imagines networks of local expertise expanding internationally, other novels make clear that local expertise can only ever remain local. It is only the privilege of the western protagonist to venture into foreign spaces to search for the truth. In James Becker's *The Lost Testament* (2013), the second Gospel Thriller featuring the British couple Bronson (an ex-cop) and Angela (his ex-wife and love interest, a museum curator), a secret account of Jesus's true parentage has turned up in the markets of Cairo. Stolen decades earlier from the inner vaults of the Vatican, the parchment ends up in the hands of a clever antiquities dealer named Amun Husani. Because the document is written in Latin, he recognizes its value and begins to work on authenticating it, ideally for sale to a western buyer. His able navigation of the local antiquities market has not prepared him to confront the violent tenacity of the European conspirators out to keep this secret buried. Tipped off by internet searches (a favorite theme of Becker's novels), organized crime members from Italy working on behalf of the Vatican hire their own local Egyptian experts – assassins – to quash Husani's efforts and recover the parchment. Husani's friends and colleagues are killed, but Husani himself makes it with great difficulty to Europe. He meets up with Angela, who has been authorized to spend a fortune on the "lost testament"; before they can set a price, a Spanish assassin kills Husani. Angela flees with the parchment, more able to navigate the twists and turns of European espionage than the "native" antiquities dealer out of his element.

The travels of Gospel Thrillers protagonists take them around the world following a trail of secrets and conspiracies: across Europe, North America, the Middle East, Africa, and east Asia. Yet some destinations and their local experts are more tightly linked with gospel secrets – even when they don't know it. Toward the end of the global race for the "Testament of Christ" in Alan Gold's *The Lost Testament*, it becomes clear that the Testament left the Dead Sea region in the second century and ended up in Ethiopia, among the ancient and dwindling community of Jews there. The various characters race to Addis Ababa in the hopes of finding the precious document. When Michael and Judith, the protagonists, disembark they see how out of place the western traveler is: "Images pressed themselves onto Michael's mind. Tall black Cushite men and women in brilliant multi-coloured robes walked proudly along streets as shorter unkempt men and women in long white linen jackets and jodhpurs scurried in between" (pp. 473–74). The white foreigners in colonialist garb ("white linen and jodhpurs") stand out awkwardly.

Michal and Judith first consult with the Catholic "bishop of Ethiopia," an old friend of Michael's, and learn how difficult it will be to find the truth among the local experts:

"Do you know how many bounty hunters we have here every year? Dozens. All of them land in great secrecy, thinking they've discovered the source of the Ark of the Covenant. They all pay great bribes, vast sums of money to the officials in the Ministry of the Interior to get a permit. And they all go to the monasteries built on the island in the middle of the lake ... And the priests love taking their money." (p. 475)

Fortunately, their own local expert, the bishop, guides them through the thicket of misleading local "expertise": he has a lead on a mysterious Ethiopian Jew imprisoned in the city of Gondar who might have the information they seek.

The prisoner, Wossen, is taken into their care and leads them to yet a third local expert: the Guardian Binyussef (whose name, in an evocation of Jesus, means *son of Joseph*). Posed like a holy man – "sitting like Mahatma Ghandi [*sic*] crosslegged" – Binyussef at first lies, refusing to acknowledge that he is the guardian they seek. Michael persists; Binyussef relents. He admits to guarding Jewish treasures of the Temple priests – but "'not the Ark of the Covenant. This was lost'" – and expresses utter uninterest in the Testament of Jesus: "'Things of Jesus are not treasures for us.'" The expertise Binyussef provides is technical – where to find the jar containing the testament – but in the end the crucial expertise about the lost gospel rests with the western travelers. Eventually Michael and Judith convince Binyussef to trust them with the location of the treasures, including the Testament, by reciting Genesis in Hebrew: their key to this foreign local expertise is a demonstration of shared tradition. Even then, however, Binyussef remains distinctly foreign and nonwestern: "Michael was becoming increasingly irritated with the Ethiopian's inscrutable smile, as though he were a Buddhist monk, possessed of knowledge but refusing to divulge it to the uninitiated" (p. 533).

Even in the days of the Bible Hunters, western travelers established relationships with their local experts, who could in turn broker the knowledge necessary to dislodge new biblical truths: the "Sinai Sisters," Margaret Gibson and Agnes Lewis, befriended the monks at St. Catherine's Monastery who cordially granted access to their ancient manuscripts. But the transplantation of the western seeker into foreign lands is never frictionless; the local expert can ease that friction but also keeps the distance between "western" and "native" front and center. In Gospel Thrillers, local experts can be helpful, guileless, treacherous, or cunning, but ultimately they remain in place while the westerner departs with knowledge in hand.[3]

"A Smallish, Frail Greek": On Mount Athos

One foreign site requiring local expertise is closer to the Euro-American sensibilities of Gospel Thriller protagonists (and readers) but still exotic and mysterious enough to be a suitable waystation on the hunt for hidden gospel secrets: the monasteries of Mount Athos in Greece. Perched precariously and tantalizingly between East and West, past and present, Mount Athos figured early in the hunt for ancient gospels. Robert Curzon was one of the first Bible Hunters to get permission to explore Mount Athos in the 1830s; in his memoir he lamented that the monks had no idea of the value of their library collections ("What can be the use of looking at such old books as these?" they asked him) and yet those same "obdurate monks" refused to sell any of their precious manuscripts to him. Konstaninos Simonides made an early name for himself in London with classical Greek manuscripts he claimed to have found "in one of the caves at the foot of Mount Athos"; these were soon after determined to be forgeries. A decade later Simonides published his audacious claim to have produced the ancient biblical codex that Constantin Tischendorf extracted from St. Catherine's Monastery in Egypt (*Codex*

---

[3] Janet Soskice, *The Sisters of Sinai: How Two Lady Adventurers Discovered the Hidden Gospels* (New York: Vintage, 2009), 122–33.

Sinaiticus); he asserted that he did so at Mount Athos at the bequest of
one of the abbots there, his uncle Benedict. What's more, he elaborated
that the codex of the Bible and "remaining apostolic fathers" was
produced in 1839 as a gift for Czar Nicholas I. Simonides's tweaking
of Tischendorf's "discovery" effectively reversed the flow of biblical
knowledge: the precious ancient manuscript "liberated" to the West
was rewritten as an artifact of modern Orthodoxy directed toward
the East.[4]

The picturesque pastness of the Mount Athos monastic complexes
also captured the touristic imagination of US readers in the twentieth
century. A 1985 pictorial essay about Mount Athos in *National
Geographic* took its readers in its first line "far away from the rest of
humanity," where "pious men retreat from the world in a tradition
dating back to the start of the Byzantine era." In a 2009 pictorial,
another *National Geographic* writer described the anachronistic
monks: "In their heavy beards and black garb – worn to signify their
death to the world – the monks seem to recede into a Byzantine fresco,
an ageless brotherhood of ritual, acute simplicity, and constant
worship." If much of the travel in Gospel Thrillers focuses on the
contemporary and exotic – "Cushite men and women in brilliant
multi-coloured robes" – travel to Mount Athos is a journey into a
(European, Christian) past. It still requires expertise to navigate, but
the knowledge there stands in closer proximity to the modern West.[5]

This collection of twenty-odd Eastern Orthodox monasteries, many
dating back a thousand years, is probably most famous for its total ban
on women in its communities (including female animals). This factoid
becomes a crucial piece of information for Steve Randall in *The Word*
in his quest to prove that the newly discovered "Gospel of James" is a
forgery. Late in the novel, when he has already grown suspicious of the
gospel's authenticity, Randall tries to figure out how the writing on the
gospel was authenticated to the first century. He wonders why Monti,

---

[4] Robert Curzon, *A Visit to the Monasteries of the Levant* (New York: George
G. Putnam, 1852), 333, 337, during a visit to the monastery of Iveron. On
Simonides's early discovery: "Our Weekly Gossip," *The Athenaeum* 1224 (April
12, 1851): 408; George Finlay, "Foreign Correspondence," *The Athenaeum*
1240 (August 2, 1851): 831. On Simonides and *Sinaiticus*, see my discussion
in Chapter 1.
[5] James L. Stanfield, "Mount Athos," *National Geographic* 164.6 (December
1983): 739–47; Robert Draper, "Called to the Holy Mountain," *National
Geographic* 216.6 (December 2009): 134, 137–41, 145, 147–58.

the discoverer of the papyrus, didn't consult "the foremost Aramaic scholar in the world ... Abbot Mitros Petropoulos, head of one of the monasteries of Mount Athos in Greece." Monti's daughter Angela (Randall's love interest) tells a bold lie: "'Abbot Petropoulos? Of course. I have met him personally. My father knew that the abbot was the outstanding scholar in Aramaic, and five years ago my father and I went to Mount Athos to see the abbot.'" She even adds a colorful detail: "'It was an unforgettable experience. The monastery – I forget which one – was so picturesque ... My father and I had to stay overnight and eat that horrible food – I think there was cooked octopus'" (p. 414).

Randall learns almost immediately that Angela lied to him (she later blames Randall's cynicism for her deception [pp. 467–68]) and he rushes off to consult with the abbot himself. Passing through the monastic boundary at "Daphni, the official port of Mount Athos," where a monk verifies his gender by "prodding his chest," Randall acquires a "guide," a "Greek youth, Vlahos, both guide and muleteer ... plainly dressed except for shoes made of automobile tires" (p. 422). Vlahos's resourceful transformation of a modern amenity into a rustic utility (the shoes "make climbing easier") presages Randall's journey from modernity into the primitive Christian past: first in a "light skiff" with a "ratty tarpaulin," then on two rented mules up the cliffsides: "All this exotic nightmare, Randall thought" (p. 423). When he meets Father Petropoulos, he finds the exotic and bygone version of the weedy academics he encountered in the UK:

He wore a fezlike black hat, a heavy black robe with a small skull-and-crossbones sewn into the habit, and crude peasant's shoes. He was a smallish, frail Greek, with patches of parchment-thin brown skin showing through his long hair, despite his bushy white mustache and beard. Odd rimless spectacles sat low on his thin nose. (p. 424)

As his "parchment-thin skin" suggests, Father Petropoulos's expertise is not merely the acquired knowledge of a learned scholar (like Jeffries or Knight); it's deeply embedded in his premodern person. After a long conversation that does not settle Randall's doubts (with several pages describing the production of ancient papyrus), Randall stays the night at Mount Athos (dining on the threatened "boiled octopus") and arranges for Petropoulos to inspect the manuscript in person.

The local expertise of the Middle East in Gospel Thrillers highlights the yawning gap between the Christian past and an Arabic present.

Mount Athos, on the other hand, takes our protagonists further along the byzantine byways of Christian history that have, over time, obscured those lost biblical origins. In the 1983 novel *Keepers of the Secret*, the protagonist Jason van Cleve has learned about a secret gospel from an old man who was subsequently murdered to hide his discovery. With some difficulty he tracks down the old man's daughter, now a nun. She explains to Jason:

"All through my father's life he was tortured by those blasphemous scrolls ... First he went to Mount Athos to become a monk, hoping to strengthen his faith in the True Church. He entered the secluded monastery of Vatopedi. Finally he showed the scrolls to Abbot Constantine, hoping to be given an explanation that would allay his doubts once and for all. The abbot denounced them as blasphemy, confiscated them, and expelled my father." (p. 111)

Hot on the trail of the final pieces of the lost gospel, Jason sets off for Mount Athos to question Abbot Constantine. Stopping in Athens, he looks up an old friend, Yanni, who provides information on Constantine, "the most powerful man in the Greek Orthodox Church" (p. 115). Jason's next guide is a rough rustic named Andoni who – for a large sum of money – agrees to get Jason onto Mount Athos. After a shot of morning ouzo ("'that's slow poison!' he gasped" [p. 141]) they set off. To evade the conspirators out to stop him, Jason travels under a pseudonym.[6]

The character of Andoni is perfectly poised to guide Jason across the geographic and temporal divide from modern Greece to premodern Athos: his "best friend" is a burro named Mangas who accompanies them on the small motorboat to Athos to carry their food and ouzo. Andoni claims to have learned English fighting in World War II ("'once I strangle two Nazis with my bare hands'" [p. 171]) and so can act as a tour guide to Anglophone tourists (he delivers much of his rehearsed spiel to Jason on the ride over); he explains all the minute customs involved in procuring permission for Jason (who is pretending to be a

---

[6] Although *Keepers of the Secret* was coauthored by a US and a Greek writer, a *Los Angeles Times* columnist who was friends with the US author, Barnaby Conrad, claimed that the Greek coauthor, Nico Mastorakis, "evidently assisted in historical, geographical, and religious research," effectively transforming a coauthor into the same kind of "local expert" featured as characters in Gospel Thrillers (Jack Smith, "Parthenogenesis," *Los Angeles Times* [May 19, 1983]: I1).

professor) to explore the monasteries. Only later does Andoni confess that he learned his English at one of the monasteries of Athos, during a quickly aborted novitiate ("'I needed woman. I not made to be monk'" [p. 198]), although he stayed long enough to be able to guide Jason to the monastery's crypt of treasures. Andoni is both "native" to Athos and able to translate its esoteric ways for outsiders.

A series of misadventures plagues Jason and Andoni on Mount Athos: a trap set at the library in the first monastery gets their travel permission revoked; while attempting to sneak into the next monastery, the hired gun sent to kill them attacks (and is fended off by a mysterious figure who has been trailing them along the way); finally, just as they have recovered the scrolls from their hiding place, a deadly confrontation with Constantine ends in death and fire. But Andoni guides Jason to safety: "'Come back to save you, boss!'" he chirps. When outside help arrives to retrieve Jason in a helicopter, Andoni remains behind to return the way he came, by old boat: "'How can I go on flying machine? I have to take care of Mangas!'" (pp. 236–38). Andoni dissolves back into the premodern past, like a monk receding into a Byzantine fresco.

A character like Andoni is chauvinistic comic relief but also serves to categorize the different types of knowledge brokered at a site like Mount Athos, where the artless know-how of locals stands next to the deceptively savvy knowledge of the monks. There is a sharp contrast, for instance, between the peasant Andoni, whose best friend is a donkey and who speaks in broken English, and Constantine, the powerful abbot who speaks eloquently and even philosophically as he tries to convince Jason to abandon his quest to reveal the lost gospel:

"Whose truth?" asked Constantine contemptuously. "Yours or mine?"
    "There can only be one truth," Jason said.
    "Wrong, Mr. Van Cleve," Constantine replied. "Truth wears many faces. Some of them are deceiving." (p. 231)

The liminal space of Mount Athos offers up two kinds of knowledge brokers: the revealer and the concealer. The innocent path to truth is opened up by the failed monk, the nonclerical "local," while "the most powerful man in the Orthodox church" counsels a cover-up. Native simplicity and transparency sit uncomfortably alongside religious institutional secrecy, both embodied in the ancient "holy mountain" of monasteries.

Athos also figures as a site of native simplicity and clerical duplicity in Rabb's *The Book of Q*. A series of serendipitously discovered
letters has led the protagonist, US Jesuit scholar Ian Pearse, to Mount
Athos. Pearse, a researcher based in Rome, travels under a pseudonym (like Van Cleve in *Keepers of the Secret*) to avoid the violent
conspirators who, he suspects, are also based in the Vatican.
An Italian colleague in Rome outfits him for his secular disguise
("'A Catholic priest on Athos ... now that wouldn't make much
sense, would it?'" [p. 126]) and puts him in touch with Greek
colleagues in Salonika who secure the appropriate paperwork to visit
Mount Athos.

Pearse's first sight of Athos is inspiring, his first welcome cheerful
and bright: "Brother Gennadios laughed as he approached ... He wore
the classic black robe of Greek Orthodoxy, the bonnet on his head
tilted at a somewhat daring angle" (p. 150). They travel to the monastery, first by truck and then by arduous footpath, literally shedding
modernity as they go. At their destination they are greeted by the
diminutive librarian of the monastery of St. Photinus, Brother
Nikotheos: "There was an almost feminine quality to his face, delicate
olive-shaped eyes, soft white skin amid the wrinkles. Even his beard
seemed to soften its texture. His hands, however, betrayed his years,
browned and bony" (p. 155).

At first St. Photinus monastery seems likewise "delicate" and serene:
"A breeze lifted off the water, more of the olive and mint, a gentle
reminder of the world he now inhabited" (p. 157). But like the
network of dark passages and hidden codes Pearse navigates to find
the secret gospel beneath the monastery grounds, the kindly monk is
not what he seems. In a hidden chamber decorated with heretical
tapestries, Pearse finds a hidden book and another surprise: "There,
peering down at him from the steps, stood Brother Nikotheos, a small
revolver in his hand" (p. 172). The "delicate" monk is a hardened
servant of the *summus princeps* – a notably Latin title disrupting the
Greek antiquity of Mount Athos – who is also a Roman Catholic
cardinal, a Manichean heretic whose underground sect long ago
infiltrated the serenity of Mount Athos. Fittingly, Pearse slips out of
the monastery and flees Mount Athos disguised as a monk, replicat-
ing the masquerade of the heretical monks of Photinus. Having found
there another clue on his quest, he leaves the false serenity of Mount
Athos behind.

"The Multitude of Secrets": Inside the Secret Archive

The Jesuit disguised as an Athonite monk embodies the different kinds of clerical knowledge brokers we see in Gospel Thrillers. The difference between the "heavy black robe ... and fezlike hat" of the Orthodox monk and the trim cassock and discreet collar of the Roman Catholic priest makes visible the difference between knowledge that beckons from the past, foreign and mysterious, and knowledge that lives in the present, only lightly covered by an anachronistic costume. Two years after its 1983 piece on Mount Athos, replete with gauzy landscapes and monks living in premodern simplicity, *National Geographic* ran a piece (with the same photographer) on Vatican City, "the powerful heart and headquarters of the Roman Catholic Church." While the inhabitants of Mount Athos were constantly drifting into a distant past, this article notes that "the Vatican's aura of timelessness is an illusion." Photos show Swiss Guards in their fanciful Renaissance costumes alongside images of those same guards in a karate class; on one page readers see the ancient tunnels that might lead to Saint Peter's tomb and on the next the state-of-the-art recording studio used to produce "Vatican Radio." Restoration of Renaissance frescoes, readers learn, is funded "by a Japanese TV network, which is paying three million dollars for the rights to chronicle the restoration." The monks of Mount Athos stand closer to the same primitive past as the gospel secrets being sought; the priests of the Vatican inhabit a modern world disguised in accessories hearkening back to that primitive past.[7]

Roman Catholic priests appear in almost every Gospel Thriller: as protagonists, conspirators, background players, best friends, confidants, betrayers. The omnipresence of men in collars reminds readers of the tense and often antagonistic relationship between traditional institutional religion and the potentially earth-shattering secrets of lost and rediscovered first-century gospels. As I explored in Chapter 4, Roman Catholicism represents all that is objectionable to the default white Protestant sensibility of the novels: hierarchical formality rising from priest to Pope, privileging pomp and splendor over spirituality and independence. Vatican City, the heart of this global Catholic

---

[7] James Fallows and James L. Stanfield, "Vatican City," *National Geographic* 168.6 (December 1985): 720–61; the same issue included a photospread of the "Treasures of the Vatican" by Stanfield.

spiderweb, disguises itself behind an Old World façade that is more brittle and less benign than the primitive isolation of Mount Athos.

The kind of knowledge brokered by the clerics here is not found on the musty shelves of the forgotten monastic library, as Bible Hunters and Gospel Thrillers imagine in the Orthodox monasteries of Athos. It lies instead on cold metal shelves, behind locked steel doors secured with numbered keypads under the watchful eye of closed-circuit cameras, deep in the heart of the Vatican "secret archives." As the protagonist of Gold's *Lost Testament* remarks when pondering a possible modern location for Jesus's testament: "There are great libraries in the Vatican. Somewhere, assuming it's still in existence, a librarian in Rome has it locked at the bottom of the drawer" (p. 179). It goes without saying that this "librarian in Rome" sports a priest's collar and rarely, if ever, allows anyone to see the bottom of that drawer.

Several novels send our protagonists to the evocatively named "Vatican Secret Archive," the central secure collection of the papal see. The original Latin *secretum* meant something more like "private" or even "closed," but the fantasy of *secrecy*, documents so deeply hidden that even the pope might not be aware of them, is irresistible to popular imagination and to Gospel Thrillers. Technically, since 2019, the archive has been officially renamed the "Vatican Apostolic Archive." But just as renaming the papal "Office of the Inquisition" the "Congregation for the Doctrine in the Faith" has done little to soften the pernicious reputation of the Roman Catholic church as repressive and intolerant, no name change will dispel the idea that this age-old, wealthy, and globally powerful institution has hoarded dangerous secrets buried deep within its bibliographic fortress.

Like Mount Athos, the Vatican Secret Archive requires special permission – or a crafty break-in – and special guidance – or hapless wandering and serendipitous discovery. In *The Negev Project*, retired biblical studies scholar Jack Winslow is a kindly senior scholar drawn out of retirement by his protégé on the trail of lost documents about the historical Jesus. Winslow happens to be old friends with the Director of the Vatican Library, a US bishop whom he knew decades earlier during World War II: "The night before, Winslow had read about the Vatican and its library; he knew he was getting privileged access" (p. 254).

Winslow's visit is revelatory but straightforward: after a brief tour of some library facilities (including manuscript restoration) and several pages of exposition on early Christological heresies, the bishop simply hands Winslow a manila envelope with the background information he has requested: "'This is everything I know ...'" he explains, and continues to complain about the Church's undeserved reputation for suppression and secrecy:

"Every time something is found, poor Mother Church gets in trouble ... When Catholic scholars get involved in the Dead Sea Scrolls, they get blamed for trying to put a spin on their meaning. When the Nag Hammadi writings of the Gnostics were discovered, the feminists said the male bishops had suppressed the helpless feminist gnostics ... I don't think it's fair." (p. 263)

Winslow and the bishop part ways after a more extensive tour of the library and a light Italian lunch.

Other novels are less sanguine about the Vatican Library's "unfair" reputation for suppression and secrecy. James Becker wrote a series of novels featuring ex-cop Chris Bronson and his ex-wife, museum curator Angela Lewis, who get entangled in various antiquities conspiracies. Two of these novels, *The First Apostle* and *The Lost Testament*, revolve around secrets hidden in and extracted from the Vatican Secret Archives. In Becker's imagination, the Vatican Secret Archives exist precisely to hide and suppress documents dangerous to the institutional authority of the Roman Catholic church.

In *The First Apostle*, a chance uncovering of ancient fresco in the UK links back to "the Vitalian Codex ... the darkest of all the multitude of secrets hidden in the Apostolic Penitentiary," which is later described as "the most secret and secure of the Vatican's numerous repositories" (pp. 41, 60). The Vitalian Codex, written by a seventh-century pope, is the only written evidence of documents that could undermine the entire foundation of Christianity and includes instructions on eliminating anyone who might stumble upon those secrets. In *The Lost Testament*, a document stolen from the *"Archivum Secretum Vaticanum"* (p. 27) during a robbery in the 1960s has resurfaced in the antiquities markets of Cairo in the 2010s, setting off a race against time to secure it. Readers learn, at the death of one prefect of the "Secret Archives" and the appointment of his successor, that for decades only the prefect and the pope were made aware of the existence of this document, and its shocking secrets, so that they might be on the lookout for its recovery.

In his Author's Note to *The First Apostle*, Becker reinforces the suppressive secrecy of the Vatican: "This book is, of course, a novel and *to the best of my knowledge* no documents resembling the Vitalian Codex or the Exomologesis exist, or have ever existed, *though without doubt* there are numerous dark secrets lurking within the Vatican Library's 75,000 manuscripts and the estimated 150,000 items now held in the Secret Archives" (p. 335, emphasis added). Becker suggests that while the *specific* explosive document he imagines in his novel may not exist, surely some other equally explosive document exists in the Secret Archives because suppressing explosive secrets are their raison d'être; similarly, the raison d'être of the "prefects" and directors of those archives is to ensure those secrets stay hidden.

The drama of Meade's *The Second Messiah* is split between Israel, where dangerous Dead Sea Scrolls are found and suppressed, and the Vatican, where a newly elected Pope has promised to throw upon the vaults of the Secret Archives and reveal all the Church's secrets: theological, financial, and political. (This new Pope, once a US priest working on a Qumran dig in the 1990s, has his own Dead Sea secrets to reveal.) The Vatican hierarchy is rocked; some few cardinals feigning loyalty to the new Pope sneak into the Archives and steal documents before they can be revealed. One of them, a senior cardinal, even decides the only way to keep the Secret Archives secret is through violence: "an age-old Vatican practice that hasn't been in fashion for years: kill the reigning pope" (p. 420). The existence of the Secret Archive symbolizes the secrecy of biblical knowledge, bound up in conspiracy and practically impossible to untangle.

One of the most surprising and perhaps even subversive appearances of a "local expert" in the Vatican Secret Archives comes in Dan Silva's *The Order* (2020). Silva's protagonist Gabriel Allon (who has appeared in more than twenty Silva novels to date) is an Israeli intelligence officer who has come back to Rome at the request of his friend Donati, a former papal chief of staff, during the contested deliberations to choose a new pope. The previous pope, Paul VII, died in suspicious circumstances after retrieving some mysterious book from the Vatican Secret Archives. Hoping to find evidence of this dangerous book (which, it will turn out, is a first-person account by Pilate exculpating the Jews for the death of Christ), Allon has his Israeli intelligence team remotely shut off the power and disable the security for the Vatican Secret Archives. Disguised as a priest, with a Beretta concealed in his waistband, Allon sneaks with Donati into the Secret Archives.

While Allon sets to picking one of the "professional grade locks" they encounter barring their entry, a mysterious and surprisingly friendly stranger appears in the darkness:

Donati aimed his phone's flashlight into the void. It illuminated a man in a cassock. No, thought Gabriel. Not a cassock. A robe. The man moved forward, soundlessly, on sandaled feet. He was identical to Gabriel in height and build ... His hair was black and curly, his skin was dark. He had an ancient face, like an icon come to life. (p. 158)

The stranger introduces himself as "Father Joshua," speaking in "fluent Italian, the language of the Vatican, but it is obviously not his native tongue." Assuring them that the book they seek is not in the archives, he hands them a "manila envelope" promising that it will tell them "everything" they "need to know" (p. 159). Father Joshua alerts them that security guards sent by the perfidious Cardinal Albanese are approaching; he leads them wordlessly to the exit: "It opened at Father Joshua's touch. He raised a hand in farewell and then melted once more into the gloom" (p. 160). The manila envelope contains a single sheet from the missing book, pointing them to the lost account of Pilate for which the Pope was killed.

Allon later learns that no one remembers a "Father Joshua" working in the Vatican Secret Archives, a fact confirmed once Donati can check the official records. Nonetheless it eventually comes to light that Father Joshua also directed Paul VII to the account by Pilate. By the time Allon encounters Father Joshua again in the Piazza San Marco in Venice it is clear that readers are meant to believe he is Jesus himself, returned to help reveal the truth: he "seemed to move across the floodwaters" in the Piazza "without disturbing the surface," as if walking on water, and tells Allon that he is from "the Galilee" (pp. 407–09; earlier, when Allon and Donati encountered Father Joshua in the Secret Archives, Allon noticed that both of his hands were "heavily bandaged").

The supernatural presence of "Father Joshua" in his robe ("not a cassock") in the Vatican Secret Archives highlights by contrast how the site's cassocked gatekeepers function to block the truth of Christian origins from seeing the light of day (we can recall similar accusations against the Roman Catholic experts who worked on the Dead Sea Scrolls, as I discussed in Chapter 3). The role of "Father Joshua" in literally unlocking the Secret Archive's secrets makes readers aware of the constantly mediated status of this dangerous knowledge: the truths revealed through hidden gospels is never inert, it is always being mobilized by a range of actors intent on revealing, or concealing, their secrets.

Bibles Codes and the Myth of Unbrokered Knowledge

I focus on knowledge brokers, the agents of revelation or concealment in Gospel Thrillers, to show how these novels engage with the problems and possibilities created by the fact that biblical knowledge is always brokered by human agents, whose motives and goals call into question their knowledge-making (and the Bible that results from it). By contrast, in the real world outside of the novels, professional biblical studies tend to operate in a depersonalized fashion, insisting on "scientific" rules and methods that would theoretically remove (or at least diminish) human interference. We might call this the myth of unbrokered biblical knowledge, a myth that exploded in a surprising way into public consciousness in the late 1990s, with the publication of *The Bible Code*.[8]

In the early 1990s, three Israeli academics – Eliyahu Rips, Doron Witztum, and Yoav Rosenberg – began experimenting with "equidistant letter sequences" (known in espionage lingo as "skip codes"); they found the names of famous rabbis from the ancient to modern periods embedded in statistically significant ways in the sequential Hebrew letters of the Torah. Rips and his colleagues published their rather arcane results in the academic journal *Statistical Science* in 1994. Two years before that, they met a US journalist who would popularize their work in a bestselling series of books.

As Michael Drosnin recounts the story in the first chapter of *The Bible Code*, he was in Israel "meeting with the chief of Israel intelligence about the future of warfare":

As I was leaving intelligence headquarters, a young officer I'd met stopped me. "There's a mathematician in Jerusalem you should see," he said. "He found the exact date the Gulf War would begin. In the Bible."

"I'm not religious," I said, getting into my car.

---

[8] Michael Drosnin, *The Bible Code* (New York: Simon & Schuster, 1997).

"Neither am I," said the officer. "But he found a code in the Bible with the exact date, three weeks before the war started."[9]

As in so many Gospel Thrillers (see Chapter 3), the officious and efficient Israeli technocracy – represented by the military and the university – unveiled for the US explorer a shocking new biblical secret. Rips showed Drosnin his computer program (devised by Witztum, a physicist) and a preprint of the article. Drosnin told a codebreaker at the National Security Agency (NSA) about the Bible code; the codebreaker not only replicated Rips's results but found additional "encoded" names.

Working sometimes with Rips (who spent time in the 1990s as a visiting scholar in the United States), sometimes with his codebreaker friends, Drosnin uncovered more codes: *Clinton* near the Hebrew word for *President*; a prediction of a comet colliding with Jupiter; and, most distressing, a prediction that Israeli Prime Minister Yitzhak Rabin would be assassinated (Drosnin opens *The Bible Code* with his fruitless attempts to warn Rabin). The Bible, Drosnin learns, holds an almost infinite amount of encoded information: "We have always thought of the Bible as a book," Drosnin writes. "It is also a computer program." In 1997, *The Bible Code* hit the shelves, full of decoded predictions from the past, the present, and the future. It rocketed up the bestseller lists.[10]

There were, of course, skeptics. (Even Rips, initially cooperative with Drosnin, told *Time* magazine that Drosnin's efforts to use the code to predict the future were "futile.") Mathematicians decried the decoding process; an Australian computer scientist took up Drosnin's challenge in *Newsweek* to "find a message about the assassination of a prime minister encrypted in *Moby Dick*" and found "predicted" deaths of more than half-dozen world leaders, including Diana, the Princess of Wales.[11]

Experts in religion and theology tried to push back against Drosnin's claims on the Bible, too. Appearing on *The Charlie Rose Show* a week after Drosnin himself, scholar of Jewish philosophy Shaul Magid

---

[9] Drosnin, *Bible Code*, 18.   [10] Drosnin, *Bible Code*, 45.
[11] David van Biema and Lisa McLaughlin, "Deciphering God's Plan," *Time* 149.23 (June 9, 1997): 56; Brendan McKay, "Assassinations Foretold in Moby Dick!" online at http://users.cecs.anu.edu.au/~bdm/dilugim/moby.html.

linked the demystification of the sacred texts to a "destructive" quest for certainty:

There is a perennial quest in human civilization for certainty and I think that that quest is in small measure healthy, but has the potential to be tragic and very destructive ... When it manifests itself in the way it's manifesting itself with these codes, that becomes the beginning and the potential for false prophecy because false prophecy is always very seductive and oftentimes very convincing and almost always very interesting ... and always wrong.[12]

The "seduction" of false prophecy is that it seems to come from outside, from a source removed from human interests and motivations (the "prophet" is, after all, a direct conduit with divine truth). The codebreaker is merely deciphering knowledge that is already "there": the myth of unbrokered biblical knowledge. Charlie Rose dedicated multiple episodes of his PBS (Public Broadcasting Service) show to the idea; articles appeared in *Time*, *Newsweek*, and *People*; Drosnin made the bestseller list again in 2003 with his follow-up *Bible Code II: The Countdown* (a third volume, published by a smaller press, failed to make the list). Other attempts to "decode" the Bible followed in turn.

We can ascribe Drosnin's success in part to the perennial public fascination with "secrets of the Bible" that generates endless basic cable specials and series. But there is also the very specific approach to the Bible as a puzzle, full of secrets waiting to be decoded, that animates a US reading public and, of course, finds elaborate expression in Gospel Thrillers. Like all good conspiracy thrillers, *The Bible Code* assumes there is a secret truth that is hidden and waiting to be revealed. In this case, however, the secrecy happens without any human agency. Drosnin is fuzzy on how the "code" ended up in the Hebrew Scriptures, using passive language ("the Bible was encoded" [pp. 24, 174]), at one point asking: "Had a non-human intelligence actually encoded the Bible?" (p. 38) and admitting "I do not know if it is God" (p. 51). (Most reviews of the time infer divine origins for the code). Likewise, the means of extracting the code happens through computer automation (once the correct program has been written, with the help of a resourceful military in Israel and the United States). The Bible of *The Bible Code* is a perpetual motion revelation machine ("a computer

---

[12] *The Charlie Rose Show*, June 25, 1997, online at https://charlierose.com/videos/ 12287.

program"), concealing its own secrets until new decoding technology from biblical lands allows the intrepid US "detective" to crack the code. It embodies a fantasy of impersonal and unbrokered biblical knowledge.[13]

This idea of the Bible as a *code*, to be cracked by the right program without any further human interference, is not so alien to the basic techniques of modern biblical studies, which I discussed in Chapter 1 and to which I return in Chapter 6: that is, the constant quest for new evidence and improved methods for "restoring" the original form of the Bible. The Bible produced by modern biblical criticism is already conceived of as the always-almost-solved puzzle pieced together through serendipitous discovery, scholarly ingenuity, and a determination to unlock the hidden truth of the biblical text. "Methods" are devised (labeled as various kinds of "criticism") that are wielded by scholarly experts but which also ostensibly operate without interference from those experts. Drosnin's *Bible Code* pressed the logic of biblical decoding to a fantastical level by removing from his narrative any trace of human agents brokering that hidden truth.

Gospel Thrillers, like most conspiracy thrillers, are not averse to using codes to propel the search for biblical truth (or lies). These codes are, however, produced and unlocked by characters in the novel whose interest and motives are made clear and central. A US archaeologist helps unravel a mysterious list of newly discovered scrolls in caves in Peters's *The Dead Sea Cipher*. A mathematician unlocks the codes embedded in French Gothic cathedrals in Sandom's *Gospel Truths* (1992). In *The Book of Q*, an Italian academic assists a Jesuit scholar in piecing together acrostics hidden in ancient letters that, in turn, reveal "an ingeniously coded map" (p. 110). In both *Gospel Truths* and *Book of Q* the "secret code" is explicitly linked to hidden theological truths concealed through the centuries: "secret knowledge ... that lies at the heart of any kind of Gnosticism" (*Book of Q*, p. 108). *The Second Messiah*'s Dead Sea Scroll is also composed in a code, called "Atbash Cipher," a simple code that switches the first letter of an alphabet and the last, the second letter and second-to-last, and so on

[13] In his sequel to *The Bible Code*, *The Bible Code II: The Countdown* (New York: Viking, 2002), Drosnin offers the novel theory that the Code was left by extraterrestrial visitors to Earth thousands of years ago. These aliens also left the genetic code for humanity and, Drosnin believes, physical evidence of their presence buried in the Middle East.

("Atbash" comes from *aleph*, *tav*, *bet*, and *shin*, the first, last, second, and second-to-last letters of the Hebrew alphabet). The protagonist, Jack Cane, figures this out (his mentor thought the Aramaic looked like "gibberish"), based on his memory of the books of Hugh Schonfield (author of, among other conspiracy-minded spiritualist works, *The Passover Plot*). *The Masada Scroll* (2007) goes so far as to imagine that its newly discovered "Gospel of Dismas," curiously written in Hebrew and Greek, contains predictive codes similar to *The Bible Code*: even the murder of one of the archaeologists deciphering the gospel is predicted before his very eyes.[14]

The recent real-world discovery of a mutilated and partial Gospel of Judas inspired two different novels to imagine the crafty work of codebreakers filling in the missing pieces. In *The Dead Sea Deception* a group of internet sleuths led by a British paleographer use some unspecified fragment of a Dead Sea Scroll to decode the "Rotgut Codex," a medieval translation of the Gospel of John that actually conceals a full and outlandish version of the Gospel of Judas. Lisa Stasi's *Book of Judas* (2017) also links recovered pages of the Gospel of Judas (in the novel stolen from the same Long Island bank where the real codex was stored in the 1980s) with a mysterious medieval "decoding" text (here the real, and likely meaningless, Voynich Manuscript). But in a turn toward the paranormal that echoes *The Bible Code* and its sequels, the protagonists of *Book of Judas* deduce the hidden biblical secrets not from these stolen pages but from the providential gaps and holes left in the surviving, published version of the Gospel of Judas.[15]

Setting aside the inexplicably produced and deduced code at the climax of *Book of Judas*, these examples of coding and decoding incorporate, and critique, the dream of unbrokered biblical knowledge freed of human motivations. Codes cannot be self-generating and self-revealing; codes must be produced by humans, just as they must be decoded by humans. *The Bible Code* indulges in a fantasy of secrets revealing themselves through computer magic; Gospel Thrillers reveal

---

[14] Schonfield first suggested the presence of the *Atbash* cipher in Qumran in *Secrets of the Dead Sea Scrolls* (London: Valentine, 1956); from there it was picked up by esoteric conspiracists and ended up in *The Da Vinci Code*.

[15] Also like *The Bible Code: Countdown*, *Book of Judas* introduces the possibility of alien visitors and "panspermia" (seeding of life on Earth by extraterrestrials).

a more cynical view of technologies, codes, and biblical secrets in the public imagination.

In Becker's *The Lost Testament*, the suppressive tendencies of the Vatican Secret Archives have extended outward into cyberspace: no longer content to keep their secrets hidden under lock and key, the upper echelon of Roman Catholic leadership has extended their surveillance outward:

> There were a fair number of skeletons in the Vatican's closets, documents and objects which, if they ever saw the light of day, would cripple – or at least very severely damage – the Church's credibility. And it made sense that anyone who discovered even a hint about any such dark secret would very probably use an online search engine to research the topic. A kind of early-warning system was needed. (p. 46)

The result, modeled on the eavesdropping technologies of "Western Europe and America," is "Codex S" (named after *Codex Sinaiticus*), "programmed to detect certain words being entered into the search engines … The date and time would be noted, and the search team recorded, the information then being fed back to the Vatican" (p. 47). Throughout the novel, Codex S is used by the nefarious Vatican forces out to recover the precious document stolen from their Secret Archives decades earlier, wending its way from Cairo to Europe. The protagonists, realizing their searches are being tracked, must work to evade this global surveillance tool to arrive at the truth. Like his not-quite-disclaimer about the Vitalian Codex in *The First Apostle*, Becker writes in his Author's Note: "The monitoring system employed by the Vatican to monitor Internet searching, and which I named Codex S, is a figment of my imagination. *But that doesn't mean* that the Vatican doesn't actually have some system that works in a similar fashion" (p. 421, emphasis added).

Becker had in fact trotted out a lower-tech version of Codex S in *The First Apostle*: here it was a group of *mafiosi*, contracted by the Vatican decades earlier to keep an eye out for discovery of their secrets, who worked directly with translators and online program moderators to send word when certain terms in various ancient languages were entered into their systems. Although less automated than Codex S, this hands-on approach to internet surveillance has much the same effect: it allows the veil of Vatican secrecy to extend outward through the information superhighway, obstructing the circuits of knowledge transmission.

The advent of computer learning and the internet has added new complications to those knowledge circuits, more points at which knowledge can be brokered by actors with motives ranging from the benign to the maleficent. Already in the 1990s, in her novel *The Prophetess*, Barbara Wood had begun grappling with the implications of the early internet: in the days before Google, Wood's heroine is stymied in her attempts to use the primitive World Wide Web for information by the antagonist, a billionaire computer mogul who has total access to the cyberworld. The journey from Lycos searches and Internet Relay Chat (IRC) chat rooms in 1996 to automated surveillance system of Codex S in 2013 may feel momentous from a technological standpoint. But like the musty libraries of Mount Athos, the high-tech stacks of the Vatican Secret Archive, or the libraries of scholars, the cyber age has merely added another site where we can watch the knowledge brokers at work, wielding sophisticated tools to reveal or conceal biblical truths.

In the 1990s, Michael Drosnin described the Bible as "computer program," generating prophetic codes waiting to be decoded by other computer programs. But biblical knowledge is never self-generated in Gospel Thrillers: there are no impersonal or objective pathways along which new biblical truths can travel. Behind every library shelf, academic tome, monastic cell, or computer terminal lies a knowledge seeker and the various knowledge brokers with multifarious motives and interests: scholars, "natives," monks, priests, and, ultimately, we the readers. When the narrative of Gospel Thrillers enters the real world, in scandals and controversies over biblical "discoveries," it is those motives and interests that take center stage.

6 | *Academic Thrillers*

Q Times 3

Q1: In the opening chapter of Irving Wallace's 1972 novel *The Word*, fictional US Bible publisher George Wheeler invites jaded public relations specialist Steve Randall to his New York City office for a meeting. There he tells Randall about plans to publish a new translation of the New Testament, mounted by an international conglomerate of Bible publishers in the United States, Great Britain, France, Germany, and Italy: "'After six years of toiling in absolute secrecy, the time had arrived for the final step – the mounting of the gigantic publicity campaign, one based on hard news rather than puffery, that would guarantee the success of the International New Testament.'" Randall expresses skepticism: "'I should think there are enough versions of the Bible around. Why would anyone ever want to publish a new one?'" (pp. 71–72)

The affable publisher then dismisses his staff from the room and reveals to Randall that the international conglomerate has been "'sitting on a keg of dynamite, keeping the lid on the hottest, most tremendous news story of all time'" (p. 75). Wheeler explains that the International New Testament is not merely a new translation, but includes a fifth gospel pieced together from papyri recently discovered by an Italian archaeologist:

"The papyri that were found – that we now possess – are the lost source for the Synoptic Gospels, the so-called Q document, a fifth but actually the first and original gospel – the Gospel According to James – written by James, James the Just, the younger brother of Jesus, to record the life of the real Jesus Christ as He walked the earth as a man among men, a human being as well as the Messiah, in the first century of our world. Now we have it all, all of it." (p. 79)

This Q document reveals a liberal Jesus with "uncanny relevance for the world today," including sayings concerning the exploitation of the poor by the wealthy and the ruling class, sayings concerning the need for a compact among nations to end war and colonialism, sayings on the necessity of education for all, sayings that disapproved of superstition, dogma, ritual, and two sayings that actually prophesied that one day men would stride the planets of heaven at a time when the earth verged on self-destruction. (p. 226)

When this new gospel is published its effects are profound. Even the deeply jaded Randall finds that "the Word had penetrated his cynicism" (p. 217).

Q2: In the year 2000, a nonfictional group of scholars called "The International Q Project" unveiled its own version of Q after years of work. *The Critical Edition of Q* promised in its preface: "The text of Q need no longer be just an imaginary black box lurking somewhere behind certain Matthean and Lukan verses as a source, but can emerge as a text in its own right." In painstaking detail, across eight columns, over 500 pages, the text "emerges" in highly annotated Greek (with English, German, and French translations), ready for scholars to recapture in its earliest form the teachings of Jesus, stripped of miracles, apocalypse, and resurrection.[1]

The theory of Q has been around for a long time. Taking its initial "Q" from the German word *Quelle* (source), Q is a hypothetical collection of Jesus's sayings fundamental to understanding the relationship of the three synoptic gospels (Matthew, Mark, and Luke). "Higher critics" beginning in the nineteenth century worked backwards from our existing gospel texts: those passages that Matthew and Luke had in common with each other, but which were absent from Mark, were believed to have derived from this non-extant source: Q.

In the 1960s and 1970s interest primarily from US academics turned to recovering and codifying Q. In 1985, James M. Robinson (whom we have met several times already as a leader in the work on the Nag Hammadi texts) established the "Q Seminar" at the annual meeting of the Society of Biblical Literature; soon after, in 1987, John Kloppenborg published his highly influential study *The Formation of Q*. Kloppenborg argued that Q was edited and reworked over time, allowing scholars to trace the development of this earliest community of Jesus's followers: that is, within the Q derived from Matthew and

---

[1] James M. Robinson, Paul Hoffmann, and John S. Kloppenborg, *The Critical Edition of Q*, Hermeneia (Minneapolis, MN: Augsburg/Fortress, 2000), at xv.

Luke were traces of earlier versions of Q, edited before its use by later gospel-writers. (We saw a similar approach to the Gospel of Thomas in Chapter 4). Kloppenborg and Robinson formed the International Q Project in 1989, completing their work eleven years later.[2]

Q3: Before the International Q Project could unveil its complex, almost mathematical work, Q was revealed in more reader-friendly fashion in 1993 by Burton Mack, a prominent biblical studies scholar in Claremont, California (where Robinson was also based). Mack's *The Lost Gospel: The Book of Q & Christian Origins* provided a highly readable (if occasionally idiosyncratic) translation of Q, an accessible and colorful account of Q's "discovery" (he compares it to "finding the shards" of a broken piece of ancient pottery), and an interpretation of what the oldest strata of Q could tell us about the earliest followers of Jesus.[3]

For Mack, Q reveals a Jesus freed from the later mythologies that congealed into the canonical gospels and (lamentable) orthodox Christian dogma. The early followers of Jesus who preserved this sayings gospel "thought of him as a teacher whose teachings made it possible to live with verve in troubled times." This original community was inspired by the multicultural and humanistic message of Jesus, now available for all in Q:[4]

The Jesus movement was attractive as a place to experiment with novel social notions and life-styles. It was generated by a sensitive and considered aware-ness of the times and a critical posture toward reigning cultural values ... People were encouraged to free themselves from traditional social constraints and think of themselves as belonging to a larger human family. As Q puts it, "If you embrace only your brothers, what more are you doing than others?"[5]

This countercultural Jesus (Mack characterizes him as a "Cynic philosopher"; others describe him as a "hippie") does not sound so different from the liberal Jesus unveiled in the fictional Q of *The Word*.

---

[2] John Kloppenborg, *The Formation of Q: Trajectories in Ancient Wisdom* (Minneapolis, MN: Fortress Press, 1987). The leaders of the International Q Project were Kloppenborg in Toronto, James Robinson in Claremont, California, and Paul Hoffman in Bamberg, Germany.

[3] Burton L. Mack, *The Lost Gospel: The Book of Q & Christian Origins* (San Francisco, CA: HarperSanFrancisco, 1993). Mack notes that his translation explicitly avoids the "familiar ring" of biblical language (p. 71).

[4] Mack, *Lost Gospel*, 4.   [5] Mack, *Lost Gospel*, 9.

He also recalls the potentially heretical Jesus of fact and fiction we met in Chapter 4.[6]

Mack's "lost gospel" sold widely. When he published his follow-up in 1995, *Who Wrote the New Testament?: The Making of Christian Myth*, he become the subject of a splashy feature on Q in *The Atlantic* magazine by conservative writer Charlotte Allen: "Q: The Search for a No-Frills Jesus." Allen laid out the various claims about, for, and against Q as a more authentic portrayal of Jesus and she gave plenty of room for Mack's "truculent and colorful" claims about the sharp break between the Jesus revealed by Q and the Christian religion that followed. While Robinson, the leader of the International Q Project, is more temperate in his claims in the article, Mack is clear in his aims: "It's over . . . We've had enough martyrs. Christianity has had a two-thousand year run, and it's over." Like the fictional International New Testament of *The Word*, Mack's rediscovery of the lost gospel Q has the potential to transform humankind.[7]

The Logi(sti)cs of Q

I begin this final chapter with these three revelations (or unveilings) of the hypothetical source document Q to bring together two threads which have woven together throughout this book: the fictional biblical fantasies spun out in Gospel Thrillers and the academic fantasies that fuel the modern Euro-American profession of biblical studies. The two are deeply intertwined and mutually revelatory: modern biblical studies provides the raw material for Gospel Thrillers (sometimes creatively transformed); Gospel Thrillers reveal unspoken fears and desires that continue to animate modern biblical studies, particularly surrounding the endless possibility of new discovery and new revision. Q, which appears in several Gospel Thrillers and has been a bedrock of modern

[6] John Dominic Crossan, who also embraced Mack's theory of a "peasant Cynic" Jesus, described Jesus and his followers as "hippies in a world of Augustan yuppies" (*Jesus: A Revolutionary Biography* [San Francisco, CA: HarperSanFrancisco, 1994], 198).

[7] Burton L. Mack, *Who Wrote the New Testament? The Making of Christian Myth* (San Francisco, CA: HarperSanFrancisco, 1995). Charlotte Allen, "Q: The Search for a No-Frills Jesus," *The Atlantic* 27.6 (December 1996): 51–68, later expanded as part of the more critical book *The Human Christ: The Search for the Historical Jesus* (New York: The Free Press, 1998).

New Testament studies, illuminates the shared aesthetic and cultural logics of biblical fiction and fact.[8]

I discussed in Chapter 1 the rise of two central planks of academic research into the Bible that rendered the academics' Bible always open to revision. One the one hand, critical approaches to the composition history of the biblical text – what was once called "Higher Criticism" but has splintered into multiple kinds of source critical methods – conjure up and scrutinize the possible sources (oral or written) that lie behind our books of the Bible. On the other hand, philological advances and new textual discoveries allow experts to amend and "correct" the text of the New Testament.

Both of these efforts are continuous and ongoing; they have no logical or foreseeable endpoint. New theories of biblical composition and new approaches to textual reconstruction give academic biblical studies the illusion of a stable Bible that is, in reality, constantly (and necessarily) in flux. (The standard Greek "critical edition" of the New Testament used by scholars has gone through twenty-eight editions since it first appeared in 1898.) Scholars also tend to frame this work as impersonal and even quasi-scientific, as sources and methods are "refined" over time like laboratory instruments. While some professional practitioners of biblical studies, particularly scholars originating outside of the Euro-American context, eschew this impersonal "view from nowhere," this scientized myth of the Bible persists as a common view.[9]

Q in many ways epitomizes these approaches and assumptions of modern critical biblical studies. Q-skeptical New Testament scholar Mark Goodacre has pointed out that Q scholars draw on both the text critical language of the "new discovery" (Mack's reconstructed "shards") as well as the source critical effort to derive Q from its existing descendants (Matthew and Luke). The result is the "discovery" of a "lost gospel" through academic ingenuity.[10]

---

[8] Q is the central gospel of only a few Gospel Thrillers (whether real or forged), all of which I have discussed in other chapters: *The Q Document* (1964), *The Word* (1972), *Gospel Truths* (1992), *The Book of Q* (2001), and *Q: Awakening* (2012).

[9] See Ekaputra Tupamahu, "The Stubborn Invisibility of Whiteness in Biblical Scholarship," *Political Theology Network*, online at https://politicaltheology .com/the-stubborn-invisibility-of-whiteness-in-biblical-scholarship.

[10] Mark S. Goodacre, "When Is a Text not a Text? The Quasi Text-Critical Approach of the International Q Project," in *Questioning Q:*

It is significant that Robinson and Kloppenborg, as well as other pro-Q scholars, referred to Q as a *gospel* rather than a *source*. Kloppenborg wrote in an essay collection published in 1994:

The SBL Q Seminar has introduced "Sayings Gospel," in part to avoid the term *source*, which inevitably obscures Q as a document of intrinsic interest in its own right (much like calling the second Gospel "the Markan source"). And in part, this designation is intended to convey the notion that Q represents a "gospel" as much as do the narrative Gospels.[11]

For Robinson, Kloppenborg, Mack, and their fellow travelers, the gospel Q is as real as the Gospel of Mark, even though it was only "discovered" in the nineteenth century and "reconstructed" toward the end of the twentieth century. Its reality, between the covers of a book (indeed, several books by the year 2000), affirms the centrality of textual discovery, reconstruction, and revision to the endeavor of biblical studies.

The logic of Q is not just technical but also aesthetic, a sense about the historical (and, ultimately, theological) inadequacy of the Bible as it presently exists. These ongoing processes of reconstruction presuppose that the (Christian) Bible as we have it is not telling us the whole story about Jesus and Christian origins and so we must dig deeper to uncover that story. (Archaeological metaphors abound in biblical criticism, like Mack's invocation of pottery shards.) There is a hidden history and a lost text (or fragment, or variant, or reconstruction) that will reveal the truth if scholars' tools can just be more accurately calibrated.

It is no coincidence, I think, that the rise of "the Q gospel" in biblical studies tracks chronologically and thematically with the flourishing of Gospel Thrillers in US popular culture since the 1960s. Bringing the

---

A Multidimensional Critique, eds. Mark S. Goodacre and Nicholas Perrin (Downers Grove: IVP Academic, 2004), 115–26. On Goodacre's critique of the Q-theory, see *The Case Against Q: Studies in Markan Priority and the Synoptic Problem* (Harrisburg, PA: Trinity Press, 2002). The standard critical edition of the Greek New Testament is *Novum Testamentum Graece* (also known as the Nestle-Aland edition), in its 28th printing as of 2012.

[11] John S. Kloppenborg, "Introduction," in *The Shape of Q: Signal Essays on the Sayings Gospel* (Minneapolis, MN: Fortress Press, 1994), 1–21, at 1; cited by Frans Neirynck, "Q: From Source to Gospel," *Ephemerides Theologicae Lovenienses* 71 (1995): 421–30, at 425. Robinson includes a lengthy chapter on "The History of Q Research" in *The Critical Edition of Q*, xix–lxxi.

two into conversation can reveal some unspoken assumptions of professional biblical studies. Like the imaginary finds of the Gospel
Thrillers, the production of a discrete "gospel" text of Q was inspired
in part by new textual discoveries. The Gospel of Thomas, a complete
version of which was found among the Nag Hammadi codices,
confirmed the existence of "sayings gospels" among early Christian
communities, removing one potential argument against the probability
of a sayings gospel like Q. As we saw in Chapter 4, the Gospel of
Thomas also took up the mantle of lost gospel that might potentially
reveal the real Jesus obscured by the canonical gospel-writers, as
scholars have continued to argue that core sayings ("kernels") of
Thomas predated the canonical gospels. Both Q and Thomas have
become swept up in a desire to recover an original Jesus suited to the
times: a countercultural wisdom teacher amenable to progressive
(Christian or non-Christian) ideals.

Like Gospel Thrillers, however, these academic desires to recover the
lost gospel derive their energy not just from new textual discoveries but
also from a broader cultural atmosphere of conspiratorial thinking.
Imagining a secret, even suppressed, history of the Bible and Christian
origins was not limited during this period to the world of fiction. This
same view of the Bible as either victim or perpetrator of a cover-up
imbues biblical studies, as well. We see this clearly in the production of
Q as a "recovered" gospel which had been "lost." To make sense of
this project of historical recovery necessitates not only reconstructing
the text but also presuming a process by which it was lost. If the Jesus
of Q is more historically authentic, what else are the canonical gospels
but attempts to misrepresent that authentic Jesus? How can we not see
continued resistance to Q as a willful attempt to keep that truth
hidden? Q is more than a *source* for the canonical gospels; it is itself
a *counter-gospel*, an unveiling of a long-concealed truth.

To be sure, it is rare to see academics speak in such stark terms
(although Mack probably comes closest in his iconoclastic popular
writings). But a lost gospel is not lost due to natural causes, like the
Lost Continent of Atlantis; it is lost through human action and
inaction. Acts of recovery in the present counteract acts of destruction
or concealment in the past. Despite Mack's fervor in the 1990s, the
actual impact of the lost gospel Q has been rather muted outside of
academia. Because Q can only ever exist as a reconstruction it remains
ultimately unthreatening to the canonical status quo. Q exists in a

strange quantum state, a lost gospel "recovered" by scholars that will never actually be found. In this way Q resembles the fictional lost gospels of Gospel Thrillers, safely contained within the covers of a novel.

The Vulnerable Bible Meets the Jesus Seminar

I have, throughout this book, attended to the political, theological, and personal stakes elucidated by Gospel Thrillers. To bring these fictions back into conversation with the fact-based world of academic biblical studies is to uncover how these three themes also animate a scholarly guild that has, for centuries, cloaked itself in scientizing rhetoric. It is rare (although not unheard of) for biblical studies scholars to critique each other's work on political, theological, or personal grounds: academic book reviews are not typically filled with accusations of treason, heresy, or immorality. Typically, the guild of biblical studies protects the Bible against undesirable textual and historical revisions through professional tools and protocols, safeguarded through the disciplinary mechanisms of academia: peer review, debate, and (when necessary) rejection. Yet there are times when these themes that are so central to Gospel Thrillers also reveal themselves as deeply embedded in academic anxieties about the vulnerability of a Christian Bible that is constantly undergoing revision.

One recent example of scholarship that highlighted this sense of biblical vulnerability is the Jesus Seminar, which produced its own gospel revision in the last decades of the twentieth century, the period of Q's ascendancy. The Seminar was founded by retired biblical studies scholar Robert Funk as the first major project of his nonprofit Westar Institute in Northern California. Funk established Westar (which remains an active research institute even after Funk's death in 2005) to produce academically rigorous scholarship on Christian origins for a wider public. In his opening remarks at a dinner of thirty invited scholars in 1985 (which still provide the mission statement for Westar), Funk insisted both on the professional "rigor" and "public accountability" of what would come to be called the Jesus Seminar:[12]

---

[12] The "mission statement" citing Funk's remarks is found on their website: www .westarinstitute.org/about. Full disclosure: in 2021, I gave a paid talk to the scholarly Fellows of Westar on topics related to early Jewish–Christian relations.

We are about to embark on a momentous enterprise. We are going to inquire simply, rigorously after the voice of Jesus, after what he really said ... We are not embarking on this venture in a corner. We are going to carry out our work in full public view; we will not only honor the freedom of information, we will insist on the public disclosure of our work and, insofar as it lies within our power, we shall see to it that the public is informed of our judgments.[13]

The Jesus Seminar relied on established criteria of historical Jesus scholarship and the collective judgment of the scholars who gathered twice a year to recover "the voice of Jesus." More than 1500 "sayings of Jesus" (which included variants of similar sayings) were culled from the four canonical gospels as well as any source of Jesus's sayings dating from the first three centuries.[14]

The most famous aspect of the Jesus Seminar is their process of deliberation. Scholars had four colored beads they used to cast their vote: red indicated certainty that Jesus said something; pink, likelihood; gray, unlikelihood; and black, that Jesus certainly did not say something. Votes were tabulated and the results scaled from .00 to 1.00, with everything scoring above .75 considered "red," i.e., an authentic saying of Jesus. In 1994, almost a decade into the Seminar's work, Funk told the magazine *Christianity Today* that the unusual voting method "is designed to attract attention."[15]

This unusual process of voting did follow the presentation of academic papers and arguments by the Fellows and, while it might differ

[13] Robert Funk, "Jesus Seminar Opening Remarks," 1985, archived online at web .archive.org/web/20220119043008/https://www.westarinstitute.org/projects/ jesus-seminar-opening-remarks.

[14] The Jesus Seminar used about a dozen gospels, including different "versions" of gospels and of non-extant "sources" (such as Q), along with Coptic texts with early Greek witnesses (such as the Gospel of Thomas and Gospel of Mary): see Robert Funk, Roy Hoover, and the Jesus Seminar, *The Five Gospels: What Did Jesus Really Say? A Search For the Authentic Words of Jesus* (Santa Rosa, CA: Polebridge, 1993; San Francisco, CA: HarperSanFrancisco, 1997), listed in a chart on p. 128 (although this publication sticks to the four canonical gospels and Thomas).

[15] Mark Kellner, "Away with the Manger: The New Jesus Seminar Discounts the Virgin Birth," *Christianity Today* (November 14, 1994): 92–93, at 92. In the same article Kellner reports that Hollywood director Paul Verhoeven (*Basic Instinct*, *Showgirls*), who had also become a Jesus Seminar Fellow, hoped to produce a film based on the Jesus Seminar's work entitled *Fully Human*. Although such a film has not yet come to pass, it is the kind of flashy detail frequently mentioned in discussions of the Jesus Seminar.

aesthetically from the process of academic peer review, it did not reject any scholarly norms of biblical studies. Funk's point in using such a mechanical process was not to ensure certainty (despite the use of a numerical scale to imply statistical likelihood). Rather he insisted that such a process was less prone to individual idiosyncrasy (or theology) since it took into account the learned opinions of all present. Furthermore, making transparent the tabulated votes and the criteria used in voting created the kind of public accountability that was the Seminar's goal. The first fruits of the Jesus Seminar, *The Five Gospels: What Did Jesus Really Say?* appeared in the same year as Mack's *The Lost Gospel* (indeed, Mack was a Jesus Seminar Fellow), published first by Westar's house press, Polebridge, and then soon after by mainstream trade press HarperCollins. The "five gospels" of the title are the four canonical gospels and Thomas, all of which are retranslated and color-coded (black, gray, pink, red) according to the Seminar's tabulations. In the same 1994 *Christianity Today* article I cited above, Funk boasted: "Quite a few [church] groups are using *The Five Gospels* to raise the literacy of their members." One demonstration of the Jesus Seminar's place in public consciousness is its recurrence (under its own name or fictional pseudonym) in several Gospel Thrillers.[16]

Among the early Fellows were some of the Q-scholars we have already met – Burton Mack, John Kloppenborg, James Robinson – along with other scholars who were writing their own public-facing calls for a broader, often noncanonical view of Christian origins. (It is therefore perhaps unsurprising that the Jesus Seminar concluded that pre- or noncanonical texts, such as Q and the Gospel of Thomas, provided more authentic sayings of Jesus.) Fellow Marcus Borg published his own version of *The Lost Gospel Q* with a small press in 1996, "deliberately designed to make Q available to the reading public." John Dominic Crossan, who had been publishing successful books on noncanonical texts and the historical Jesus since the 1980s, came out in 1994 with *The Essential Jesus: Original Sayings and*

---

[16] Kellner, "Away with the Manger," 92. The Jesus Seminar appears in Winfield Williams, *The Judas Conspiracy* (2010), 67; Witham, *The Negev Project* (1994), 56–57, 77, 112, 213 calls it the Jesus Colloquium; Wood, *The Prophetess* (1996), 180, calls it the Historical Jesus Society; Silva, *The Order* (2020), 192, calls it the Jesus Task Force.

Earliest Images, his own attempt at reconstructing the "original" Jesus's words.[17]

Stephen Prothero, a historian of US religion, places the Jesus of the Seminar in a direct line with other Enlightenment efforts to mold the messiah to modern times. The result evokes shades of Q (fictional and nonfictional): "Their Jesus was a cross between a 1770s *philosophe* and a 1970s hippie," Prothero writes, adding: "More poet than prophet, more iconoclast than icon, he was a Dharma Bum of the Galilean variety." Prothero credits the Jesus Seminar with touching off the "Jesus Wars" of the 1990s, a protracted public struggle between liberal and conservative scholars over the historical Jesus. While the Seminar's Jesus was soundly and predictably rejected by conservative Christians, Prothero notes that "the sharpest attacks came from New Testament scholars."[18]

The variety and quality of critiques has varied, but we can see clearly the centrality of political, theological, and personal concerns. The Fellows were accused of political bias, magically producing a Jesus sympathetic to the Seminar's California liberalism veiled in a cloak of statistical reliability. Theological objections stemmed from the perception that many participants (like Mack) were determined to find a Jesus in opposition to mainstream institutional Christianity.[19]

The splashy and public nature of the Jesus Seminar's work led to personal criticisms, as well. Philip Jenkins, in a work pushing back against the modern obsession with "hidden gospels," writes of Funk and fellow "radical scholars": "Even more promising for journalists, Funk offers a melodramatic and conspiratorial picture of the

[17] Marcus Borg (ed.), *The Lost Gospel Q: The Original Sayings of Jesus* (Berkeley, CA: Ulysses Press, 1996); John Dominic Crossan, *The Essential Jesus: Original Sayings and Earliest Images* (San Francisco, CA: HarperSanFrancisco, 1994).

[18] Stephen Prothero, *American Jesus: How the Son of God Became a National Icon* (New York: Farrar, Straus, and Giroux, 2004), at 38–39, 36. In their introduction, Funk, Hoover, and the Jesus Seminar, *Five Gospels*, 35, already note that Seminar members are frequently subject to "public attack."

[19] On the statistical front, see Sean F. Everton, "What are the Odds? The Jesus Seminar's Quest for Objectivity," *Journal for the Study of the Historical Jesus* 13 (2015): 24–42. For a broad criticism of the methods, politics, and theology of the Jesus Seminar, see Luke Timothy Johnson, *The Real Jesus: The Misguided Quest for the Historical Jesus and the Truth of the Traditional Gospels* (San Francisco, CA: HarperSanFrancisco, 1996). Johnson's main target throughout is the Jesus Seminar, but he includes in his critique other sensationalist (and, on his account, wrong) modern approaches to the historical Jesus.

difficulties faced by radical scholars in their quest for truth." Funk is "populist," "media-savvy," able to draw "on a rich rhetorical arsenal by invoking phrases which carry an image of heroic resistance against oppressive institutions." Jenkins's take on Funk (as on many so-called radical approaches to modern New Testament scholarship) is polemical and defensive. Jenkins is defending the Bible against what he perceives as unfair personal attacks on its historical and theological coherence.[20]

I don't intend to defend the Jesus Seminar against Jenkins, but I do think it's important to step back and understand what the Seminar was doing and why it evoked such repeated outrage. The work of the Jesus Seminar stemmed from the basic understanding of the New Testament that is fundamental to modern biblical studies: that the text and meaning of the Bible is subject to careful scholarly revision, based on agreed-upon source critical methodologies, analysis of textual variants, and consideration of new textual discoveries. The Seminar conducted this work in a different mode, through votes and statistics rather than academic peer review. In so doing, the Seminar made it clear that this standard approach renders the Bible not just revisable but vulnerable. Defense was required because the Bible seemed to be under attack; Jenkins therefore questions the Seminar's biases, its "populism," its "media-savvy."[21]

The narrative deployed by Jenkins and others should be familiar to us by now, focused as it is on the political (the "progressive" politics of the Seminar Fellows), the theological (their disdain for the traditional Christian message of revelation and resurrection), and the personal (their "populism" and hunger for attention). The conspiratorial narrative surrounding the Bible cuts both ways: for Mack, Funk, the Q scholars, and the Jesus Seminar, the Bible is the product of a conspiratorial cover-up engineered centuries ago and continuing into the present. For Jenkins and others, the Bible is the victim of conspiratorial forces out to diminish its historical and theological value for nefarious ends.

---

[20] Philip Jenkins, *Hidden Gospels: How the Search for Jesus Lost Its Way* (New York: Oxford University Press, 2001), 202–03.

[21] Even Johnson, in his book-length broadside against the Jesus Seminar, admitted in his introduction that "the Jesus Seminar has been more provocative stylistically than substantively" (*Real Jesus*, 3).

Other lost gospels published by biblical studies scholars have provoked equally volatile reactions, reproducing in whole or part the same
conspiratorial modes of thinking about biblical revision and vulnerability. Like the Jesus Seminar, these occasionally explosive affairs
bring to surface the heightened theological, political, and personal
fears and desires that come with a vulnerable Bible and which are
rarely articulated in professional biblical studies (but to which Gospel
Thrillers make us more sensitive). Unlike Q, these recent finds are
actual objects, neither fictional nor hypothetical, material fragments
about which one cannot simply agree to disagree. Because they are
real, not contained and framed by fiction, these lost gospels recovered
within the guild of biblical studies can inspire genuine alarm and
fierce acrimony.

Jesus's Wife

In 2012, at a meeting of the International Congress of Coptic Studies in
Rome, Harvard professor Karen King introduced a small Coptic fragment that included the phrase "Jesus said to them: 'my wife ...'" King
had been an early member of the Jesus Seminar and had praised Funk's
call for a rigorous study of the Bible directed to the broader public. In
addition to presenting the fragment to an academic audience (both at a
rather arcane academic conference and in a scholarly article submitted
to the *Harvard Theological Review*) King also made efforts to share it
with the wider public (through prearranged newspaper and magazine
pieces, a Harvard website, and a planned special on the Smithsonian
Channel). King gave the fragment a headline-catching title:
"The Gospel of Jesus's Wife."[22]

King was interested in what this fragment might tell us about debates
concerning gender, marriage, and divinity in the first Christian centuries. She posited that this fragment, like other surviving Coptic gospels,
was a translation of a (lost) Greek original, and so placed it in the

[22] The most detailed account of King's involvement with the fragment is now Ariel
Sabar, *Veritas: A Harvard Professor, a Con Man, and the Gospel of Jesus's Wife*
(New York: Doubleday, 2020). On King's praise of Funk, see Laurie Goodstein,
"R.W. Funk, 79, Creator of Jesus Seminar, Dies," *New York Times*
(September 10, 2005): C14. (Goodstein is also the *New York Times* reporter
who will cover the Gospel of Jesus's Wife story for the paper.)

second century alongside surviving texts asserting Jesus's unmarried state. She found in the fragment evidence for a robust, but forgotten, debate about the nature of discipleship, family, marriage, and sexuality among early Christians. The fragment was *not*, King insisted to the press, evidence that the historical Jesus was married.[23]

King's insistence was (and continues to be) roundly ignored in popular press. In the same *New York Times* article in which King "repeatedly cautioned that this fragment should not be taken as proof that Jesus, the historical person, was actually married," the reporter notes that "the discovery could reignite the debate over whether Jesus was married." *USA Today* ran with the awkward and potentially confusing headline: "A MARRIED JESUS? SOME THOUGHT THAT." *Newsweek* ran a piece by New Testament scholar Bart D. Ehrman on the family life of the historical Jesus, assuming that readers would be more interested in Jesus's actual matrimonial status than second- and third-century debates over it. Comparisons to *The Da Vinci Code* abounded. The Twitter hashtag #JesusWife quickly devolved into jokes about what kind of nagging Jesus might have endured from his spouse.[24]

Scholarly reaction was equally lively. That King was unable to show detailed images of the papyrus fragment at the Rome conference (her laptop had died en route) and was unwilling to share the name of the "collector" who first contacted her about it (she said he insisted on anonymity) raised suspicions. A vocal cohort of archaeologists and papyrologists had for some time been calling for more transparency about provenance before the publication of "newly discovered" ancient manuscripts. There were also questions about the authenticity

---

[23] Karen L. King, "'Jesus Said to Them: "My Wife…"': A New Coptic Papyrus Fragment," *Harvard Theological Review* 107 (2014): 131–59.

[24] Laurie Goodstein, "A Faded Piece of Papyrus Refers to Jesus' Wife," *New York Times* (September 19, 2012): A1 and A21. Daniel Burke, "A Married Jesus? Some Thought That," *USA Today* (September 19, 2012): 2A. Bart D. Ehrman, "The Myths of Jesus," *Newsweek* 160.25 (December 17, 2021): 24–28. Goodstein, Burke, and Ehrman all refer to *The Da Vinci Code*, as did most other commentators and reporters. On the "*Da Vinci Code* context" for the fragment's reception, see Mark Goodacre, "Jesus' Wife, the Media, and *The Da Vinci Code*," in *Fakes, Forgeries, and Fictions: Writing Ancient and Modern Christian Apocrypha*, ed. Tony Burke (Eugene, OR: Cascade Books, 2017), 341–48.

of the fragment: its sloppy handwriting, its curious grammar, and, of course, its explosive content. Was it too good to be true?[25]

A lot of the initial spadework on the technical aspects of the papyrus fragment took place online and was quickly magnified through social media. Andrew Bernhard, who had studied noncanonical gospels at Oxford but left academia, uncovered that the gospel fragment was composed out of pieces of the Gospel of Thomas almost certainly derived from an interlinear (i.e., alternating Coptic and English translation) online version posted by amateur Coptologist Michael Grondin. The fragment even incorporated one of Grondin's transcription errors. Bernhard's findings were published on Mark Goodacre's popular website in October 2012. Later Bernhard was able to access the interlinear translation prepared by the fragment's owner and discovered that this, too, was cobbled together out of Grondin's online Gospel of Thomas translation (even explaining some of the bizarre Coptic grammar in the fragment).[26]

These technical questions quickly became personal and political. When papyrologist Christian Askeland discovered that another fragment offered by the same collector was an unequivocal forgery, written in the same shaky hand as the Gospel of Jesus's Wife, he published a blog post entitled "Jesus had an ugly sister-in-law." Other scholars in the comments section of the blog post objected to the "old tropes that have long alienated and shamed women" and "old-fashioned rhetoric which uses women's appearance in this way." Askeland defended himself in response: "The issue here is that a forger is playing off of hyperfeminist sensibilities . . . I did not bring the gender issue in here, the forger did and King swallowed it whole." (In a later comment Askeland apologized for his "aggressive"

---

[25] Roberta Mazza, a papyrologist at the University of Manchester, posted a piece on her blog: "Papyri, Private Collectors, and Academics: Why the Wife of Jesus and Sappho Matter" (April 17, 2014), online at https://facesandvoices .wordpress.com/2014/04/17/papyri-private-collectors-and-academics-why-the-wife-of-jesus-and-sappho-matter.

[26] For summary see Sabar, *Veritas*, 111–26, 143–49; Caroline T. Schroeder, "Gender and the Academy Online: The Authentic Revelations of the *Gospel of Jesus' Wife*," in *Fakes, Forgeries, and Fictions*, ed. Tony Burke, 304–25, and James McGrath, "Slow Scholarship: Do Bloggers Rush in Where Jesus' Wife Would Fear to Tread?" in *Fakes, Forgeries, and Fictions*, ed. Tony Burke, 326–40.

response and changed the title of the post, removing the word "ugly.")[27]

Eva Mroczek, one of the commenters on Askeland's blog post, wrote a longer response for the online publication *Religion Dispatches*. She argued that Askeland's joke and his defense fused misogynist tropes with attacks on King's scholarly good faith. Mroczek pointed out that King's physical appearance was itself already the subject of unnecessary attention in the *Smithsonian* magazine article about the papyrus fragment: "Female scholars often experience scrutiny and judgment based on their personal appearance, where a male scholar would not be subjected to such attention." The very question of gender – whether broached by King in her scholarship or Mroczek in her blog comment and subsequent essay – is deemed somehow non-objective, part of personal beliefs or political stakes.[28]

The *Smithsonian* article mentioned by Mroczek, published first online on the day of King's presentation in Rome and then updated with subsequent reactions in the November print issue, was written by freelance writer Ariel Sabar. Sabar's investigative work on the Gospel of Jesus's Wife in the years following that first assignment for *Smithsonian* has definitively shaped the public and scholarly narrative of this gospel "discovery." While academic sleuths had pieced together how the fragment was probably forged, it was Sabar who tracked down Walter Fritz, the German-American owner of the papyrus, and uncovered Fritz's serial deceptions and probable forgery of the fragment. First in a blockbuster essay for *The Atlantic* in 2016 and then in

---

[27] Christian Askeland, "Jesus Had a Sister-in-Law," *Evangelical Text Criticism* (April 24, 2014) (note the URL – https://evangelicaltextualcriticism.blogspot .com/2014/04/jesus-had-ugly-sister-in-law.html – retains the original title).

[28] Eva Mroczek, "'Gospel of Jesus' Wife' Less Durable than Sexism Surrounding It," *Religion Dispatches* (May 6, 2014), online at https://religiondispatches.org/ gospel-of-jesus-wife-less-durable-than-sexism-surrounding-it. *Smithsonian* published an online article coinciding with King's presentation in Rome and then an updated version in the next print issue incorporating reactions to her presentation: Ariel Sabar, "The Inside Story of a Controversial New Text About Jesus," *Smithsonian* (September 18, 2012), online at www.smithsonianmag .com/history/the-inside-story-of-a-controversial-new-text-about-jesus-41078791) and "The Gospel According to King," *Smithsonian* (November 2012), online at www.smithsonianmag.com/history/update-the-reaction-to-karen-kings-gospel-discovery-84250942. The description of King's hair and clothes appears in both versions, although the location is changed (from Cambridge to Rome).

his 2020 book, *Veritas: A Harvard, Professor, a Con Man, and the Gospel of Jesus's Wife,* Sabar wove together a compelling story that rehearses many of the tropes of the Gospel Thrillers.[29]

Sabar is the protagonist of the story, picking apart clues, following shadowy leads, and traveling around the world to unravel the tangle of secrets and lies. Sabar occupies the role that Fredric Jameson, in his study of conspiracy theory narratives, called "the social detective," the character who unwittingly stumbles upon some intricate, hidden plot. (The jacket copy of the paperback edition calls *Veritas* "an exhilarating, globe-straddling detective story.") Sabar was a freelance writer contacted by a *Smithsonian* editor as the magazine's sister network prepared its documentary. He thus enters the story as an outsider, a *naif* drawn into the orbit of biblical studies, revisionist histories, and sinister forgeries. Sabar was the only journalist in the room at the conference in Rome, an outside observer of the "shocking discovery" that King unleashed: "What had begun at an obscure scholarly conference," he writes, "had taken on the aspect of a Hollywood thriller." Sabar filed his story and "moved on to new assignments."[30]

While working on another story for *Smithsonian* in 2015, Sabar found himself in Migdal, "the presumed site of Magdala, the ancient fishing city said to be Mary Magdalene's home." Struck by a conversation with a Catholic priest in Migdal about truth and faith, Sabar became inspired to dig back into the story:

When faith went searching for fact, it wandered into a valley of illusion and temptation. Somewhere still in that valley was a figure who had haunted me since my 2012 stories on the Gospel of Jesus's Wife: the invisible stranger who set the entire spectacle in motion ... The time had come to find and speak his name.[31]

The allure of a truth, hidden in shadows, proved irresistible for the investigator. The long article in *The Atlantic* appeared the next year and the book, greatly expanding the research in the article, in 2020.

---

[29] Ariel Sabar, "The Unbelievable Tale of Jesus' Wife," *The Atlantic* (July/August 2016): 64–78 and *Veritas.*

[30] Sabar, *Veritas*, 81, 97, 153.

[31] Sabar, *Veritas*, 155. The article Sabar was researching in Israel was a *Smithsonian* cover story: "Unearthing the World of Jesus," *Smithsonian* (January/February 2016), online at www.smithsonianmag.com/history/unearthing-world-jesus-180957515.

Sabar throughout is tireless at finding and interpreting clues. That the forger used the word *abdicate* from the interlinear online Gospel of Thomas inspires a flash of insight: "If the forger was someone who relished wordplay … he had perhaps found in Grondin's translation the perfect double entendre. The 'king' whose abdication he sought might well have been Karen King." Fritz's first email to King about the papyri "was 114 years, to the day, after German scholars announced their discovery of the Gospel of Mary." The number 114 "is instantly recognizable to experts on noncanonical gospels" as the number of sayings in the Gospel of Thomas and the number of the final saying in which Jesus promises to "make Mary male": "The email's timing, if deliberate, was a stroke of genius by a man who'd already shown himself a master of minimalism." Such asides draw on the familiar interpretive strategies of the conspiracy narrative, in which every piece of evidence holds the potential to unlock the truth, needing only a persistent and keen eye.[32]

While the *Atlantic* article focused primarily on the quest to find the fragment's owner and putative forger, *Veritas* expands its scope. To arrive at the truth beneath the deceptions, Sabar must reconstruct the opaque motives of both main players of this story: the "Harvard professor" and the "con man" of the book's title. Sabar intersperses his investigation into the fragment, its forgery, and its aftermath with deep dives into Fritz's and King's biographies: their childhoods, their personal lives, their professional histories, their presumed psychological states. What is it that drives them – Fritz to forge the gospel and King to believe in it? Political, theological, and personal motivations quickly emerge.

Even before Fritz enters the narrative Sabar contemplates theological motives: "to goose the Church by yoking Jesus to an actual wife" with evidence that "gored Catholic tradition." In surveying popular response, he notes that some members of the public "sniffed a political [i.e., feminist] agenda." After Sabar finds Fritz other motives present themselves: "greed" or perhaps "a yearning to settle scores" (Sabar briefly speculates that Fritz's former Egyptology professor in Berlin might have been the original target). When Fritz reveals to Sabar that as a child he was raped by a priest, Sabar wonders if vengeance against a brutal church "went to the heart of motivation." Sabar uncovers that

---

[32] Sabar, *Veritas*, 150, 252.

Fritz and his wife had, at one point, operated multiple pornographic sites and that their theories on sexuality verged into New Age spiritual waters possibly influenced by *The Da Vinci Code*: Was the fragment an attempt to spread their own sexual theology?[33]

At one point Sabar runs his various forgery theories past Fritz:

But Fritz spurned all of my theories of motivation. He told me of the alleged rape … because he feared the Vatican might otherwise leak word of it to discredit the fragment. To admit motive, of course, was to admit forgery, and Fritz had no plans to confess "to some story of a brilliant genius (me) who had forged a manuscript in order to expose the bias and prejudice in the Catholic Church, and the utter ignorance of scholars."[34]

Eventually Sabar finds Fritz's motivation in a psyche shaped by childhood traumas and adult failures, inflected by sex and gender:

The Gospel of Jesus's Wife, I came to believe, had begun as a joke and ended as an exorcism. It was a settling of scores with all of the male authority figures who had robbed Fritz of his potential … If the provenance story was a reckoning with the men in his life, the papyrus itself was an homage to a woman … Fritz's mother.

Sabar concludes that the con man's motives are driven more by personal demons than by "greed" or professional jealousy (although these too are explained by Fritz's psychology).[35]

When Sabar turns to the Harvard professor, however, political considerations and professional ambition take center stage. Sabar wants to figure out why, after putting off Fritz's initial email inquiries for close to a year, King suddenly embraced the gospel fragment and went to such lengths to promote it. Sabar digs back into King's childhood, her education, and her professional trajectory to uncover a scholar whose "ideological commitments were choreographing her practice of history … She cloaked what were primarily ethical positions in the guise of empirical history." Those commitments, Sabar explains, are primarily feminist and revisionist, seeking to replace the age-old "master story" of Christian origins with a new, more inclusive vision.[36]

Sabar also pinpoints King's professional ambition as part of her motive for pushing the Gospel of Jesus's Wife for years in the face of

---

[33] Sabar, *Veritas*, 24, 97, 98, 187, 216–18, 233.   [34] Sabar, *Veritas*, 253.
[35] Sabar, *Veritas*, 256–57.   [36] Sabar, *Veritas*, 2, 324–25.

increasing scrutiny. Readers are told more than once that she is a
formidable scholar who works hard to make her voice heard. Sabar
recounts stories from her final days with the Jesus Seminar, when she
pressed to have a late text (possibly the first Christian text by a woman)
included in a *New New Testament* collection. Sabar also dwells (and
has continued to dwell in follow-up stories) on King's attempts to
control the messaging in the issue of the *Harvard Theological Review*
her article was scheduled to appear in.[37]

Most seriously, Sabar links the timing of King's embrace of Fritz's
fragment to threats to the standing of Harvard Divinity School within
Harvard University. Harvard's president, Drew Gilpin Faust, had
convened an outside panel to evaluate the effectiveness of religious
studies education across the university (which did not then and still
does not have a Department of Religious Studies in the Faculty of Arts
and Sciences). In compiling a timeline of events surrounding the Gospel
of Jesus's Wife, Sabar realized that two days after Faust announced the
outside review panel to the Divinity School faculty, King sent her first
encouraging email to Fritz expressing interest in publishing his fragment: "It felt as though a blindfold were lifted," Sabar writes. Another
piece of a shadowy puzzle falling into place.[38]

The period of the outside panel's review coincided with King's work
on the fragment and its report was essentially shelved by Faust in
September amid headlines touting the Harvard professor's explosive
discovery about Jesus's wife. "Did a forgery help save Harvard
Divinity School?" Sabar asks. No one involved in these decisions can
confirm Sabar's suspicions; Faust has since retired and King stopped
communicating with Sabar while he was writing *Veritas*. Nonetheless
Sabar believes he has tracked down King's motivation: "The Gospel of
Jesus's Wife, I came to believe, was King's boldest intervention, a
daring play for survival in a time of uncertainty."[39]

Although *Veritas* delves equally into its two main characters, the con
man and the Harvard professor, it is fair to say King bears the brunt of
Sabar's criticism for failing in her duty as "a scholar, a professional
truth seeker." If the con man twists the truth, after all, that's only to be
expected: "A con man depends for his livelihood on the propensity of

[37] Sabar, *Veritas*, 284–308, 319–21 and Ariel Sabar, "A Scholarly Screw-Up of
Biblical Proportions," *Chronicle of Higher Education* (June 29, 2021), online
at www.chronicle.com/article/a-scholarly-screw-up-of-biblical-proportions.
[38] Sabar, *Veritas*, 315.   [39] Sabar, *Veritas*, 318.

people to see what they want to see." When the *Atlantic* article appeared, Sabar writes in *Veritas*, "many readers pinned the blame squarely on the Harvard scholar at its center." At the end of his own longer deliberations, between the covers of his creative nonfiction, Sabar seems to agree with his "many readers."[40]

By now the narrative shape of Sabar's story and its cast of characters is familiar enough: a forged papyrus, shadowy motives, deep secrets, a race around the world for the truth. (To be sure, there are no Nazis or Vatican assassins, although Sabar does manage to work in a lot of Cold War intrigue with chapters set in East Berlin in the 1980s; moreover, Fritz's accusations against his childhood priest rise all the way to the Vatican.) I confess little interest in adjudicating the merits of Sabar's narrative; I have quibbles with his understanding of academic institutional politics, the nature of professional history-writing, and the role of gender in the academy. I am more interested in his insistence on King's responsibility for the five-year roller coaster of the Gospel of Jesus's Wife. Why does King make more sense to him as a historian who has betrayed her loyalty to "the truth" (the *Veritas* of his title, which is also Harvard's motto) rather than a dupe conned by a slick liar?

When the Gospel Thriller narrative enters the real world, the role of biblical studies scholars in producing a Bible vulnerable to revisions becomes a matter of acute anxiety. To let King pass as a victim, a mark unable to see past the schemes and lies of a semicompetent con man, is to concede that the Bible is defenseless against bad actors. It might be better to paint the scholar as culpable rather than to view the Bible as helpless. If only more scholars were dedicated to truth, rather than swayed by personal, theological, and professional motives, the Bible would not be at dire risk from forgery and conspiracy.

Sabar is not mounting a defense of the Bible, like Jenkins in his fulminations against the Jesus Seminar, but by zeroing in on King as the culprit in the story he echoes Jenkins's and others' anxieties about scholars taking advantage of biblical vulnerability to their own ends. Sabar's deep dive into the Gospel of Jesus's Wife brought this narrative of the supposedly irresponsible scholar and the new discovery to a popular audience; it was not the first time, however, that professional tangles over Christian origins spilled into the public square.

[40] Sabar, *Veritas*, 260, 323.

The Gospel of Judas

Conservative writer Charlotte Allen, who had earlier profiled Burton
Mack and his version of Q, began the first of two disdainful essays on
the Gospel of Jesus's Wife in *The Weekly Standard* by invoking
another recent ancient gospel discovery that made headlines:

> Jesus had a wife! It's the Gospel of Judas all over again. An exotic Gnostic
> document claimed to date from the third century, written in Coptic, contain-
> ing something startling about Jesus, and shrouded in secrecy until its sudden
> and dramatic unveiling. Next comes the *derecho* of media publicity, the
> carefully timed television documentary, the speculation that this means the
> end of Christianity as we know it, and then, with the finality of a soufflé
> collapsing as the oven door opens, the revelation that the document isn't, or
> may well not be, exactly what its promoters say it is.

Allen goes on to summarize the various scholarly debates and rancor
among scholars of Gnosticism attendant upon the spectacular
unveiling of the Gospel of Judas in 2006, debates (she points out) that
also involved Karen King.[41]

The modern story of the Gospel of Judas shows us that biblical
anxiety is not just generated by the fear of forgery. The antiquity of
the Gospel of Judas has never really been in question. No tenacious
journalist has had to track down its forger and try to divine his or her
murky motives. It is authentically ancient, written (like other gnostic
texts) in Coptic and likely a translation from a Greek original. After
initial controversy surrounding the provenance of the text, debate
around the Gospel of Judas centered around translation and interpretation. What new light might this ancient text, focused on the betrayer
of Christ, tell us about Christian origins? What motives did scholars
have to favor one interpretation over another? How could this text be
made to fit in – or perhaps challenge – ideas about the biblical past?

The Gospel of Judas was part of a Christian Coptic codex that had
been smuggled out of Egypt, probably in the twentieth century, and
supposedly languished for nearly two decades in a safety deposit box in

---

[41] Charlotte Allen, "Jesus' Ex-Wife," *The Weekly Standard* (October 8, 2012):
30–32. Allen's follow-up was "The Wife of Jesus Tale," *The Weekly Standard*
(May 5, 2014): 30–33. Karen King coauthored a translation and commentary
on the Gospel of Judas with Elaine Pagels: *Reading Judas: The Gospel of Judas
and the Shaping of Christianity* (New York: Penguin, 2007).

Hicksville, New York (just outside New York City on Long Island). Its Egyptian owner had tried to sell it in the 1980s in Europe and the United States. It was purchased, now in terrible disrepair, by an antiquities dealer from Switzerland who attempted to sell it to US academic institutions but eventually sold it to a charitable foundation operated by her attorney. In Switzerland the codex was reconstructed, transcribed, and translated.

A writer and documentary producer for the National Geographic Society named Herbert Krosney heard rumors of a Gospel of Judas, held by a Swiss collector, and managed to form a temporary partnership between the owners of the codex, the scholars working to reconstruct it, and National Geographic. In return for material support and funding, National Geographic retained sole rights of publication. While the existence of the Gospel of Judas was announced in scholarly circles in 2004 (at another meeting of the International Coptic Congress, this time in Paris) it was National Geographic's carefully coordinated release of a documentary film (complete with dramatic reenactments of the contents of the gospel and its modern recovery), an accompanying book by Krosney, and the publication of an English translation and commentary that made headlines, all less than two weeks before Easter in 2006. The headline in the *New York Times* was modest ("IN ANCIENT DOCUMENT, JUDAS, MINUS THE BETRAYAL"), but it still made the front page.[42]

The first sustained account of the Gospel of Judas was Krosney's *The Lost Gospel* (the same title used by Mack and Borg for their 1990s translations of Q). The protagonists of this "bizarre cloak-and-dagger journey" are the various figures who come into contact with the gospel: the "illiterate" locals who found the codex; the entrepreneurial Egyptian antiquities dealer who spent decades trying to sell it for

---

[42] The documentary, *The Gospel of Judas*, aired on April 9, 2006; the same week saw the publication of Herbert Krosney, *The Lost Gospel: The Quest for the Gospel of Judas Iscariot* (Washington, DC: National Geographic, 2006), Rodolphe Kasser, Marvin Meyer, and Gregor Wurst (eds.), *The Gospel of Judas from Codex Tchacos* (Washington, DC: National Geographic, 2006), John Noble Wilford and Laurie Goodstein, "In Ancient Document, Judas, Minus the Betrayal," *New York Times* (April 7, 2006): A1, plus a sidebar on the historical significance of the Gospel of Judas (Laurie Goodstein, "Document Is Genuine, But Is It True?" *New York Times* [April 7, 2006]: A20), and an op-ed by Elaine Pagels the following day ("The Gospel Truth," *New York Times* [April 8, 2006]: A13).

millions; the cosmopolitan European collectors and scholars who eventually "rescued" and recovered the text; and the US academics and journalists who came last on the scene to secure the gospel's future. Arrayed against these characters working to save the gospel are unscrupulous dealers, huckster middlemen, and even a libelous blogger, all vying for control over "one of the greatest discoveries in Judeo-Christian archaeology."[43]

Krosney begins with the typical kind of "find" narrative associated with the Dead Sea Scrolls and Nag Hammadi library: in the 1970s *fellahin* in search of antiquities to supplement their income accidentally "stumbled" upon a tomb (which Krosney unsuccessfully tries to locate years later) with the codex inside. They passed it on to a savvy local middleman who then sold it to a prosperous Coptic antiquities dealer in Cairo (given the pseudonym "Hanna Asabil"). Before Hanna could sell the codex it was stolen (along with other Egyptian antiquities) and smuggled out of Egypt, ending up in the hands of a fabulously wealthy Greek antiquities dealer in Geneva.

Soon after recovering the codex Hanna tried to set up a sale in Europe to US academics; they assembled in Geneva with Hanna's partner and translator, but when Hanna demanded $3 million the deal fell through. (I recounted this story, with its clandestine bathroom transcription, in Chapter 2.) Hanna then brought it to the United States to try to sell it ("after all, American is where millions have made their fortunes"). Unsuccessful in his venture, he left it locked in the safety deposit box in Hicksville. The year was 1984. The codex would remain in that bank box for sixteen years, moldering away.[44]

Around 2000, art dealer Frieda Tchacos Nussberger set out to track down the codex following a mysterious phone call from a nameless Greek selling a few ancient manuscript pages. She had known Hanna for decades, and even tried at one point in the 1980s to find him a buyer for the codex. Now she brought him to the United States and bought the codex from him herself. (Eventually the manuscript would be called Codex Tchacos after her family.) She tried unsuccessfully to sell it to Yale University and entered into a disastrous arrangement with an untrustworthy antiquities dealer in Ohio. When that deal fell through, she handed over the codex to her own attorney, Mario Roberty. Roberty operated a charitable foundation called Maecenas

[43] Krosney, *Lost Gospel*, 4.   [44] Krosney, *Lost Gospel*, 143.

dedicated to preserving antiquities and restoring them to their places of origin. Together they reached out to European scholars Rodolphe Kasser, Florence Dabre, and Gregor Wurst who painstakingly pieced together and restored as much of the damaged manuscript as possible. Kasser modestly announced the find at the 2004 conference; National Geographic came in soon after to fund testing, promotion, and publication of the text.[45]

Krosney intersperses this dramatic narrative with splashes of local color (from the Egyptian countryside to a Geneva villa to a Long Island bank), quick dips into early Christian history, a tour of the disreputable modern antiquities market, and lively prose snapshots of the diverse cast of characters. The Gospel of Judas is imperiled at every turn by unscrupulous dealers and the destructive forces of time, nature, and careless handling. Knowledge brokers – scholars, dealers, "natives" – play predictable roles. Nussberger, while lamenting her "mistakes," becomes the central figure of the drama as the gospel's savior. She tells Krosney:

I had the opportunity to take them [i.e., the papyrus sheets] away from people who didn't know what they were and how to handle them. I wanted to protect them and to give them to people who could read them and conserve them. I wanted to save them. It came slowly to me that there was something that was pushing me ... I was guided by Providence.[46]

How much of Krosney's story is true remains unverifiable, apart from independently attested attempts to sell the codex in the 1980s, up until the point in 2000 when Nussberger emerges as the codex's owner and then partners with her attorney and his foundation (even then questions remain). From that point on there are legal documents, outside witnesses, and public records. Before that, Krosney must rely on second- and third-hand reports from highly interested parties. That the *fellahin* found the codex and sold it on to the dealer in Cairo in the 1970s would explain why the dealer never registered it with the

---

[45] Krosney is light on the financial details (*Lost Gospel*, 228: Roberty "persuaded" Nussberger "to turn the manuscripts over to the foundation"); according to the *Los Angeles Times*, Nussberger "sold [the codex] to Roberty for $1.5 million" and National Geographic paid the Maecenas Foundation $1 million and future royalties for exclusive publishing rights: Jason Felch and Ralph Frammolino, "Judas Gospel Figure Has Tainted Past," *Los Angeles Times* (April 13, 2006): A23.

[46] Krosney, *Lost Gospel*, 175.

Egyptian Department of Antiquities, as required by a 1983 law. That it was stolen by a mysterious redhead, along with other Egyptian antiquities, explains how it left Egypt in the 1980s.[47]

Nussberger's role in the story is key to Krosney's narrative. She authenticates both the find and its expatriation to Europe. Egyptian by birth, Greek by nationality, educated in Paris, based in Switzerland, fluent in multiple languages, she seems to perfect person to "protect" the gospel which means, as it had since the days of the Bible Hunters, extracting it from the land of "illiterate *fellahin*" to the ultramodern laboratories of European scholarship.[48]

Only after Krosney's book and the National Geographic documentary spotlighting Nussberger's central role in saving Judas did some unsavory details begin to emerge. She had been recently charged by the Italian government with "trafficking in looted art." Yale officials made clear that their unwillingness to buy the codex in 2000 was due to its unverified provenance; the president of the Archaeological Institute of American denounced the codex as looted. In a scathing editorial, the *Los Angeles Times* revealed how Nussberger had financially benefited from both the nonprofit foundation and the National Geographic deal. The editorial drew a blunt parallel between greed in the Bible and in the art world: "Thirty pieces of silver then, or $1.5 million now: It's still about money."[49]

The truth of the modern history of the Gospel of Judas is factually unknowable (at least based on current evidence). What we have instead are a series of interchangeable stories all of which fit modern expectations of the lost gospel. Nussberger's narrative malleability in the tale, as either European savior or Levantine trickster, fits neatly within the tropes and stereotypes of the Gospel Thriller, along with the

---

[47] Brent Nongbri, *God's Library: The Archaeology of the Earliest Christian Manuscripts* (New Haven, CT: Yale University Press, 2018), 96: "Krosney's account, generated almost thirty years after the alleged date of the discovery, is wholly unreliable."

[48] As of June 2023, according to the Leuven Database of Ancient Books, Codex Tchacos remains on "temporary loan" to the Bodmer Fondation in Switzerland and is still listed as part the "Private Collection, Nussberger-Tchacos," online at www.trismegistos.org/text/108481.

[49] "Judas' Deal, 2000 years later," *Los Angeles Times* (April 13, 2006): B12. On his blog, Brent Nongbri has also posted evidence that Nussberger was selling pages from this cache of papyri long before she supposedly bought the codex from Hanna, online at https://brentnongbri.com/2021/03/18/further-thoughts-on-the-tchacos-ferrini-exodus.

find narrative, the exotic locales, and the cast of characters. When speculation on the find petered out, controversy turned from the circumstances of the codex to its contents: the new story about Jesus and his betrayer. The drama shifted from the world of looters, dealers, and smugglers to the more rarefied, but no less dramatic, domain of academics.

At the center of this scholarly drama was, as we might expect, the figure of Judas. The first study and translation of the text presented a radically different image of Judas: a sympathetic figure, far from the treacherous and diabolical villain of the canonical gospels. This inter-pretation was based primarily on the translation executed by Rodolphe Kassser and Gregor Wurst (who had worked to reconstruct the text) along with Marvin Meyer, a US specialist in gnostic Christianity brought in by the National Geographic team. Their initial translation presented Judas in an entirely new light: "The Judas Iscariot of the Gospel of Judas is the betrayer of Jesus, but he is simultaneously the hero of the gospel." This Judas is the only one of the apostles to recognize Jesus's true divine nature and when he does turn in Jesus to be crucified it is with Jesus's full knowledge and approval. Jesus praises Judas as a divine "spirit" and promises him a place in the "holy generation."[50]

Much of the theology of the Gospel of Judas resonated with particu-lar gnostic myths about the true spiritual realm of the divine which is separate from the plodding, material world in which humans find themselves. Jesus, as an emissary of true divinity, brings knowledge (*gnosis*) of that pure spiritual realm to those humans able to receive such knowledge (the "holy generation"). This dualistic theology was, by this time, familiar to readers of the Nag Hammadi library and, like the early studies of those texts I discussed in Chapter 4, initial inter-pretations of the Gospel of Judas also emphasized its greater theo-logical appeal to modern audiences.[51]

Although the Gospel of Judas dated from (at the earliest) the second or third century, it was nonetheless taken by many scholars to repre-sent a theological "road not taken," an alternative to the orthodox "master story" of the canonical gospels. The text didn't shed new light

[50] See Kasser et al., *Gospel of Judas*, 3–7.
[51] For the most up-to-date translation and analysis, see David Brakke, *The Gospel of Judas: A New Translation with Introduction and Commentary*, Anchor Yale Bible 45 (New Haven, CT: Yale University Press, 2022).

on the "real" Judas; but it might give insight into the diversity of views among Christians before orthodoxy took hold. In this case, the Judas who understood Jesus, who worked with him and not against him, who was promised a place in the highest heavens, might counteract centuries of anti-Jewish rhetoric that attached to the greedy traitor Judas (whose name, in many ancient and modern languages, means *Jew*). The "traditional depiction of Jesus," Meyer told the *Los Angeles Times*, "has fed the flames of anti-Semitism," suggesting that a revised Judas could help tamp those flames.[52]

Other biblical studies experts who had been specializing in theological "roads not taken" explored the implications of this new Judas, freed and freeing from the orthodox baggage of historical orthodoxy. Karen King and Elaine Pagels coauthored a volume, *Reading Judas*, in which they highlighted the gnostic celebration of the spiritual over the mundane as well as the Gospel's seeming rejection of an embrace of violent martyrdom patterned on the death of Jesus. In the *New York Review of Books*, Yale biblical studies scholar Harold Attridge (who, as he points out in a footnote, turned down the opportunity to buy Codex Tchacos at two different universities) notes that beneath King's and Pagels's historical analysis of the Gospel of Judas "lies a fairly clear theological position": "They clearly want to protest the kind of religiosity that glorifies martyrdom, a glorification they see as contrary to efforts to improve the human condition."[53]

Even as the new Judas ushered in these new takes on Christian origins, some scholars began pushing back. Multiple panels and papers at the annual meeting of the Society of Biblical Literature (SBL) in November 2007 dealt with this new discovery. (Given the lead time involved in submitting papers to the SBL, we wouldn't expect any sustained treatment at the meeting in 2006.) To get a sense of the excitement generated by the Gospel of Judas from its unveiling in

---

[52] Thomas H. Maugh II, "Judas Is No Traitor in Long-Lost Gospel," *Los Angeles Times* (April 7, 2006): A1 and A26. The Gospel of Judas has also inspired more than one Gospel Thriller. I discussed Winfield Williams, *The Judas Conspiracy* and Blake, *The Dead Sea Deception* (2011) in Chapter 4, and Stasi's rather fantastical *Book of Judas* (2017) in Chapter 5.

[53] King and Pagels, *Reading Judas*; Harold Attridge, "The Case for Judas, Continued," *New York Review of Books* 55.7 (May 1, 2008), online at www .nybooks.com/articles/2008/05/01/the-case-for-judas-continued. The universities that turned down the codex were Southern Methodist University in the 1980s and Yale University in the 2000s.

spring 2006 to this scholarly conference in fall 2007, we need only look at one special evening session featuring the authors and coauthors of the ten books on the Gospel of Judas that had been published during that brief time.[54]

Among these authors were those who were invested in the "new Judas": Meyer, Pagels, King, Ehrman (who had written his own book on Judas and the gospel and was also involved in the National Geographic rollout). James Robinson was present; angry at his former student, Meyer, for participating in a "secret" translation project, Robinson had published an unhappy volume downplaying the significance of the Gospel of Judas, decrying the sensationalist manner in which it was publicized, and detailing his own experience trying to make the codex public in the 1980s. Other participants had written books scaling back the sensational claims made for the gospel, arguing that it had very little to tell us about Christian origins since it was a later, heretical text.[55]

There were also scholars there to downplay or even argue against the National Geographic volume's reading of Judas as a "hero" in the gospel. Prominent among them was April DeConick, a specialist in Gnosticism at Rice University, whose book *The Thirteenth Apostle: What the Gospel of Judas Really Says* was scheduled to come out the following month. DeConick, with some other experts, objected to the heroic Judas that Meyer and others had produced in their translation: choosing to translate *daimon* as "spirit" instead of "demon"; interpreting Jesus's confiding in Judas as camaraderie rather than condemnation; and misinterpreting the gnostic context that actually made Judas into the worst of the worst.

---

[54] There was one panel at the 2006 SBL meeting, clearly arranged before the April 2006 media fanfare. By contrast there were two dedicated panels, the book event, and several discrete papers in other sessions at the 2007 meeting.

[55] Bart Ehrman, *The Lost Gospel of Judas Iscariot: A New Look at Betrayer and Betrayed* (Oxford: Oxford University Press, 2006); James M. Robinson, *The Secrets of Judas: The Story of the Misunderstood Disciple and His Lost Gospel* (San Francisco, CA: Harper, 2006). Among those trying to put distance between Judas and Christian orthodoxy: N.T. Wright, *Judas and the Gospel of Jesus: Have We Missed the Truth about Christianity?* (Grand Rapids, MI: Baker Books, 2006); Stanley E. Porter and Gordon L. Heath, *The Lost Gospel of Judas: Separating Fact from Fiction* (Grand Rapids, MI: Eerdmans, 2007). On this schism between Robinson and Meyer, see Louis Sahagun, "Was It Virtue or Betrayal?" *Los Angeles Times* (January 6, 2007): A1.

About two weeks after the SBL meeting, DeConick took her objections to the pages of the *New York Times* in a cutting op-ed. She accused the National Geographic-sponsored team of sloppiness in their transcription and translation practices, resulting in a pro-Judas interpretation that did violence to the meaning of the text. DeConick wonders: "How could these serious mistakes have been made? Were they genuine errors or was there something more deliberate going on? This is the question of the hour and I do not have satisfactory answers." DeConick does offer some suggestions on the genesis of these "serious mistakes": a highly damaged manuscript; a secretive process that could easily lead to error and went against best professional practices; and, perhaps most damning of all, unacceptable theological and political bias, which has also captivated her colleagues and the public at large:

I have wondered why so many scholars and writers have been inspired by the National Geographic version of the Gospel of Judas. I think it may stem from an understandable desire to reform the relationship between Jews and Christians ... Although we should work toward a reconciliation of this ancient schism, manufacturing a hero Judas is not the answer.

DeConick finds such motives "understandable" but nonetheless improper. Similar to the accusations Sabar will lodge against King a decade later, DeConick proposes that her colleagues are putting ideology before history.[56]

Unsurprisingly the scholars involved in the National Geographic project objected to DeConick's characterization of their work. The following week the *New York Times* published letters in response. Terry Garcia, the National Geographic executive overseeing the project, reasserted the scholarly expertise of those who worked on the codex and the openness of National Geographic to share images and text freely. After noting that DeConick's specific transcriptional and translational points were discussed in notes to the text, Marvin Meyer remarked:

Professor DeConick's additional insinuations of ulterior motives by her fellow scholars in the establishment of the Coptic text and the development of an appropriate translation are extremely disappointing and disturbing.

[56] April DeConick, "Gospel Truth," *New York Times* (December 1, 2007): A15.

She knows how we struggled carefully and honestly with this difficult text preserved in fragments.[57]

From Meyer's perspective, DeConick has taken matters of scholarly disagreement and turned them into personal "insinuations" of "ulterior motives." By framing DeConick's op-ed in this way, Meyer effectively turns her own objections into something suspicious and overwrought. She "knows" how much they "struggled," so why would she impute sinister motives to them?

It is unusual to see a scholarly debate over a fourth-century Coptic text take up so much real estate in the *New York Times* opinion pages. Obviously the enormous amount of press the Gospel of Judas received the previous spring made it newsworthy enough; DeConick's forthcoming book on a hot topic likewise provided sufficient justification for publishing her op-ed and the two responses. But deeper anxieties in the field of biblical studies, usually kept at bay, were also coming to the surface, anxieties surrounding the vulnerability of the Christian Bible and its story of Christian origins. The Bible is not only vulnerable to fakes and forgeries, but to the more subtle attempts by scholars to use new discoveries to "manufacture" a more desirable past.

The hubbub over the Gospel of Judas subsided fairly quickly. The scholars involved moved on to other projects, or have since passed away, and the Gospel itself has taken its place alongside other ancient gnostic texts that provide alternative views of Christ, the apostles, and cosmic salvation. Its sensational debut and subsequent fracas have left their traces, like faint footprints in the public discourse of lost gospels, to be raised again when the Gospel of Jesus's Wife began making a splash years later. Behind both of these anxious narratives of Christian origins under threat lies an older scandal, still echoing through academic corridors and even creating an unexpected bridge between the realm of academic thrillers and their fictional counterparts.

The Secret Gospel of Mark

Almost a year after National Geographic's release of the Gospel of Judas made worldwide headlines, another *New York Times* headline resurrected a much older controversy: "WAS IT A HOAX? DEBATE ON

---

[57] Marvin Meyer, "The Gospel of Judas: A Word from the Translators," *New York Times* (December 7, 2007): A30.

A 'SECRET MARK' GOSPEL RESUMES." The occasion for this piece by
Peter Steinfels, the *New York Times's* "Beliefs" columnist, was the
publication of two books accusing Morton Smith, a historian of
ancient religions who had died in 1991, of having forged a controversial ancient gospel fragment decades earlier. The saga of the Secret
Gospel of Mark has haunted biblical studies, especially in the United
States, for more than half a century.[58]

Smith's "secret" gospel first made headlines in the *New York Times*
on December 30, 1960, during the annual meeting of the SBL in New
York: "A NEW GOSPEL ASCRIBED TO MARK: COPY OF GREEK
LETTER SAYS SAINT KEPT 'MYSTERIES' OUT." Although there was
no institutional public relations machine at work, as there would be for
the Gospel of Judas and the Gospel of Jesus's Wife, Smith had taken it
upon himself to invite a handful of news outlets to hear his talk; among
them the *New York Times* found his announcement newsworthy. The
world would have to wait more than a decade for the book-length
studies that would propel this "Secret Gospel of Mark" into a seemingly endless tug-of-war over Christian origins, forgery, conspiracy,
and acrimony.[59]

The text first reported in 1960, published in 1973, and still debated
to this day was copied, probably in the eighteenth century, into the
endpapers of a seventeenth-century book kept in a library in a
Jerusalem monastery where Smith spent time as a visiting scholar in
1958. It purported to be part of a letter written by Clement of
Alexandria, an intellectual Christian living in Egypt toward the end

---

[58] Peter Steinfels, "Was It a Hoax? Debate on 'Secret Mark' Gospel Resumes,"
     New York Times (March 31, 2007): A12. The two books were Stephen Carlson,
     The Gospel Hoax: Morton Smith's Invention of Secret Mark (Waco, TX: Baylor
     University Press, 2005) and Peter Jeffery, *The Secret Gospel of Mark Unveiled:
     Imagined Rituals of Sex, Death, and Madness in a Biblical Forgery* (New Haven,
     CT: Yale University Press, 2007).

[59] Sanka Knox, "A New Gospel Ascribed to Mark: Copy of Greek Letter Says
     Saint Kept 'Mysteries' Out," *New York Times* (December 30, 1960): 1; Knox
     published a follow-up article the next day: "Expert Disputes 'Secret Gospel,'"
     New York Times (December 31, 1960): 7. Smith's archives show that he
     personally reached out to at least four media outlets in advance of his talk: see
     Geoffrey S. Smith and Brent C. Landau, *The Secret Gospel of Mark:
     A Controversial Scholar, a Scandalous Gospel of Jesus, and the Fierce Debate
     over Its Authenticity* (New Haven, CT: Yale University Press, 2023), 5, 193. My
     thanks to Drs. Smith and Landau for sharing the page proofs of their book in
     advance of its publication.

of the second century. In this letter (whose ending is missing) Clement cited two passages from a "mystical" (or "secret") version of the Gospel of Mark unavailable to everyday Christians. The first passage read like a primitive version of the resurrection of Lazarus (here unnamed), adding that the "young man" raised from the dead by Jesus "loved him" and after coming to him one night "with a linen sheet on his naked body" he learned from Jesus "the mystery of the kingdom of God." The second, shorter passage mentioned the "sister of the youth whom Jesus loved and his mother and Salome," and reported that Jesus would not "receive them."

In his initial paper and subsequent books on the "secret gospel," Smith claimed that it was not just some second-century apocryphal text but a possible witness to Jesus's own ritual activities later scrubbed from orthodox Christianity. In his more scholarly book on the text, published by Harvard University Press in 1973, overflowing with hundreds of pages of philological and technical citations, Smith hypothesized that the "mystery of the kingdom of God" was

a baptism administered by Jesus to chosen disciples, singly, and by night. In this baptism the disciple was united with Jesus. The union may have been physical ... but the essential thing was that the disciple was possessed by Jesus' spirit. One with Jesus, he participated in Jesus' ascent into the heavens; he entered the kingdom of God and was thereby set free from the laws ordained for and in the lower world.[60]

In his more popular book, published the same year by Harper & Row, Smith stated more simply (and, perhaps, provocatively) that

the disciple was possessed by Jesus' spirit and so united with Jesus. One with him, he participated by hallucination in Jesus' ascent into the heavens, he entered the kingdom of God, and was thereby set free from the laws ordained for and in the lower world. Freedom from the law may have resulted in completion of the spiritual union by physical union. This certainly occurred in many forms of gnostic Christianity; how early it began there is no telling.[61]

[60] Morton Smith, *Clement of Alexandria and a Secret Gospel of Mark* (Cambridge, MA: Harvard University Press, 1973), 251. Smith had completed his technical book by 1966 but it spent years in review and production, during which time he wrote his popular account, *The Secret Gospel: The Discovery and Interpretation of the Secret Gospel According to Mark* (New York: Harper & Row, 1973) (see pp. 76–77 on the long publication process for *Clement of Alexandria*).
[61] Smith, *Secret Gospel*, 113–14.

Most of Smith's argument in the 1970s focused on this early form of baptism that involved magical incantation and mystical possession. His repeated use of the term "physical union" become central to the scandal of the secret gospel.

Resistance to Smith's interpretation of the Secret Gospel of Mark was swift and varied. Some scholars were more comfortable categorizing Clement's strange version of Mark as late and heretical. Clement's theological *bona fides* has always been a bit marginal, particularly in his tolerance for pagan and noncanonical texts. But Smith's books appeared just as a theologically liberal cadre of scholars was gearing up to push back against canonical accounts of Christian origins. The 1980s would be the decade of the Jesus Seminar, of the International Q Project, the decade during which scholars began producing more liberally amenable Jesuses out of lost gospels of all shapes and sizes. In this context, the radicalness of Smith's Secret Gospel might find a home.[62]

In 1980, Harvard New Testament scholar Helmut Koester delivered a paper (later published in 1983) arguing, in part, that "Secret Mark" was actually older than the canonical Gospel of Mark. Koester posited a "proto-Mark" used by the writers of Matthew and Luke, later developed into the "mystical" version Clement knew, and finally edited into the version in our New Testament; in sum, "Canonical Mark is derived from Secret Mark." A few years later John Dominic Crossan endorsed and built on Koester's argument: "Canonical Mark is a very deliberate revision of *Secret Mark*." In 1990 Marvin Meyer not only accepted the priority of "Secret Mark," but restored a complex chain of scenes involving the "young man" that only made sense if the "secret" version was the original one.[63]

---

[62] On early reception of Smith's "Secret Gospel," see Tony Burke, "Introduction," in *Ancient Gospel or Modern Forgery? The Secret Gospel of Mark In Debate*, ed. Tony Burke (Eugene, OR: Cascade Books, 2013), 26–57, at 30–34; Shawn Eyer, "The Strange Case of the Secret Gospel According to Mark: How Morton Smith's Discovery of a Lost Letter by Clement of Alexandria Scandalized Biblical Scholarship," *Alexandria* 3 (1995): 103–29; Morton Smith, "Clement of Alexandria and Secret Mark: The Score at the End of the First Decade," *Harvard Theological Review* 75 (1982): 449–61. On Clement's marginal orthodoxy, Herbert Musurillo wrote in a review of Smith's two books: "Clement was a notorious collector of strange tales and traditions" ("Morton Smith's Secret Gospel," *Thought* 48 [1973]: 327–31, at 328).

[63] Helmut Koester, "History and Development of Mark's Gospel (From Mark to *Secret Mark* and 'Canonical' Mark)," in *Colloquy on New Testament Studies. A Time for Reappraisal and Fresh Approaches*, ed. Bruce C. Corley (Macon,

To be sure, most of these scholars hastily jettisoned Smith's arguments about magic, ritual, and physical union. Instead, they deduced a compelling narrative of personal discipleship embodied by the young man raised and initiated by Jesus. The Secret Gospel of Mark became part of the arsenal of countercanonical texts marshaled by (according to scholar Scott Brown) "theologically liberal scholars." Smith's recovered version of Mark was one of the texts included for consideration by the Jesus Seminar.[64]

Smith's account of his find, laid out in easy prose in his popular 1973 book, evokes (perhaps deliberately) the fading era of Bible Hunters like Agnes Lewis and Margaret Gibson. Smith gives a long and evocative description of the isolated monastery, which he first visited in 1941 and returned to in 1958 after developing an interest in "manuscript hunting." The piles of books and manuscripts in the library have fallen into disuse (the monks preferring to spend time in liturgical services). A small collection of photographs in the book – men with great big beards, aerial shots of the isolated monastery, jumbles of manuscripts used for binding – prepare us for the tale of the persistent western scholar "discovering" his treasure among the serene and stagnant remains of eastern Christians.[65]

While he may have initially styled himself as a Bible Hunter, Smith operated in the political realities that were shaping the complex work surrounding more recent finds, like the Nag Hammadi codices or the Dead Sea Scrolls. So, unlike Tischendorf, Smith left the book with the explosive Greek text where he had found it, taking with him only black and white photographs. Early reviews objected to this lack of physical artifact: How could other scholars verify his readings and interpretations (especially since Harvard University Press failed to print the full photos of the manuscript)? Very early on in the early reception of Smith's two books on the Secret Gospel attention turned to questions

GA: Mercer University Press, 1983), 35–57, at 56; John Dominic Crossan, *Four Other Gospels: Shadows on the Contours of Canon* (Minneapolis, MN: Seabury, 1985), 108; Marvin Meyer, "The Youth in the *Secret Gospel of Mark*," *Semeia* 49 (1990): 129–53. I cite Koester because of his central role in this scholarly drama, cognizant of the serious accusations of sexual assault lodged against him by his former doctoral student Elaine Pagels.

64 Scott Brown, *Mark's Other Gospel: Rethinking Morton Smith's Controversial Discovery* (Waterloo: Wilfrid Laurier University Press, 2005), 16.

65 Smith, *Secret Gospel*, 8.

of provenance and, eventually, charges of forgery, chicanery, and hoax.[66]

In an essay in the *Catholic Biblical Quarterly*, Quentin Quesnell, a biblical studies scholar at Smith College, questioned the veracity of Smith's "discovery." After a few preliminary pages bemoaning the lack of scholarly access to the physical artifact of the text, which might help determine its date and provenance, Quesnell asks "the unavoidable next question": "the possibilities of forgery." Quesnell pointed out that it would take only "ability" (a copy of the seventeenth-century book, handwriting samples, skills in forgery, mastery of Clement's vocabulary, and access to the monastery library) and "motivation" (Quesnell imagines several). Quesnell also notes some "puzzling" aspects of Smith's own interpretations which suggest Smith had a longstanding interest in Jesus, magic, and ritual before finding the possibly forged letter.[67]

Quesnell did not directly accuse Smith of forgery. Smith nonetheless, and perhaps not unreasonably, felt he had been accused. In a subsequent issue of the same journal Smith writes: "Quesnell insinuates that I forged the MS. Such accusations are customary when important MSS are discovered" (in a footnote he notes "Zeitlin's absurd attacks on the Dead Sea documents," which I discussed in Chapter 2). Smith dismisses Quesnell's objections as laughably inconsistent, requiring an "imaginary genius" who nonetheless produces an "amateurish imitation" of Mark. He likewise rebuts Quesnell's assertion that the fragment served to support interests and theories Smith already held. Quesnell was allowed space in the same issue for a brief response, in which he denies that he meant to accuse Smith ("If that had been my point, I would have stated it clearly") and reiterates that, in the absence of the actual document, its authenticity should not be assumed.[68]

---

[66] A representative collection of scholarly responses appeared in W. Wuellner (ed.), *Longer Mark: Forgery, Interpolation, or Old Tradition?* (Berkeley, CA: Center for Hermeneutical Studies, 1976).

[67] Quentin Quesnell, "The Mar Saba Clementine: A Question of Evidence," *Catholic Biblical Quarterly* 37 (1975): 48–67.

[68] Morton Smith, "On the Authenticity of the Mar Saba Letter of Clement," *Catholic Biblical Quarterly* 38 (1976): 196–99; Quentin Quesnell, "A Reply to Morton Smith," *Catholic Biblical Quarterly* 38 (1976): 200–03. Brown, *Mark's Other Gospel*, 35–36, accepts that Quesnell was careful not to accuse Smith or imply he was the forger although, in correspondence with Brown, Quesnell

A few other scholars broached the possibility of forgery during Smith's lifetime: one scholar suggested an ancient or possibly early modern forgery (perhaps copied into the seventeenth-century book in Europe before it arrived at the monastery); another pointed out places where the letter by Clement too perfectly answered all of the questions a modern reader might have about the secret gospel, providing a self-authenticating frame for a modern forgery. But while Morton Smith was still alive, even after Quesnell's article, accusations of forgery remained abstract and did not center on Smith himself.[69]

After Smith's death his former student, Jacob Neusner, a titan of Jewish Studies, took to accusing Smith routinely and flamboyantly of forging this key piece of evidence in his disgraceful narrative about Jesus. In a 1993 monograph purportedly debunking Smith's first dissertation, Neusner attacked Smith's intellectual rigor and personal character, including a brief excursus on the Secret Gospel of Mark. Smith's fabrication of Jesus in his two books as a "homosexual magician" (Neusner repeats this phrase many times) is evidence of both Smith's shoddy scholarship and his personal malice, aimed at discrediting and demeaning Jesus and Christianity. Although Neusner had offered a praiseworthy blurb to Smith's popular account – a "brilliant account" of a "major discovery" – he now disdained the fragment as "the forgery of the century."[70]

As Neusner freely admits in his introduction, his broadside against his former mentor was provoked by years of scholarly warfare; Neusner derides Smith's ineffectual attempts to destroy Neusner's career. Yet alongside his acid prose, Neusner also notes that Smith's

---

admitted: "Did I personally think Smith . . . had forged the document? Of course I did" (p. 35). Brown likewise finds Smith's response "intemperate."

[69] Musurillo, "Morton Smith's"; Charles Murgia, "Secret Mark: Real or Fake?" in Wuellner, *Longer Mark*, 35–40. See Brown, *Mark's Other Gospel*, 28–34. In the transcript of the "Minutes of the Colloquy" in *Longer Mark*, Murgia explicitly rejects the idea that Smith might have forged the text (p. 60).

[70] Jacob Neusner, *Are There Really Tannaitic Parallels to the Gospels? A Refutation of Morton Smith*, South Florida Studies in the History of Judaism 80 (Atlanta, GA: Scholars Press, 1993), 27–31. In multiple places, Neusner suggests that other scholars, including Quesnell, refused to accuse Smith of forgery for fear of lawsuits. Shaye Cohen, another Smith student attacked in *Are There Really*, published a stinging review: "Are There Tannaitic Parallels to the Gospels?" *Journal of the American Oriental Society* 116 (1996): 85–89. See also Brown, *Mark's Other Gospel*, 39–43 and Burke, "Introduction," 30–31.

act of historical predation (as he sees it) laid bare the inherent vulnerability of the New Testament in modern biblical studies:

> Now the spectacle of the quest for the historical Jesus was exposed for all to
> see. What controls of rationality, objectivity, strict rules of evidence, skepti-
> cism, and criticism protected the field as such from a brilliant forgery? ...
> Smith disgraced New Testament studies, because he showed through his
> (momentary) success that the field could not defend itself from fraud ... a
> field of learning that validates even its existence by assuming that documents
> of religious faith conceal fraud – the Gospel truth is true only some of the
> time, and we'll find out when – surely meets its match in a secret gospel no
> one is permitted to examine but everyone expected to believe.[71]

In his own work Neusner sought to disentangle literary and religious
evidence from historical evidence in rabbinic literature. The peculiar
historical critical practices of New Testament studies are merely inci-
dental to his larger point. They nonetheless help explain the persistent
and seemingly unending anxiety that Smith's secret gospel continues to
generate within biblical studies, even decades after his death: It
revealed a Bible that "could not defend itself."

Once Neusner lit the fuse the academy exploded with "proof" of
Smith's forgery. Occasionally such proof might be on technical
grounds, as in one attempt to prove forgery from a statistical analysis
of Clement's authentic writings. Increasingly the drumbeat of accusations harped on personal motivations, like Neusner's accusations of
"anti-Christianism." It did not help that – as Neusner's diatribe made
clear – Smith behaved in distinctly unpleasant ways in his professional
life and so made for many a believable villain. Additional personal
motives continued to be adduced. By the early 2000s, when several
books on the Secret Gospel of Mark began to appear, it became
uncontroversial to treat the text as a forgery likely executed by Smith
himself. Over this period, three interrelated motives for forgery have
congealed around Smith.[72]

---

[71] Neusner, *Are There Really*, 30–31.

[72] Statistical article: Andrew Criddle, "On the Mar Saba Letter Attributed to
Clement of Alexandria," *Journal of Early Christian Studies* 3 (1995): 215–20,
and Brown, *Mark's Other Gospel*, 54–57. On motivations generally, see Scott
Brown, "The Question of Motive in the Case Against Morton Smith," *Journal
of Biblical Literature* 125 (2006): 351–83. In 2003, Bart D. Ehrman assessed the
likelihood that Smith forged the text: *Lost Christianities: The Battles for
Scripture and the Faiths We Never Knew* (Oxford: Oxford University Press,

Some scholars accused Smith of acting out of professional ambition or jealousy. In the years prior to his discovery of the text, Smith had been teaching at Brown University, where he hoped to be granted a tenured position. In 1954, he was informed his contract would be ending the next year. Although by 1958 he had been hired in a permanent position at Columbia University, where he spent the remainder of his career, some have suggested this stinging rejection prompted Smith either to seek a kind of professional revenge by passing off a forgery as authentic, or to bolster his own "vulnerable" career with a blockbuster find.[73]

Other theories of personal motive delve into Smith's biography, perhaps to discern theological motives. Smith had been ordained as an Episcopalian priest in the 1940s but later stopped any ministerial service (although he remained in the rosters of the priesthood for his whole career). Perhaps, some posit, he broke with the conservative religion of his upbringing and early career and wanted either to strike a blow against conservative Christianity or, more generously, provide a vision of Christ centered on personal intimacy rather than stern remoteness. Or, as one particularly lurid account posited, perhaps the disjunction between his religious upbringing and later beliefs caused a kind of psychological break that pushed him into forgery and deception.[74]

Almost all recent accusations against Smith explicitly or implicitly find motive in Smith's own sexuality. Scholars speculated during his lifetime that Smith was gay. Biblical studies scholar Bruce Chilton recalled a time in the 1970s when a conference chair, during a lunch break, "went into a loud harangue about Smith, complete with disparaging remarks about homosexuals and homosexuality" (Chilton also notes that Smith, standing nearby, "had heard every word that had been said"). When Quentin Quesnell traveled to Jerusalem in 1983 to personally inspect the book containing the secret gospel,

2003), 67–89. By 2021, Simon Gathercole unequivocally described the text as a "modern forgery" likely executed by Smith: *The Apocryphal Gospels* (London: Penguin, 2021), 403–04.

[73] Carlson, *Gospel Hoax*, 79–80; Pierluigi Piovanelli, "Halfway Between Sabbatai Tzevi and Aleister Crowley," in *Ancient Gospel*, ed. Tony Burke, 202–35.

[74] Psychological speculation is key to Jeffery, *Secret Gospel*, 149–84, 243–44. Scott Brown, *Mark's Other Gospel*, 13, remarks: "Scholars tended to trade stories about Smith's character, which was something they knew firsthand or had heard a great deal about."

he had a meeting with Hebrew University professor David Flusser during which the two of them wondered about Smith's homosexuality and whether it might have prompted his forgery. In more recent arguments for forgery, it seems almost taken for granted that a gay scholar would want to circulate a gay Jesus, either as revenge for his experiences of homophobia or in a sincere theological interest in liberation.[75]

In their quest to prove the gospel a forgery, scholars dissect large and small clues, much as Sabar would later contemplate the number 114 or the significance of the word *abdication*: in the conspiracy (even of one man's hoax) no clue is insignificant. We read about handwriting analysis (based on old photographs), hidden messages (is a line about "salt" a wink from *Morton* Smith?), opaque context clues (when did baptism take place in second-century Alexandria? what about that "linen sheet"?), and letters from Smith to colleagues on seemingly unrelated topics. In an impassioned defense of Smith, *Biblical Archaeology Review* publisher Hershel Shanks complained: "No matter how many arguments for forgery that you refute, you can never prove that the letter is authentic. There will always be some other flaw that you haven't yet found that would expose the letter as a modern forgery."[76]

Gospel Thrillers even make an appearance. In *Hidden Gospels*, Philip Jenkins was the first to point out that Smith discovered his gospel at Mar Saba Monastery, "the scene of the forgery described only a few years before in the then-popular novel *The Mystery of Mar Saba*." Jenkins continues: The "fact that Secret Mark came from Mar

---

[75] Bruce Chilton, "Review of Stephen C. Carlson, *The Gospel Hoax: Morton Smith's Invention of* Secret Mark," *The Review of Rabbinic Judaism* 10 (2007): 122–28, at 127. Quesnell recorded his conversation with Flusser in a journal kept during a *sub rosa* trip to Jerusalem: see Stephan Hüller and Daniel N. Gullota, "Quentin Quesnell's *Secret Mark* Secret," *Vigiliae Christianae* 71 (2017): 353–78. Carlson, *Gospel Hoax*, 85–86 hints coyly at Smith's sexuality; see also Javier Martinez, "Cheap Fictions and Gospel Truths," in *Splendide Mendax: Rethinking Fakes and Forgeries in Classical, Late Antique, and Early Christian Literature*, eds. Edmund P. Cueva and Javier Martinez (Groningen: Barkhuis, 2016), 3–20, at 5–8. In an unpublished response to Scott Brown's review of his book, Peter Jeffery made the distasteful claim that "I resisted the temptation to publish any of the jaw-dropping oral traditions I have heard about Smith, even though some (if accurate) would be quite revealing," online at https://music2.princeton.edu/jeffery/Review of Biblical Literature-Jeffery reply to Brown.pdf and cited in Martinez, "Cheap Fictions," 8.

[76] Hershel Shanks, "Was Morton Smith the Bernie Madoff of the Academy?" in *Ancient Gospel*, ed. Tony Burke, 177–87, at 179.

Saba is either strong proof of a thing in the 1950's, or else it is a tribute to the unabashed *chutzpah* of a forger." Others quickly hopped on the *Mar Saba* bandwagon, piling up more supposed clues from the novel. By 2010, New Testament studies scholar Francis Watson could assert that "there is no alternative but to conclude that Smith is dependent on the novel." Even the son of the novel's author weighed in on the matter.[77]

It is fitting that the prototype of Gospel Thrillers should make an appearance in the seemingly endless debate over a real-life story of a secret, shocking gospel. The story that biblical studies specialists keep telling about Morton Smith and his secret gospel reenacts the same theological, geopolitical, and personal anxieties revealed by the novels. By assuming that Smith was able to use and abuse the resources of the Mar Saba monastery to perpetrate his fraud, Smith's accusers frame the geopolitical location of the monastery in much the same way as Gospel Thrillers imagined the politically dangerous yet biblically fruitful sands of the Dead Sea: as an unreliable outpost of biblical colonialism. Moreover, the theological security of the Bible comes under threat from this wild colonial space; Smith's "homosexual magician" Jesus is more disruptive than anything imagined by fictional Gospel Thrillers. Above all, the personal motives of the scholar, endlessly scrutinized, animate both fictional Gospel Thrillers and their real-world counterparts: a fear of deviation from a straight, white, male norm that should (but can never fully) secure the truth of the Bible.[78]

In a thoughtful essay on the modern history of the Secret Gospel of Mark, Alexis Waller has read the decades of debate as part of an affective archive, a history of emotional encounter, response, and

---

[77] Jenkins, *Hidden Gospels*, 102; Francis Watson, "Beyond Suspicion: On the Authorship of the Mar Saba Letter and the Secret Gospel of Mark," *Journal of Theological Studies* 61 (2010): 128–70, at 163–70; Ian Hunter, "The (Continuing) Mystery of Mar Saba," *National Post* (June 30, 2005): A22. See also Robert M. Price, "Second Thoughts on the Secret Gospel," *Bulletin for Biblical Research* 14 (2004): 127–32, at 131 and Gathercole, *Apocryphal Gospels*, 403–04. For problems with Smith's supposed use of *The Mystery of Mar Saba*, see Allan J. Pantuck, MD, "Solving the *Mystereion* of Morton Smith and the Secret Gospel of Mark," online at www.biblicalarchaeology.org/wp-content/uploads/secret-mark-handwriting-response-pantuck.pdf.

[78] The Secret Gospel of Mark itself appears in only one Gospel Thriller: Lustbader, *The Testament* (2006) assumes the fragment found by Smith was authentic.

resistance that illuminates broader issues in the historical and theological approach to the Christian Bible that predominates in biblical studies. Waller writes:

The exaggerated responses to Smith's so-called "homosexual" designs on the Christian past might be felt, however, as speaking *symptomatically* to a kind of panic reverberating across the field. They point not only to anxiety about some scholarship touching the historical Jesus in inappropriate ways but also to the anxiety New Testament scholars generally feel about their own desires to make contact with the past. People on both sides of the argument seem to hold out hope that stabilizing the reputation of *Secret Mark* as definitively forged or authentic will shut down uncomfortable uncertainties and, perhaps, alleviate anxiety about their own theological, imaginative, perverse, relations with the past.[79]

As Waller suggests, no amount of rational argument or proof-texting, no compilation of clues and evidence, will "shut down" these "uncertainties" because they are endemic to the vulnerability of the modern Bible produced and circulated by biblical studies.[80]

The saga of Smith and his secret gospel has chugged alongside the production of Gospel Thrillers since the 1960s, taking many of the same twists and turns, and structuring future debates in the academy over new discoveries and reimaginations of Christian origins and biblical authenticity. Every "exciting" new biblical discovery falls under the shadow of Smith's "homosexual magician," a term coined by his detractors that underscores the moral panic attendant upon the vulnerability of a revisable Bible. (Sabar spends several pages on Smith in *Veritas*.)[81]

The parallels between academic thrillers and their novelistic counterparts, I have been arguing, are not merely aesthetic. These extraordinary moments of public controversy and debate, some lasting for decades, enact in a kind of repetitive panic anxieties that are

---

[79] Alexis G. Waller, "The 'Unspeakable Teachings' of *The Secret Gospel of Mark*: Feelings and Fantasies in the Making of Christian Histories," in *Religion, Emotion, Sensation: Affect Theories and Theologies*, eds. Karen Bray and Stephen Moore (New York: Fordham University Press, 2019), 145–173, at 155–56, emphasis in original.

[80] See Smith and Landau who, in *Secret Gospel of Mark*, assess the story of Smith's discovery and the controversy around the text in great detail and offer their own theory of the late ancient origins of the text.

[81] Sabar, *Veritas*, 33–36.

normally kept at bay in professional biblical studies: in a guild that has constructed a revisable, and so vulnerable, Bible, what political, theological, and personal motivations and stakes are being occluded under the cloak of scholarly expertise and acumen? While modern biblical studies can only acknowledge these anxieties in the most extreme and spectacular cases, Gospel Thrillers can, and do, address them head-on.

7 | Conclusions

The fact that new biblical discoveries continue to make national and international headlines speaks to the particular desires and fears for a new biblical truth that might just change everything we think we know about Christian origins, religious truth, and western (i.e., white, US) identity. The fundamental revisability of the Bible as constructed by modern biblical studies makes possible this hope for, and fear of, such a radical discovery.

Gospel Thrillers offer an enclosed space to explore the fears and desires of a vulnerable Bible, made palatable by the fictionality of their new "discovery." Here we see the value, perhaps even the genius, of this quirky genre that has persisted for almost sixty years. As I lay out in Chapter 6, the real world of biblical studies offers no consolation for the unending vulnerability of the Bible: the case of Morton Smith has been endlessly litigated for the past thirty years not because of the magnitude of the purported "hoax" but precisely because it gives space for readers to attend to the anxious vulnerability of the modern Bible.

If we can puzzle a bit at the ongoing anxiety over the Secret Gospel of Mark, Gospel Thrillers leave us little doubt as to the magnitude of *their* discoveries:

"It's a theological H-bomb" (Kiefer, *Pontius Pilate Papers*, p. 281).

"A moral A-bomb" (Conrad and Mastorakis, *Keepers of the Secret*, p. 90).

"The academics froze in their chairs, instantly realizing the meaning of the bombshell" (Gold, *The Lost Testament*, p. 7).

"You'll have to take my word, Inspector, that it's certainly a bombshell" (Meade, *The Second Messiah*, p. 225).

"This scroll is a time bomb. It could tear the Church apart" (Van Greenaway, *The Judas Testament*, p. 427).

"They're living with a time bomb. They know that everything they have established is based on a lie" (Rocha, *The Pope's Assassin*, pp. 287–88).

As we've seen, these metaphorical bombs are often accompanied by literal bombs in these novels to underscore that this new discovery is not only momentous but dangerous.

Yet, as we've also seen throughout, and as I especially noted in Chapter 4, these novels that delve so deeply and thoroughly into the "bombshell" possibilities of a new first-century gospel more often than not pull their punches at the end: we rarely, if ever, see that metaphorical bomb explode. The Bible, and the various religious, political, and cultural institutions that derive authority from it, remain intact. Status quo persists; the bombshells are duds.

One novel out of dozens does imagine life after the bomb goes off: perhaps the most successful of the genre to date, Irving Wallace's *The Word*. Wallace worked on this novel for close to a decade, jotting down his first ideas for the novel in 1961 and sending back his final galleys to his publisher in 1971. Wallace's self-curated archives, stored in the Special Collections of Honnold-Mudd Library at the Claremont Colleges in southern California, preserve the journey his novel took from early conception to final execution.

It's clear from a two-page document written in May 1961 that Wallace knew right from the start where his novel would end (even though almost every other detail changed):

Hero has evidence, says hoax. Then in showdown, informer or forger found murdered, a "suicide" ... evidence missing ... only hero to protest ... and he hooted down ... and new bible goes out, and hero sees it quoted and sermons preached from it ... realizes then it makes men happy, like all religion, and doesn't matter ... and he is freed to go on with new maturity.[1]

Over the years Wallace changed the details leading to this ending. In 1961, the "hero" was a "small college instructor, expert in Aramaic or Greek"; by publication he is a slick and cynical PR executive. The contents of the gospel change, as well. In 1961, he imagines that Jesus "went to Rome, how he looked, lived in Egypt, his brother James." (The first and last details remain.) By April 1970, Wallace has grown more ambitious:

---

[1] Wallace Archives BGI WO7 1961 (typescript, May 17, 1961) (Wallace archive folders contain multiple items; the folder is dated according to the oldest item in that folder, so I include dates of individual documents when available).

New discovery will prove –

Jesus was relevant today – a young rebel who preached a new social order and utopia on earth, which suits what is going on right now.

Conveniently approved of divorce, disapproved of celibacy for all the clergy, approved of abortion, equality between the sexes, approved of blacks and browns and yellows as one with whites.

Jesus traveled widely in lost years, from Palestine to Rome to Near and Far East including ####### India and possibly China.[2]

Almost none of this makes it into Wallace's version of "Q," a Gospel of James that readers see little of but which is generically comforting and reassuring:

James had set down numerous sayings of his brother Jesus that had uncanny relevance for the world today, sayings concerning the exploitation of the poor by the wealthy and the ruling class, sayings concerning the need for a compact among nations to end war and colonialism, sayings on the necessity of education for all, sayings that disapproved of superstition, dogma, ritual, and two sayings that actually prophesied that one day men would stride the planets of heaven at a time when the earth verged on self-destruction. (p. 226)

The biggest bombshell in this gospel is that Jesus survived his first crucifixion in Jerusalem and went on to teach on Rome; there he was eventually crucified again and really did rise from the dead (leading the whole project of translation and publication to be code-named "Resurrection Two.").

As I've noted elsewhere, the protagonist Randall suspects and confirms that Q is a forgery, but (as Wallace already planned in 1961) his warnings to the Bible publishers who have hired him go unheeded. A new translation of the New Testament is published with the Gospel of James as an appendix. The results are transformative:

If you went shopping, visited a bar, dined in a restaurant, attended a party, you heard it discussed. The drums beat, and the charismatic new Christ was gathering souls again, souls without number. The decrease in violence was being attributed by some to the return to Christ. The improvement in the

---

[2] Wallace Archives BGI WO7 1961 (typescript, April 13, 1970); the hashmarks are in the ms., probably correcting a typo.

economy was being credited by others to Christ. The drop in drug usage was owing to Christ. The end of this war, the beginning of that peace talk, the general well-being and euphoria and brotherhood sweeping the earth were heralded by the recently awakened as the work of Christ. (p. 661)

The spiritual transformation wrought by the fake Gospel of James ends geopolitical strife and ushers in an era of "euphoria and brotherhood." While upon initially reading the Gospel Randall had also felt its euphoric effects, in the wake of its publication he goes on a bender of self-pity, righteous indignation, booze, and "meaningless" sex (pp. 663–64). Yet even cynical Randall, at the end, finds himself at home, in his childhood church, watching the transformative effects of the forged gospel and beginning, once more, to feel them himself.

It should not escape our attention that the one Gospel Thriller actually to narrate the bombshell transformative effects of a newly discovered first-century gospel depicts that gospel as a deceitful forgery created by a vicious ex-convict bent on revenge and retaliation. Its publication was enabled by greedy publishers and power-hungry clerics. The conspiracy at the heart of this Gospel Thriller has succeeded but, as Wallace noted to himself in 1961, "it makes men happy, like all religion, and doesn't matter." The conspiracy can be thwarted, the conspiracy can succeed, and either way the result is still the status quo: a world in which the Bible possesses the power to shape the way we see the world.

Thrillers are fictions that probe the possibilities – fearsome, exciting, outrageous, provocative – of a struggle over hidden knowledge. Conspiracy theories, as I discuss in Chapter 2, unspool endlessly, producing "clue" after "clue" for the intrepid seeker to decode. By their very nature conspiracy theories never end: they fade, they mutate, they persist. Thrillers are vehicles of narrative containment, in which readers can experience the thrill of conspiratorial secrecy and revelation without that attendant anxiety of a new clue or threat or secret around the corner: the anxiety of *unending*.

In the novels I have explored, the Christian Bible is conjured as a site of conspiracy, revealed to protagonists by new "discoveries"; but that conspiracy is – for the moment, at least – resolved as the specific dangers posed by the new "discovery" are averted. By making biblical conspiracy into a fictional *thriller*, Gospel Thrillers offer what real-world professional biblical studies cannot: finitude and closure over the political, theological, and personal challenges posed by an authoritative yet vulnerable Bible. Of course, once the covers of the book are closed the reader returns to that real world, in which *the Bible* is once more both an imagined pillar of the West and endlessly susceptible to revision and distortion. Perhaps as long as the Bible remains both totemic and vulnerable, Gospel Thrillers will keep appearing to assuage US readers' anxiety and contain their biblical fears and desires.

Appendix
The Novels

I provide information on the first printed version of each novel and, where applicable, information on the version I cite in brackets. Books are listed in chronological order.

James Hogg Hunter. *The Mystery of Mar Saba*. Toronto: Evangelical Publishers, 1940.

James Hall Roberts. *The Q Document*. New York: Morrow, 1964. [James Hall Roberts (Robert Duncan). *The Q Document*. New York: Ballantine, 1979.]

Elizabeth Peters. *The Dead Sea Cipher*. New York: Harper, 1970. [Elizabeth Peters. *The Dead Sea Cipher*. New York: HarperSuspense, 2012.]

Peter van Greenaway. *Judas!* London: Gollancz, 1972. [Peter van Greenaway. *The Judas Gospel*. New York: Dell, 1973.]

Irving Wallace. *The Word*. New York: Simon & Schuster, 1972. [Irving Wallace. *The Word*. New York: Pockets Books, 1973.]

Warren Kiefer. *The Pontius Pilate Papers*. New York: Harper, 1976. [Warren Kiefer. *The Pontius Pilate Papers*. New York: Jove/HBJ, 1977.]

Robert Ludlum. *The Gemini Contenders*. New York: Doubleday, 1976. [Robert Ludlum. *The Gemini Contenders*. New York: Bantam Books, 1989.]

Barnaby Conrad and Nico Mastorakis. *Keepers of the Secret*. New York: Jove Books, 1983.

Alan Gold. *The Lost Testament*. New York: Harper, 1992. [Alan Gold. *The Lost Testament*. New York: HarperPaperbacks, 1994.]

J. G. Sandom. *Gospel Truths*. New York: Doubleday, 1992. [J. G. Sandom. *Gospel Truths*. Bantam Books, 1993.]

Daniel Easterman. *The Judas Testament*. New York: HarperCollins, 1994. [Daniel Easterman. *The Judas Testament*. London: HarperCollins, 1995.]

Larry Witham. *The Negev Project*. College Park: Meridian Books, 1994.

Barbara Wood. *The Prophetess*. Boston: Little, Brown, and Co., 1996.

Jonathan Rabb. *The Book of Q*. New York: Crown Publishers, 2001.

Paul Christopher. *The Lucifer Gospel*. New York: Onyx, 2006.

Eric Van Lustbader. *The Testament*. New York: Forge, 2006. [Eric Van Lustbader. *The Testament*. Forge, 2017.]

Paul Block and Robert Vaughan. *The Masada Scroll*. New York: Tor, 2007.

Richard and Rachael Heller. *The 13th Apostle*. New York: Harper, 2007.

James Becker. *The First Apostle*. New York: Signet, 2008.

Ronald Cutler. *The Secret Scroll*. New York: Beaufort Books, 2008.

David Gibbins. *The Last Gospel*. London: Headline, 2008. [David Gibbins. *The Lost Tomb*. New York: Dell, 2008.]

Greg Loomis. *The Coptic Secret*. New York: Dorchester, 2009.

Adam Blake. *The Dead Sea Deception*. New York: Little, Brown, and Co., 2011. [Adam Blake. *The Dead Sea Deception*. London: Sphere, 2011.]

Glenn Meade. *The Second Messiah*. New York: Howard Books, 2011.

Luis Rocha. *The Pope's Assassin*. Trans. Robin McAllister. New York: G. P. Putnam's Sons, 2011.

Leslie Winfield Williams. *The Judas Conspiracy*. Tomball: JoSara MeDia, 2010.

G. M. Lawrence. *Q: Awakening*. Online only: Variance, 2012.

James Becker. *The Lost Testament*. New York: Signet, 2013.

Paul Christopher. *Secret of the Templars*. New York: Signet, 2015.

Linda Stasi. *Book of Judas*. New York: Tor, 2017.

Daniel Silva. *The Order*. New York: HarperCollins, 2020.

References

Allegro, John. *The Dead Sea Scrolls: A Reappraisal*. Rev. ed. London: Penguin, 1963.

The Sacred Mushroom and the Cross: A Study of the Nature and Origins of Christianity within the Fertility Cults of the Ancient Near East. London: Hodder and Stoughton, 1970.

Allen, Charlotte. *The Human Christ: The Search for the Historical Jesus*. New York: The Free Press, 1998.

"Jesus' Ex-Wife," *The Weekly Standard* (October 8, 2012): 30–32.

"Q: The Search for a No-Frills Jesus," *The Atlantic* 27.6 (December 1996): 51–68.

"The Wife of Jesus Tale," *The Weekly Standard* (May 5, 2014): 30–33.

Allen, Jr., John. "Power, Secrecy Feed Conspiracy Theories in Vatican City," *National Catholic Reporter* 34.35 (July 31, 1998): 15–18.

Almog, Oz. *The Sabra: The Creation of the New Jew*. Trans. Haim Watzman. Berkeley, CA: University of California Press, 2000.

[Anonymous.] "Best Sellers: The Year of the Bird and the Bible," *Publishers Weekly* 203.6 (February 5, 1973): 41.

"Judas' Deal, 2000 years later," *Los Angeles Times* (April 13, 2006): B12.

"Our Weekly Gossip," *The Athenaeum* 1224 (April 12, 1851): 408.

"The Revised Standard Version of the Bible: A Symposium," *Religious Education* 47 (1951): 243–77.

"A Syrian Text of the Gospels," *London Echo* (April 13, 1893): 2.

Ariel, Yaakov. *An Unusual Relationship: Evangelical Christians and Jews*. New York: NYU Press, 2013.

Askeland, Christian. "Jesus Had a Sister-in-Law," *Evangelical Text Criticism* (April 24, 2014). https://evangelicaltextualcriticism.blogspot.com/2014/04/jesus-had-ugly-sister-in-law.html.

Attridge, Harold. "The Case for Judas, Continued," *New York Review of Books* 55.7 (May 1, 2008). www.nybooks.com/articles/2008/05/01/the-case-for-judas-continued.

Baigent, Michael and Richard Leigh. *The Dead Sea Scrolls Deception*. London: Jonathan Cape, 1991.

Baigent, Michael, Richard Leigh, and Henry Lincoln. *The Holy Blood and the Holy Grail*. London: Jonathan Cape, 1982.

The Messianic Legacy. London: Jonathan Cape, 1986.

Barnhardt, Wilton. *Gospel*. New York: Picador, 1993.

Barnstone, Willis. *The Other Bible: Jewish Pseudepigrapha, Christian Apocrypha, Gnostic Scriptures, Kabbalah, Dead Sea Scrolls*. San Francisco, CA: HarperSanFrancisco, 1984.

Bauer, Walter. *Rechtglaübkeit und Ketzerei im ältesten Christentum*. Tübingen: J. C. B. Mohr, 1934. [*Orthodoxy and Heresy in Earliest Christianity*. Trans. Robert A. Kraft, Gerhard Kroedel, and a team from the Philadelphia Seminar on Christian Origins. Philadelphia, PA: Fortress Press, 1971.]

Becke, Johannes. "Dismantling the Villa in the Jungle: Matzpen, Zochrot, and the Whitening of Israel," *Interventions: International Journal of Postcolonial Studies* 21 (2019): 874–91.

Becker, James. *The Messiah Secret*. Berkeley, CA: Onyx, 2010.

The Moses Stone. Berkeley, CA: Onyx, 2009.

Ben-zvi, Yael. "Blind Spots in Portraiture: On Oz Almog's *Ha-tsabar – Dyokan, Sabra: The Creation of the New Jew*," *Jewish Social Studies* 7 (2000): 167–74.

Berzon, Todd. *Classifying Christians: Ethnography, Heresy, and the Limits of Knowledge in Late Antiquity*. Oakland, CA: University of California Press, 2016.

Blake, Adam. *The Demon Code*. London: Little, Brown and Co., 2012.

Borg, Marcus (ed.). *The Lost Gospel Q: The Original Sayings of Jesus*. Berkeley, CA: Ulysses Press, 1996.

Brakke, David. *The Gnostics*. Cambridge, MA: Harvard University Press, 2010.

The Gospel of Judas: A New Translation with Introduction and Commentary. Anchor Yale Bible 45. New Haven, CT: Yale University Press, 2022.

Brennan, Terry. *The Sacred Cipher*. Grand Rapids, MI: Kregel Publications, 2009.

Brier, Bob. *Cleopatra's Needles: The Lost Obelisks of Egypt*. London: Bloomsbury, 2016.

Brodkin, Karen. *How Jews Became White and What That Says About Race in America*. New Brunswick, NJ: Rutgers University Press, 1998.

Brody, David. "EXCLUSIVE: Franklin Graham Tells CBN News He Thinks Democratic Party Is 'Opposed to Faith.'" *CBNNews.com* (August 28, 2020). www1.cbn.com/cbnnews/2020/august/exclusive-franklin-graham-tells-news-he-thinks-democrats-are-opposed-to-faith.

Brown, Dan. *The Da Vinci Code*. New York: Doubleday, 2003.

Brown, Scott. *Mark's Other Gospel: Rethinking Morton Smith's Controversial Discovery*. Waterloo: Wilfrid Laurier University Press, 2005.

"The Question of Motive in the Case against Morton Smith," *Journal of Biblical Literature* 125 (2006): 351–83.

Bruce, James. *Travels to Discover the Source of the Nile*. London: G. G. J. and J. Robinson, 1790.

Burke, Daniel. "A Married Jesus? Some Thought That," *USA Today* (September 19, 2012): 2A.

Burke, Tony (ed.). *Ancient Gospel or Modern Forgery? The Secret Gospel of Mark in Debate*. Eugene, OR: Cascade Books, 2013.

(ed.). *Fakes, Forgeries, and Fictions: Writing Ancient and Modern Christian Apocrypha*. Eugene, OR: Cascade Books, 2017.

"Introduction." In *Ancient Gospel or Modern Forgery?* 26–57.

Burke, Tony and Gregory Peter Fewster. "*Opera Evangelica*: A Lost Collection of Christian Apocrypha," *New Testament Studies* 67 (2021): 356–87.

Burns, Dylan. *Apocalypse of the Alien God: Platonism and the Exile of Sethian Gnosticism*. Divinations. Philadelphia, PA: University of Pennsylvania, 2014.

Burrows, Millar.*The Dead Sea Scrolls of St. Mark's Monastery*. New Haven, CT: American Schools of Oriental Research, 1950–1951.

Butler, Anthea. *White Evangelical Racism: The Politics of Morality in America*. Chapel Hill, NC: University of North Carolina Press, 2021.

Campbell, Richard, Christopher R. Martin, and Bettina Fabos. *Media and Culture: An Introduction to Mass Communication*. 8th ed. Boston/New York: Bedford/St. Martins, 2012.

Carlson, Stephen. *The Gospel Hoax: Morton Smith's Invention of Secret Mark*. Waco, TX: Baylor University Press, 2005.

Chancey, Mark. "The Bible and American Public Schools," in *The Oxford Handbook of Religion and American Education*, 271–82. Eds. Michael D. Waggoner and Nathan C. Walker. New York: Oxford University Press, 2018.

"Bible Bills, Bible Curricula, and Controversies of Biblical Proportions: Legislative Efforts to Promote Bible Courses in Public Schools," *Religion and Education* 34 (2007): 28–47.

Chidester, David. *Empire of Religion: Imperialism and Comparative Religion*. Chicago, IL: University of Chicago Press, 2014.

Chilton, Bruce. "Review of Stephen C. Carlson, *The Gospel Hoax: Morton Smith's Invention of* Secret Mark," *The Review of Rabbinic Judaism* 10 (2007): 122–28.

Clark, Mary Higgins. *The Lost Years*. New York: Simon & Schuster, 2012.

Cobley, Paul. "The Semiotics of Paranoia: The Thriller, Abduction, and the Self," *Semiotica* 148 (2004): 317–36.

Coffman, Christopher K. "Taming Paranoia: Underground Cinema and the Domestication of the Thriller in McElroy, DeLillo, Wallace, and Danielewski," *Genre* 42 (2009): 119–43.

Cohen, Shaye. "Are There Tannaitic Parallels to the Gospels?" *Journal of the American Oriental Society* 116 (1996): 85–89.

Cohn, Bernard. *Colonialism and Its Forms of Knowledge: The British in India*. Princeton, NJ: Princeton University Press, 1996.

Collins, John J. *The Dead Sea Scrolls: A Biography*. Lives of Great Religious Books. Princeton, NJ: Princeton University Press, 2013.

Conan Doyle, Arthur. "The Adventure of the Golden Pince-Nez." In *The Return of Sherlock Holmes*, 260–90. New York: McClure, Philips, and Co., 1905.

Criddle, Andrew. "On the Mar Saba Letter Attributed to Clement of Alexandria," *Journal of Early Christian Studies* 3 (1995): 215–20.

Crossan, John Dominic. *The Essential Jesus: Original Sayings and Earliest Images*. San Francisco, CA: HarperSanFrancisco, 1994.

Four Other Gospels: Shadows on the Contours of Canon. Minneapolis, MN: Seabury, 1985.

Jesus: A Revolutionary Biography. San Francisco, CA: HarperSanFrancisco, 1994.

Crossley, James G. "A 'Very Jewish' Jesus: Perpetuating the Myth of Superiority," *Journal for the Study of the Historical Jesus* 11 (2013): 109–29.

Crum, Bartley C. *Behind the Silken Curtain: A Personal Account of Anglo-American Diplomacy in Palestine and the Middle East*. New York: Simon & Schuster, 1947.

Cuéllar, Gregory Lee. *Empire, the British Museum, and the Making of the Biblical Scholar in the Nineteenth Century: Archival Fever*. Cham: Palgrave Macmillan, 2019.

Curzon, Robert. *Visits to the Monasteries of the Levant*. London: John Murray, 1849.

Dart, John. *The Jesus of Heresy and History: The Discovery and Meaning of the Nag Hammadi Gnostic Library*. New York: Harper & Row, 1988.

The Laughing Savior: The Discovery and Significance of the Nag Hammadi Library. New York: Harper & Row, 1976.

Davies, Stevan. "Thomas: The Fourth Synoptic Gospel," *Biblical Archaeologist* 46 (1983): 6–14.

De Groot, Jerome. *Consuming History: Historians and Heritage in Popular Culture*. London: Routledge, 2008.

DeConick, April D. "Gospel Truth," *New York Times* (December 1, 2007): A15.

"The Original *Gospel of Thomas*," *Vigiliae Christianae* 56 (2002): 167–99.

Denzey Lewis, Nicola. "(Still) Rethinking the Origins of the Nag Hammadi Codices," *Marginalia Review of Books* (July 6, 2018). https://themarginaliareview.com/still-rethinking-the-origins-of-the-nag-hammadi-codices.

Denzey Lewis, Nicola and Justin Ariel Blount. "Rethinking the Origins of the Nag Hammadi Codices," *Journal of Biblical Literature* 133 (2014): 399–419.

Dershowitz, Idan. *The Valediction of Moses: A Proto-Biblical Book.* Tübingen: Mohr-Siebeck, 2021.

Diamantopoulou, Lilia. "Konstantinos Simonides: Leben und Werk. Ein tabellarischer Überblick." In *Die getäuschte Wissenschaft: Ein Genie betrügt Europa – Konstantinos Simonides*, 305–25. Eds. Andreas Müller, Lilia Diamantopoulou, Christian Gastgeber, and Athanasia Katsiakiori-Rankl. Vienna: Vienna University Press, 2017.

Douglas, Christopher. *If God Meant to Interfere: American Literature and the Rise of the Christian Right.* Ithaca, NY: Cornell University Press, 2016.

Draper, Robert. "Called to the Holy Mountain," *National Geographic* 216. 6 (December 2009): 134, 137–41, 145, 147–58.

Drosnin, Michael. *The Bible Code.* New York: Simon & Schuster, 1997.

The Bible Code II: The Countdown. New York: Viking, 2002.

Du Mez, Kristin K. *Jesus and John Wayne: How White Evangelicals Corrupted a Faith and Fractured a Nation.* New York: Liveright, 2020.

Ehrman, Bart D. *Lost Christianities: The Battle for Scripture and the Faiths We Never Knew.* New York: Oxford University Press, 2003.

The Lost Gospel of Judas Iscariot: A New Look at Betrayer and Betrayed. Oxford: Oxford University Press, 2006.

Lost Scriptures: Books that Did Not Make It into the New Testament. New York: Oxford University Press, 2003.

"The Myths of Jesus," *Newsweek* 160.25 (December 17, 2021): 24–28.

Truth and Fiction in The Da Vinci Code. New York: Oxford University Press, 2004.

Eisenman, Robert. *James the Just in the Habakkuk Pesher.* Leiden: Brill, 1986.

Maccabees, Zadokites, Christians and Qumran: A New Hypothesis of Qumran Origins. Leiden: Brill, 1984.

Elliott, J. K. *Codex Sinaiticus and the Simonides Affair.* Analecta Vlatadon 33. Thessaloniki: Patriarchal Institute for Patristic Studies, 1982.

Ellsberg, Daniel. *Secrets: A Memoir of Vietnam and the Pentagon Papers.* New York: Penguin, 2003.

Elson, John. "Toward a Hidden God," *Time* 87.14 (April 8, 1966): 82–87.

Evans, G. R. *A Short History of Heresy.* Oxford: Blackwell, 2003.

Everton, Sean F. "What are the Odds? The Jesus Seminar's Quest for Objectivity," *Journal for the Study of the Historical Jesus* 13 (2015): 24–42.

Eyer, Shawn. "The Strange Case of the Secret Gospel According to Mark: How Morton Smith's Discovery of a Lost Letter by Clement of Alexandria Scandalized Biblical Scholarship," *Alexandria* 3 (1995): 103–29.

Fallows, James and James L. Stanfield. "Vatican City," *National Geographic* 168.6 (December 1985): 720–61.

Fanon, Frantz. *Black Skin, White Masks*. New York: Grove Press, 1967.

Farrelly, Maura Jane. *Anti-Catholicism in America, 1620–1860*. Cambridge: Cambridge University Press, 2018.

Felch, Jason and Ralph Frammolino. "Judas Gospel Figure Has Tainted Past," *Los Angeles Times* (April 13, 2006): A23.

Fenster, Mark. *Conspiracy Theories: Secrecy and Power in American Culture*. Rev. ed. Minneapolis, MN: University of Minnesota Press, 2008.

Fields, Weston W. *The Dead Sea Scrolls: A Full History. Vol. 1: 1947–1960*. Leiden: Brill, 2009.

Finlay, George. "Foreign Correspondence," *The Athenaeum* 1240 (August 2, 1851): 831.

François, Wim and August den Hollander (eds.). *Vernacular Bible and Religious Reform in the Middle Ages and the Early Modern Era*. Bibliotheca Ephemeridum Lovaniensium, 287. Leuven: Peeters, 2017.

Fraser, Ian. *The Heir of Parham: Robert Curzon, 14th Baron Zouche*. Norfolk: Paradigm Press, 1986.

Fredriksen, Paula and Adele Reinhartz (eds.). *Jesus, Judaism, and Christian Anti-Judaism: Reading the New Testament after the Holocaust*. Louisville, KY: Westminster/John Knox Press, 2002.

Frykholm, Amy Johnson. *Rapture Culture: Left Behind in Evangelical America*. New York: Oxford University Press, 2004.

Fuller, Robert. *Spiritual, But Not Religious: Understanding Unchurched America*. New York: Oxford University Press, 2001.

Funk, Robert. "Jesus Seminar Opening Remarks," 1985. https://web.archive.org/web/20220119043008/https://www.westarinstitute.org/projects/jesus-seminar-opening-remarks.

Funk, Robert, Roy Hoover, and the Jesus Seminar. *The Five Gospels: What Did Jesus Really Say? A Search For the Authentic Words of Jesus*. Santa Rosa: Polebridge, 1993; San Francisco, CA: HarperSanFrancisco, 1997.

Gathercole, Simon. *The Apocryphal Gospels*. London: Penguin, 2021.

George, Alan. "'Making the Desert Bloom': A Myth Examined," *Journal of Palestine Studies* 8 (1979): 88–100.

Gin Lum, Kathryn. *Heathen: Religion and Race in American History.* Cambridge, MA: Harvard University Press, 2022.

Given, J. Gregory. "'Finding' the *Gospel of Thomas* in Edessa," *Journal of Early Christian Studies* 25 (2017): 501–30.

Goff, Philip, Arthur Farnsley, and Peter Thuesen (eds.). *The Bible in American Life.* New York: Oxford University Press, 2017.

Goldberg, Jeffrey. "The Conspiracy Theorists Are Winning," *The Atlantic.* www.theatlantic.com/ideas/archive/2020/05/shadowland-introduction/610840.

Goldstein, Eric. *The Price of Whiteness: Jews, Race, and American Identity.* Princeton, NJ: Princeton University Press, 2006.

Goodacre, Mark S. *The Case against Q: Studies in Markan Priority and the Synoptic Problem.* Harrisburg, PA: Trinity Press, 2002.

"How Reliable Is the Story of Nag Hammadi?" *Journal for the Study of the New Testament* 35 (2013): 303–22.

"Jesus' Wife, the Media, and The Da Vinci Code." In *Fakes, Forgeries, and Fictions: Writing Ancient and Modern Christian Apocrypha.* 341–48. Ed. Tony Burke. Eugene, OR: Cascade Books, 2017.

"When Is a Text not a Text? The Quasi Text-Critical Approach of the International Q Project." In *Questioning Q: A Multidimensional Critique*, 115–26. Eds. Mark S. Goodacre and Nicholas Perrin. Downers Grove, IL: IVP Academic, 2004.

Goodstein, Laurie. "Document Is Genuine, But Is It True?" *New York Times* (April 7, 2006): A20.

"A Faded Piece of Papyrus Refers to Jesus' Wife," *New York Times* (September 19, 2012): A1, A21.

"R.W. Funk, 79, Creator of Jesus Seminar, Dies," *New York Times* (September 10, 2005): C14.

Grafton, Anthony. *Forgers and Critics: Creativity and Duplicity in Western Scholarship.* New ed. Foreword by Ann Bair. Princeton, NJ: Princeton University Press, 2019.

Grafton, Anthony and Megan H. Williams. *Origen, Eusebius, and the Library of Caesarea.* Cambridge, MA: Harvard University Press, 2006.

Green, Jackie and Steve Green. *This Dangerous Book: How the Bible Has Shaped Our World and Why It Matters Today.* Grand Rapids, MI: Zondervan, 2017.

Greshko, Michael. "'Dead Sea Scrolls' at the Museum of the Bible Are All Forgeries," *National Geographic Magazine* (March 13, 2020). www.nationalgeographic.com/history/article/museum-of-the-bible-dead-sea-scrolls-forgeries.

Guil, Shlomo. "The Shapira Scroll Was an Authentic Dead Sea Scroll," *Palestine Exploration Quarterly* 149 (2017): 6–27.

Gutjahr, Paul C. "Protestant English-Language Bible Publishing and Translation." In *The Oxford Handbook of the Bible in America*, 3–18. Ed. Paul C. Gutjahr. New York: Oxford University Press, 2018.

Hammer, Olav. "The Jungian Gnosticism of the Ecclesia Gnostica," *International Journal for the Study of New Religions* 9 (2018): 33–56.

Hargis, Billy James. *Communist America – Must It Be?* Tulsa, OK: Christian Crusade, 1960.

Harris, Harriet. "Fundamentalist Readings of the Bible." In *The New Cambridge History of the Bible. Vol. 4: From 1750 to the Present*, 328–43. Ed. John Riches. Cambridge: Cambridge University Press, 2015.

Hawk, Brandon. *Apocrypha for Beginners: A Guide to Understanding and Exploring Scriptures Beyond the Bible*. Emeryville, CA: Rockbridge Press, 2021.

Heschel, Susannah. *The Aryan Jesus: Christian Theologians and the Bible in Nazi Germany*. Princeton, NJ: Princeton University Press, 2008.

Hicks-Keeton, Jill. "The Fantasy of 'the Bible' in the Museum of the Bible and Academic Biblical Studies," *Journal for Interdisciplinary Biblical Studies* 4.3 (2022): 1–18. https://hcommons.org/deposits/item/hc:46903.

Hicks-Keeton, Jill and Cavan Concannon. *Does Scripture Speak for Itself? The Museum of the Bible and the Politics of Interpretation*. Cambridge: Cambridge University Press, 2022.

(eds.). *The Museum of the Bible: A Critical Introduction*. London: Rowan & Littlefield, 2019.

Hoffman, Michael L. "Gnostic Gospels of 150 A.D. Found: Throw Light on Early Christianity," *New York Times* (November 16, 1953): 1.

Hofstadter, Richard. "The Paranoid Style in American Politics," *Harpers Magazine* (November 1964): 77–86.

The Paranoid Style in American Politics. Introduction by Sean Wilentz. New York: Vintage Books, 2008.

Hone, William. *The Apocryphal New Testament*. London: Ludgate Hill, 1820.

Howard, Evan Drake. *The Galilean Secret*. New York: Guideposts, 2010.

Hüller, Stephan and Daniel N. Gullota. "Quentin Quesnell's *Secret Mark* Secret," *Vigiliae Christianae* 71 (2017): 353–78.

Hunter, Ian. "The (Continuing) Mystery of Mar Saba," *National Post* (June 30, 2005): A22.

Jacobs, Andrew S. *Epiphanius of Cyprus: A Cultural Biography of Late Antiquity*. Christianity in Late Antiquity 2. Oakland, CA: University of California Press, 2016.

"Gospel Thrillers," *Postscripts* 1 (2005): 125–42.

"'This Piece of Parchment Will Shake the World': *The Mystery of Mar Saba* and the Evangelical Prototype of a Secular Fiction Genre," *Christianity & Literature* 69 (2020): 91–106.

James, M. R. *The Apocryphal New Testament*. Oxford: Clarendon Press, 1924.

Jameson, Frederic. *The Geopolitical Aesthetic*. Bloomington, IN: Indiana University Press, 1992.

Jefferson, Rebecca J.W. *The Cairo Genizah and the Age of Discovery in Egypt*. London: I. B. Tauris, 2022.

"Deconstructing the 'Cairo Genizah': A Fresh Look at Manuscript Discoveries in Cairo before 1897," *Jewish Quarterly Review* 108 (2018): 422–48.

Jeffery, Peter. *The Secret Gospel of Mark Unveiled: Imagined Rituals of Sex, Death, and Madness in a Biblical Forgery*. New Haven, CT: Yale University Press, 2007.

Jemison, Elizabeth L. *Christian Citizens: Reading the Bible in Black and White in the Postemancipation South*. Chapel Hill, NC: University of North Carolina Press, 2020.

Jenkins, Jerry. *Dead Sea Rising*. Franklin, TN: Worthy Press, 2018.

Jenkins, Philip. *Hidden Gospels: How the Search for Jesus Lost Its Way*. New York: Oxford University Press, 2001.

Johnson, Luke Timothy. *The Real Jesus: The Misguided Quest for the Historical Jesus and the Truth of the Traditional Gospels*. San Francisco, CA: HarperSanFrancisco, 1996.

Joyce, Donovan. *The Jesus Scroll*. Sydney: Angus and Robertson, 1972.

Kaplan, Amy. *Our American Israel: The Story of an Entangled Alliance*. Cambridge, MA: Harvard University Press, 2018.

Kaplan, Steven. "Can the Ethiopian Change His Skin? The Beta Israel (Ethiopian Jews) and Racial Discourse," *African Affairs* 98 (1999): 535–50.

Kasser, Rodolphe, Marvin Meyer, and Gregor Wurst (eds.). *The Gospel of Judas from Codex Tchacos*. Washington, DC: National Geographic, 2006.

Kellner, Mark. "Away with the Manger: The New Jesus Seminar Discounts the Virgin Birth," *Christianity Today* (November 14, 1994): 92–93.

Kerby, Lauren R. *Saving History: How White Evangelicals Tour the Nation's Capital and Redeem a Christian America*. Chapel Hill, NC: University of North Carolina Press, 2020.

"White Nationalists Want More than Just Political Power," *The Atlantic* (January 15, 2021). www.theatlantic.com/ideas/archive/2021/01/white-evangelicals-fixation-on-washington-dc/617690.

Kershner, Isabel. "Israeli Researchers Show Dead Sea Scrolls Artifacts," *New York Times* (March 16, 2021): A9.

Kessler, Edward. "'I Am Joseph, Your Brother': A Jewish Perspective on Christian-Jewish Relations since Nostra Aetate 4," *Theological Studies* 74 (2013): 48–72.

King, Karen L. (ed.). *Images of the Feminine in Gnosticism.* Studies in Antiquity and Christianity. Philadelphia, PA: Fortress Press, 1988.

"'Jesus Said to Them: "My Wife…"': A New Coptic Papyrus Fragment," *Harvard Theological Review* 107 (2014): 131–59.

What Is Gnosticism? Cambridge, MA: Harvard University Press, 2003.

King, Karen L. and Elaine Pagels. *Reading Judas: The Gospel of Judas and the Shaping of Christianity.* New York: Penguin, 2007.

King, Laurie R. *A Letter of Mary.* New York: St. Martin's Press, 1996.

Kissinger, John. "Archaeology as 'Wild Magic': The Dead Sea Scrolls in Popular Fiction," *Journal of American Culture* 21.3 (1998): 75–81.

Kloppenborg, John S. *The Formation of Q: Trajectories in Ancient Wisdom.* Minneapolis, MN: Fortress Press, 1987.

"Introduction." In *The Shape of Q: Signal Essays on the Sayings Gospel,* 1–21. Ed. John S. Kloppenborg. Minneapolis, MN: Fortress Press, 1994.

Knox, Sanka. "Expert Disputes 'Secret Gospel.'" *New York Times* (December 31, 1960): 7.

"A New Gospel Ascribed to Mark: Copy of Greek Letter Says Saint Kept 'Mysteries' Out," *New York Times* (December 30, 1960): 1.

Koester, Helmut. "ΓΝΩΜΑΙ ΔΙΑΦΟΡΟΙ: The Origin and Nature of Diversification in the History of Early Christianity," *Harvard Theological Review* 58 (1965): 160–203.

"History and Development of Mark's Gospel (From Mark to *Secret Mark* and 'Canonical' Mark)." In *Colloquy on New Testament Studies. A Time for Reappraisal and Fresh Approaches,* 35–57. Ed. Bruce C. Corley. Macon, GA: Mercer University Press, 1983.

Kotrosits, Maia. "Romance and Danger at Nag Hammadi," *The Bible and Critical Theory* 8 (2012): 39–52.

Krosney, Herbert. *The Lost Gospel: The Quest for the Gospel of Judas Iscariot.* Washington, DC: National Geographic, 2006.

LaFrance, Adrienne. "Nothing Can Stop What Is Coming," *The Atlantic* (June 2020): 27–38.

Lerner, Gerda. *The Creation of Patriarchy.* New York: Oxford University Press, 1986.

Levine-Rasky, Cynthia. *Whiteness Fractured.* New York: Routledge, 2013.

Levine, Amy-Jill. "Supersessionism: Admit and Address rather than Debate or Deny," *Religions* 13.155 (2022): 1–12.

Lin, Yii-Jan. *The Erotic Life of Manuscripts: New Testament Textual Criticism and the Biological Sciences.* New York: Oxford University Press, 2016.

Lingeman, Richard R. "Happy Irving Wallace Day!" *New York Times* (March 15, 1972): 45.

Little, Douglas. *American Orientalism: The United States and the Middle East since 1945.* Chapel Hill, NC: University of North Carolina Press, 2009.

Longmuir, Anne. "Genre and Gender in Don DeLillo's *Players* and *Running Dog*," *Journal of Narrative Theory* 37 (2007): 128–45.

Mack, Burton L. *The Lost Gospel: The Book of Q & Christian Origins.* San Francisco, CA: HarperSanFrancisco, 1993.

  Who Wrote the New Testament? The Making of Christian Myth. San Francisco, CA: HarperSanFrancisco, 1995.

Mączyńska, Magdalena. *The Gospel According to the Novelist: Religious Scripture and Contemporary Fiction.* New Directions in Religion and Literature. London: Bloomsbury, 2015.

Magness, Jodi. *Masada: From Jewish Revolt to Modern Myth.* Princeton, NJ: Princeton University Press, 2019.

Maier, Paul. *The Constantine Codex.* Carol Stream, IL: Tyndale House Publishers, 2011.

Maloney, Sean M. *Deconstructing Dr. Strangelove: The Secret History of Nuclear War Films.* Lincoln, NE: Potomac Books, 2020.

Marcus, Greil. "Pagels Says: Don't Knock the Gnostics," *Rolling Stone* 312 (March 6, 1980): 36.

Marsden, George M. *Fundamentalism and American Cultures.* 2nd ed. Oxford: Oxford University Press, 2006.

Marsh, Jan. "Icon of the Age: Victoria and *The Secret of England's Greatness.*" In *Black Victorians: Black People and British Art*, 57–67. Ed. Jan Marsh. Manchester Art Gallery: Manchester, 2005.

Martin, William. *With God on Our Side: The Rise of the Religious Right in America.* New York: Broadway Books, 1996.

Martinez, Javier. "Cheap Fictions and Gospel Truths." In *Splendide Mendax: Rethinking Fakes and Forgeries in Classical, Late Antique, and Early Christian Literature*, 3–20. Eds. Edmund P. Cueva and Javier Martinez. Groningen: Barkhuis, 2016.

Massa, Mark. *Anti-Catholicism in America: The Last Acceptable Prejudice.* New York: Crossroad, 2003.

  "Anti-Catholicism in the United States." In *The Cambridge Companion to American Catholicism*, 197–215. Eds. Margaret M. McGuinness and Thomas F. Rzeznik. Cambridge: Cambridge University Press, 2021.

Masuzawa, Tomoko. *The Invention of World Religions: Or, How European Universalism Was Preserved in the Language of Pluralism*. Chicago, IL: University of Chicago Press, 2005.

Maugh II, Thomas H. "Judas Is No Traitor in Long-Lost Gospel," *Los Angeles Times* (April 7, 2006): A1, A26.

Mawer, Simon. *The Gospel of Judas*. New York: Little, Brown and Co., 2002.

Mazza, Roberta. "Papyri, Private Collectors, and Academics: Why the Wife of Jesus and Sappho Matter," *Faces and Voices* (April 17, 2014). https://facesandvoices.wordpress.com/2014/04/17/papyri-private-collectors-and-academics-why-the-wife-of-jesus-and-sappho-matter.

McGowan, Todd. "Hitchcock's Ethics of Suspense: Psychoanalysis and the Devaluation of the Object." In *A Companion to Alfred Hitchcock*, 493–528. Eds. Thomas Leitch and Leland Poague. Malden, MA: Wiley Blackwell, 2011.

McGrath, James. "Slow Scholarship: Do Bloggers Rush in Where Jesus' Wife Would Fear to Tread?" In *Fakes, Forgeries, and Fictions: Writing Ancient and Modern Christian Apocrypha*. 326–40. Ed. Tony Burke. Eugene, OR: Cascade Books, 2017.

Melley, Timothy. *Empire of Conspiracy: The Culture of Paranoia in Postwar America*. Ithaca, NY: Cornell University Press, 2000.

Melton, Jr., William R. "Duncan's Pen Mightier than His Typewriter," *Los Angeles Times* (June 19, 1966): B18.

Meyer, Barbara U. *Jesus the Jew in Christian Memory: Theological and Philosophical Explorations*. Cambridge: Cambridge University Press, 2020.

Meyer, Marvin. "The Gospel of Judas: A Word from the Translators," *New York Times* (December 7, 2007): A30.

"The Youth in the *Secret Gospel of Mark*," *Semeia* 49 (1990): 129–53.

Mitchell, Timothy. *Colonising Egypt*. Berkeley, CA: University of California Press, 1991.

Mitsein, Rebekah. "'Come and Triumph with Your Don Quixote': or, How James Bruce Travelled to Discover the Nile but Found Scotland Instead," *Studies in Travel Writing* 18 (2014): 1–17.

Mortenson, Erik. "A Journey into the Shadows: *The Twilight Zone*'s Visual Critique of the Cold War," *Science Fiction Film and Television* 7 (2014): 55–76.

Moss, Candida R. and Joel S. Baden. *Bible Nation: The United States of Hobby Lobby*. Princeton, NJ: Princeton University Press, 2017.

Mroczek, Eva. "'Gospel of Jesus' Wife' Less Durable than Sexism Surrounding It," *Religion Dispatches* (May 6, 2014). https://religiondispatches.org/gospel-of-jesus-wife-less-durable-than-sexism-surrounding-it.

"True Stories and the Poetics of Textual Discovery," *Bulletin for the Study of Religion* 45.2 (2016): 21–31.

"Truth and Doubt in Discovery Narratives." In *Rethinking "Authority" in Late Antiquity: Authorship, Law, and Transmission in Jewish and Christian Tradition*, 139–60. Routledge Monographs in Classical Studies. Eds. A. J. Berkovitz and Mark Letteney. London: Routledge, 2018.

Muirhead, Russell and Nancy L. Rosenblum. *A Lot of People Are Saying: The New Conspiracism and the Assault on Democracy*. Princeton, NJ: Princeton University Press, 2019.

Müller, Andreas, Lilia Diamantopoulou, Christian Gastgeber, and Athanasia Katsiakiori-Rankl (eds). *Die getäuschte Wissenschaft: Ein Genie betrügt Europa—Konstantinos Simonides*. Vienna: Vienna University Press, 2017.

Murgia, Charles. "Secret Mark: Real or Fake?" In *Longer Mark: Forgery, Interpolation, or Old Tradition?* 35–40. Ed. W. Wuellner. Berkeley, CA: Center for Hermeneutical Studies, 1976.

Musurillo, Herbert. "Morton Smith's Secret Gospel," *Thought* 48 (1973): 327–31.

Mykoniati, Anna. "Biographische Bemerkungen zu Konstantinos Simonides." In *Die getäuschte Wissenschaft: Ein Genie betrügt Europa – Konstantinos Simonides*, 87–106. Eds. Andreas Müller, Lilia Diamantopoulou, Christian Gastgeber, and Athanasia Katsiakiori-Rankl. Vienna: Vienna University Press, 2017.

Nead, Lynda. "The Secret of England's Greatness," *Journal of Victorian Culture* 19 (2014): 161–82.

Neirynck, Frans. "Q: From Source to Gospel," *Ephemerides Theologicae Lovenienses* 71 (1995): 421–30.

Neklason, Annika. "The Conspiracy Theories That Fueled the Civil War," *The Atlantic* (May 29, 2020). www.theatlantic.com/politics/archive/2020/05/conspiracy-theories-civil-war/612283.

Neusner, Jacob. *Are There Really Tannaitic Parallels to the Gospels? A Refutation of Morton Smith*. South Florida Studies in the History of Judaism 80. Atlanta, GA: Scholars Press, 1993.

Nigro, Paul. *Q: A Novel*. Tulsa, OK: River Oak Publishing, 2002.

Nongbri, Brent. "Finding Early Christian Books at Nag Hammadi and Beyond," *Bulletin for the Study of Religion* 45 (2016): 11–19.

"Further Thoughts on the Tchacos-Ferrini Exodus," *Variant Readings* (March 18, 2021). https://brentnongbri.com/2021/03/18/further-thoughts-on-the-tchacos-ferrini-exodus.

God's Library: The Archaeology of the Earliest Christian Manuscripts. New Haven, CT: Yale University Press, 2018.

O'Donnell, Patrick. "Obvious Paranoia: The Politics of Don DeLillo's *Running Dog*," *Centennial Review* 34 (1990): 56–72.

Obenzinger, Hilton. *American Palestine: Melville, Twain, and the Holy Land*. Princeton, NJ: Princeton University Press, 1999.

Pagels, Elaine. *Beyond Belief: The Secret Gospel of Thomas*. New York: Random House, 2004.

    The Gnostic Gospels. New York: Random House, 1979.

    "The Gospel Truth," *New York Times* (April 8, 2006): A13.

    Why Religion? A Personal Story. New York: HarperCollins, 2018.

Pantuck, Allan J., MD. "Solving the *Mystereion* of Morton Smith and the Secret Gospel of Mark," *Biblical Archaeology Society* (October 14, 2009). www.biblicalarchaeology.org/wp-content/uploads/secret-mark-handwriting-response-pantuck.pdf.

Parfitt, Tudor. *Black Jews in Africa and the Americas*. Cambridge, MA: Harvard University Press, 2013.

Parker, David. *Codex Sinaiticus: The Story of the World's Oldest Bible*. London: British Library, 2010.

Parker, Gary. *The Ephesus Fragment*. Minneapolis, MN: Bethany House, 1999.

Pinto, Pasquale Massimo. "Simonides in England: A Forger's Progress." In *Die getäuschte Wissenschaft: Ein Genie betrügt Europa – Konstantinos Simonides*, 109–26. Eds. Andreas Müller, Lilia Diamantopoulou, Christian Gastgeber, and Athanasia Katsiakiori-Rankl. Vienna: Vienna University Press, 2017.

Piovanelli, Pierluigi. "Halfway Between Sabbatai Tzevi and Aleister Crowley." In *Ancient Gospel or Modern Forgery? The Secret Gospel of Mark in Debate*, 202–35. Ed. Tony Burke. Eugene, OR: Cascade Books, 2013.

Plaksow, Judith. "The Coming of Lilith." In *Religion and Sexism: Images of Women in the Jewish and Christian Traditions*, 341–43. Ed. Rosemary Radford Ruether. New York: Simon & Schuster, 1974. Republished with an extended introduction in *The Coming of Lilith: Essays on Feminism, Judaism, and Sexual Ethics, 1972–2003*, 23–33. Ed. Judith Plaskow with Donna Berman. Boston: Beacon Press, 2005.

Porter, Stanley E. *Constantine Tischendorf: The Life and Work of a 19th Century Bible Hunter*. London: Bloomsbury, 2015.

Porter, Stanley E. and Gordon L. Heath. *The Lost Gospel of Judas: Separating Fact from Fiction*. Grand Rapids, MI: Eerdmans, 2007.

Prescott, Orville. "Ingenious Plot Makes Implausible Tale," *New York Times* (June 5, 1964): 29.

Press, Michael. "The Career of Moses Shapira, Bookseller and Antiquarian," *Palestine Exploration Quarterly*, forthcoming.

Price, Robert M. "Second Thoughts on the Secret Gospel," *Bulletin for Biblical Research* 14 (2004): 127–32.

Secret Scrolls: Revelations from the Lost Gospel Novels. Eugene, OR: Wipf & Stock, 2011.

Prothero, Stephen. *American Jesus: How the Son of God Became a National Icon.* New York: Farrar, Straus, and Giroux, 2004.

Quesnell, Quentin. "The Mar Saba Clementine: A Question of Evidence," *Catholic Biblical Quarterly* 37 (1975): 48–67.

"A Reply to Morton Smith," *Catholic Biblical Quarterly* 38 (1976): 200–203.

Quispel, Gilles. "The Gospel of Thomas and the New Testament," *Vigiliae Christianae* 11 (1957): 189–207.

Reed, Annette Yoshiko. "The Afterlives of New Testament Apocrypha," *Journal of Biblical Literature* 133 (2015): 401–25.

Jewish-Christianity and the History of Judaism. Texts and Studies in Ancient Judaism 171. Tübingen: Mohr Siebeck, 2018.

Reid, Donald M. *Contesting Antiquity in Egypt: Archaeologies, Museums, and the Struggle for Identities from World War I to Nasser.* Cairo: American University in Cairo Press, 2015.

Whose Pharaohs? Archaeology, Museums, and Egyptian National Identity from Napoleon to World War I. Berkeley, CA: University of California Press, 2002.

Reif, Stefan C. "Giblews, Jews and Genizah Views," *Journal of Jewish Studies* 55 (2004): 332–46.

Reiner, Fred N. "C. D. Ginsburg and the Shapira Affair: A Nineteenth-Century Dead Sea Scroll Controversy," *The British Library Journal* 21 (1995): 109–27.

Robinson, James M. *The Nag Hammadi Story.* 2 vols. Nag Hammadi and Manichaean Studies 86. Leiden: Brill, 2014.

The Secrets of Judas: The Story of the Misunderstood Disciple and His Lost Gospel. San Francisco, CA: Harper, 2006.

Robinson, James M., Paul Hoffmann, and John S. Kloppenborg. *The Critical Edition of Q.* Hermeneia. Minneapolis, MN: Augsburg/Fortress, 2000.

Rogerson, John. *Old Testament Criticism in the Nineteenth Century: England and Germany.* London: SPCK, 1984.

Rose, Kenneth. *One Nation Underground: The Fallout Shelter in American Culture.* New York: NYU Press, 2001.

Rubin, Martin. *Thrillers.* Cambridge: Cambridge University Press, 1999.

Sabar, Ariel. "The Gospel According to King," *Smithsonian* (November 2012). www.smithsonianmag.com/history/update-the-reaction-to-karen-kings-gospel-discovery-84250942.

"The Inside Story of a Controversial New Text About Jesus," *Smithsonian* (September 18, 2012). www.smithsonianmag.com/history/the-inside-story-of-a-controversial-new-text-about-jesus-41078791.

"A Scholarly Screw-Up of Biblical Proportions," *Chronicle of Higher Education* (June 29, 2021). www.chronicle.com/article/a-scholarly-screw-up-of-biblical-proportions.

"The Unbelievable Tale of Jesus' Wife," *The Atlantic* (July/August 2016): 64–78.

"Unearthing the World of Jesus," *Smithsonian* (January/February 2016). www.smithsonianmag.com/history/unearthing-world-jesus-180957515.

Veritas: A Harvard Professor, a Con Man, and the Gospel of Jesus's Wife. New York: Doubleday, 2020.

Sahagun, Louis. "Was It Virtue or Betrayal?" *Los Angeles Times* (January 6, 2007): A1.

Sandom, J. G. *The God Machine.* New York: Bantam Book, 2009.

Sasson-Levy, Orna. "A Different Kind of Whiteness: Marking and Unmarking of Social Boundaries in the Construction of Hegemonic Ethnicity," *Sociological Forum* 28 (2013): 27–50.

Schonfield, Hugh G. *The Passover Plot.* New York: Random House, 1965.

Secrets of the Dead Sea Scrolls. London: Valentine, 1956.

Schroeder, Caroline T. "Gender and the Academy Online: The Authentic Revelations of the Gospel of Jesus' Wife." In *Fakes, Forgeries, and Fictions: Writing Ancient and Modern Christian Apocrypha*, 304–25. Ed. Tony Burke. Eugene, OR: Cascade Books, 2017.

Schröter, Jens. "The Quest for the Historical Jesus: Current Debates and Prospects," *Early Christianity* 11 (2020): 283–96.

Schweitzer, Albert. *The Quest of the Historical Jesus: A Critical Study of its Progress from Reimarus to Wrede.* 2nd ed. Trans. W. Montgomery. London: Adam and Charles Black, 1911.

Scott, Peter Dale. *The War Conspiracy: The Secret Road to the Second Indochina War.* Indianapolis, IN: Bobbs-Merrill, 1972.

Shanks, Hershel. "Was Morton Smith the Bernie Madoff of the Academy?" In *Ancient Gospel or Modern Forgery? The Secret Gospel of Mark in Debate*, 177–87. Ed. Tony Burke. Eugene, OR: Cascade Books, 2013.

Shapira, Anna. "The Bible and Israeli Identity," *AJS Review* 28 (2004): 11–42.

Sheehan, Jonathan. *The Enlightenment Bible: Translation, Scholarship, Culture.* Princeton, NJ: Princeton University Press, 2005.

Sherwood, Yvonne with Anna Fisk. *The Bible and Feminism: Remapping the Field.* New York: Oxford University Press, 2017.

Silberman, Neil Asher. *A Prophet From Amongst You: The Life of Yigael Yadin: Soldier, Scholar, and Mythmaker of Modern Israel.* Reading: Addison-Wesley, 1993.

Silliman, Daniel. *Reading Evangelicals: How Christian Fiction Shaped a Culture and a Faith*. Grand Rapids, MI: Eerdmans, 2021.

Simon, Reeva S. *The Middle East in Crime Fiction: Mysteries, Spies, Novels, and Thrillers From 1916 to the 1980s*. New York: Lilian Barber Press, 1989.

Spies and Holy Wars: The Middle East in 20th-Century Crime Fiction. Austin, TX: University of Texas Press, 2010.

Simonides, K. (ed.). *The Periplus of Hannon, King of the Karchedonians*. London: Trübner & Co., 1864.

Smith, Geoffrey S. and Brent C. Landau. *The Secret Gospel of Mark: A Controversial Scholar, a Scandalous Gospel of Jesus, and the Fierce Debate over Its Authenticity*. New Haven, CT: Yale University Press, 2023.

Smith, Jack. "Parthenogenesis," *Los Angeles Times* (May 19, 1983): I1.

Smith, Morton. *Clement of Alexandria and a Secret Gospel of Mark*. Cambridge, MA: Harvard University Press, 1973.

"Clement of Alexandria and Secret Mark: The Score at the End of the First Decade," *Harvard Theological Review* 75 (1982): 449–61.

"On the Authenticity of the Mar Saba Letter of Clement," *Catholic Biblical Quarterly* 38 (1976): 196–99.

The Secret Gospel: The Discovery and Interpretation of the Secret Gospel According to Mark. New York: Harper & Row, 1973.

Smith, Robert O. *More Desired than Our Owne Salvation: The Roots of Christian Zionism*. Oxford: Oxford University Press, 2013.

Solomon, Stephen D. *Ellery's Protest: How One Young Man Defied Tradition and Sparked the Battle over School Prayer*. Rev. ed. Ann Arbor, MI: University of Michigan Press, 2010.

Soskice, Janet. *The Sisters of Sinai: How Two Lady Adventurers Discovered the Hidden Gospels*. New York: Vintage Books, 2009.

Stanfield, James L. "Mount Athos," *National Geographic* 164.6 (December 1983): 739–47.

Steinfels, Peter. "Was It A Hoax? Debate on 'Secret Mark' Gospel Resumes," *New York Times* (March 31, 2007): A12.

Stroumsa, Guy G. *Another Seed: Studies in Gnostic Mythology*. Nag Hammadi Studies 24. Leiden: Brill, 1984.

Tercatin, Rosella. "Are the Newest Dead Sea Scrolls Just the Beginning?" *The Jerusalem Post* (March 18, 2021). www.jpost.com/archaeology/dead-sea-scrolls-many-caves-left-more-biblical-texts-may-emerge-662327.

Thuesen, Peter J. *In Discordance with the Scriptures: American Protestant Battles over Translating the Bible*. New York: Oxford University Press, 1999.

Tigay, Chanan. *The Lost Book of Moses: The Hunt for the World's Oldest Bible*. New York: Harper, 2016.

Tigchelaar, Eibert. "A Provisional List of Unprovenanced, Twenty-First Century, Dead Sea Scroll-Like Fragments," *Dead Sea Discoveries* 24 (2017): 173–88.

Tischendorf, Constantin. *Travels in the East by a Pilgrim*. Trans. W. E. Schukard. London: Longman, Brown, Green, and Longmans, 1851.

Tischendorf, Constantine [*sic*]. *When Were Our Gospels Written? An Argument by Constantine Tischendorf with a Narrative of the Discovery of the Sinaitic Manuscript*. 2nd ed. London: Religious Tract Society, 1867.

Tite, Philip L. "Windows and Mirrors: Texts, Religions, and Stories of Origin," *Bulletin for the Study of Religion* 45 (2016): 2–3.

Toland, John. *Amyntor, or: A Defence of Milton's Life*. London: Booksellers of London & Westminster, 1699.

    Nazarenus, or: Jewish, Gentile, and Mahometan Christianity. London: J. Brown without Temple-Bar, 1718.

Train, Arthur Cheney. "The Lost Gospel," *The Saturday Evening Post* 196.49 (June 7, 1924): 3–5, 216–18, 220–22.

Tupamahu, Ekaputra. "The Stubborn Invisibility of Whiteness in Biblical Scholarship," *Political Theology Network*. http://politicaltheology.com/the-stubborn-invisibility-of-whiteness-in-biblical-scholarship.

Twain, Mark. *Innocents Abroad or, The New Pilgrim's Progress; Being Some Account of the Steamship Quaker City's Pleasure Excursion to Europe and the Holy Land*. Hartford, CT: American Publishing Company, 1869.

Tyrell, George. *Christianity at the Crossroads*. London: Longmans, Green, & Co., 1909.

Ullmann-Margalit, Edna. *Out of the Cave: A Philosophical Inquiry into the Dead Sea Scrolls Research*. Cambridge, MA: Harvard University Press, 2006.

Vaca, Daniel. *Evangelicals Incorporated: Books and the Business of Religion in America*. Cambridge, MA: Harvard University Press, 2019.

Van Biema, David and Lisa McLaughlin. "Deciphering God's Plan," *Time* 149.23 (June 9, 1997): 56.

Vermes, Geza. *The Story of the Scrolls*. New York: Penguin, 2010.

Walker, Jesse. *The United States of Paranoia: A Conspiracy Theory*. New York: Harper Perennial, 2013.

Waller, Alexis G. "The 'Unspeakable Teachings' of *The Secret Gospel of Mark*: Feelings and Fantasies in the Making of Christian Histories." In *Religion, Emotion, Sensation: Affect Theories and Theologies*, 145–73. Ed. Karen Bray and Stephen Moore. New York: Fordham University Press, 2019.

Wasserman, Tommy. "Simonides' New Testament Papyri: Their Production and Purported Provenance," *Marginalia: LA Review of Books*,

July 6, 2018. https://themarginaliareview.com/simonides-new-testa ment-papyri-their-production-and-purported-provenance.

Watson, Francis. "Beyond Suspicion: On the Authorship of the Mar Saba Letter and the Secret Gospel of Mark," *Journal of Theological Studies* 61 (2010): 128–70.

Weigert, A. J. "Christian Eschatological Identities and the Nuclear Context," *Journal for the Scientific Study of Religion* 27 (1988): 175–91.

Wharton, Annabel Jane. *Selling Jerusalem: Relics, Replicas, Theme Parks.* Chicago, IL: University of Chicago Press, 2006.

Wilford, John Noble and Laurie Goodstein. "In Ancient Document, Judas, Minus the Betrayal," *New York Times* (April 7, 2006): A1.

Williams, Daniel. *God's Own Party: The Making of the Christian Right.* New York: Oxford University Press, 2010.

Williams, Michael A. *Rethinking "Gnosticism": An Argument for Dismantling a Dubious Category.* Princeton, NJ: Princeton University Press, 1996.

Wilson, Edmund. *The Dead Sea Scrolls: 1947–1969.* New York: Farrar, Straus, Giroux, 1969.

"A Reporter at Large: The Scrolls from the Dead Sea," *New Yorker* (May 14, 1955): 45–131.

The Scrolls from the Dead Sea. New York: Oxford University Press, 1955.

Wood, Gordon. "Conspiracy and the Paranoid Style: Causality and Deceit in the Eighteenth Century," *William and Mary Quarterly* 39 (1982): 401–41.

Wright, N. T. *Judas and the Gospel of Jesus: Have We Missed the Truth about Christianity?* Grand Rapids, MI: Baker Books, 2006.

Wuellner, W. (ed.). *Longer Mark: Forgery, Interpolation, or Old Tradition?* Berkeley, CA: Center for Hermeneutical Studies, 1976.

Yadin, Yigael. *Masada: Herod's Fortress and the Zealots' Last Stand.* Trans. Moshe Pearlman. New York: Random House, 1966.

Yosef, Raz. *Beyond Flesh: Queer Masculinities and Nationalism in Israeli Cinema.* New Brunswick, NJ: Rutgers University Press, 2004.

Zeitlin, Solomon. "The Hebrew Scrolls: Once More and Finally," *Jewish Quarterly Review* 41 (1950): 1–58.

"The Propaganda of the Hebrew Scrolls and the Falsification of History," *Jewish Quarterly Review* 46 (1955): 1–39, 116–80; 46 (1956): 209–58.

Index